DETLING AIRFIELD

A HISTORY
1915–1959

DETLING AIRFIELD

A HISTORY
1915–1959

ANTHONY J. MOOR

AMBERLEY

First published 2011

Amberley Publishing
The Hill, Stroud
Gloucestershire GL5 4EP

www.amberleybooks.com

British Library Cataloguing in Publication Data.
A catalogue record for this book is available from the British Library.

ISBN 978-1-4456-0346-9

Typeset in 10pt on 12pt Sabon.
Typesetting and Origination by Amberley Publishing.
Printed in the UK.

Contents

Acknowledgements

On reflection, this book should have been published some time ago, when many of the people featured, both military and civilian, were still able to recall tales of their time at Detling airfield. Sadly that is not the case, but I have been lucky in finding a few who served at various times in the airfield's history. I would like to thank them for their contributions. There are also several publications, articles and documents written by pilots, airmen and civilians which can be located in museums and libraries in the UK and abroad. Their authors and families must be congratulated for preserving them for historians to read and ponder over.

We remember those who lost their lives working and flying from Detling. They must never be forgotten, and I hope this book sheds some light on another of the airfields in the UK that played a major role in both world wars, as well as on the county of Kent, which was so embroiled in the history of aviation. I would like to mention some of the individuals and organisations who have helped me with research and photographs: Imperial War Museum; RAF Museum Hendon; Fleet Air Arm Museum; Museum of Army Flying; Kent Gliding Club; C. Bunyan; Royal Mid-Surrey Golf Course; *Kent Messenger*; Brooklands Museum; The National Archives, Kew; Kent Aviation Historical Research Society; R .Walton; J. Duay; D. King; B. Read; F. J. Baldwin; A. F. Kennett; P. Kingman; P. Newman; S. R. Chambers; T. Spencer; F. Conn; K. H. Hyatt; W. Mayes; Mrs D. Marr; S. Williams; R. J. Brooks; A. E. Wright; P. Grundy; L. Pilkington; J. E. Williams; E. F. Cheesman; G. S. Leslie; A. Thomas; L. Tedder; S. Burdett; E. Day OBE; J. Hubbard OBE; N. Forder; Sqn Ldr I. Blair DFM; Mrs D. H. Clarke; K. J. Clarke; P. G. Listeman; Australian War Memorial; J. F. Garlinge; Mrs C. Grandi and the Malloch family; Veterans Memorial Military Museum, Canada; J. M. C. Manson; E. Edwards; Cross & Cockade; F. Baldwin; P. Sikora, Mrs F. Tuke; Fleet

Air Arm Officers' Association; 446th Bomb Group; 401st Bomb Group; 385th Bomb Group; 381st Bomb Group; P. Walton; P. D. Cornwell; *Air Mail Magazine* (RAF Benevolent Fund); Zorn Collection; I. MacLaclan; C. Shores; C.Thomas; D. G. Collyer; D. Minterne; and S. G. A Brook.

Introduction

Kent's North Downs were selected as the location for an airfield as early as 1915 by the Directorate of Works, and levelling the fields chosen was still in progress when the first aircraft arrived in June of that year. The Royal Naval Air Service was initially based at Detling until it moved to Manston in May 1916.

The airfield then remained unused until the Royal Flying Corps arrived in April 1917, when Bessonneau hangars were erected. Various units were based there until 31 October 1919. 143 Squadron was the first RFC unit, arriving on 8 February 1918, shortly before the RAF was formed in April 1918. Detling was again abandoned the following December, although during the following years there was some civilian aviation activity, including gliding.

However, it was not until the late 1930s that the airfield was selected to be part of an Expansion Scheme and rebuilt, with technical and domestic sites located near Binbury Manor. Detling's grass airfield was developed with a maximum landing run of 4,200 feet NE/SW and reopened on 14 September 1938 for 16 Group Coastal Command.

When the Second World War began, the airfield became home to 500 (County of Kent) Squadron RAuxAF in March 1939. In 1940, the year of Dunkirk and the Battle of Britain, many varied units, including some Fleet Air Arm squadrons, were based at Detling.

An extremely active airfield was developing, and Detling took on the role of an aircraft delivery park: machines were repaired and modified before being passed on to operational units and other squadrons.

Detling was targeted as a frontline airfield by the Germans, but in fact it was never a 'Battle of Britain' airfield. Nevertheless, it was attacked during this period and suffered much damage. Many servicemen and women were killed and injured, notably on 13 August 1940, or 'Eagle Day', when the Luftwaffe tried to destroy RAF airfields in the South East. Throughout the war, there were several dramatic events at the airfield, many tragic, and some involving returning bombers of the RAF and 8th USAAF.

Following the war, in 1945, grass airfields such as Detling became surplus to requirements and were reduced to Care and Maintenance. Bomb Disposal Flights and a Signals Wing later used the site. Units of the RAF Regiment and Gliding Schools, plus the Home Command Gliding School, remained there until 1955, when an Army Observation Post unit returning from Korea moved onto the airfield. In 1956, Detling was again reduced to Care and Maintenance.

However, the Kent Gliding Club, which was seeking a new home, used the airfield until 1956. It eventually found a permanent home at Challock, also on the North Downs, and not far from Detling. On 1 October 1959, the historic airfield was de-requisitioned; Kent County Council bought some of the land for the County Showground. The electronics company Pye established a wireless transmitter station and an airways navigation beacon was located on the site.

Today, the visitor can still see pillboxes and overgrown air-raid shelters; Bellman hangar is one of the buildings used for various events. I am pleased to say that there are two memorials at Detling. One is located on the County Showground; the other, more impressive, is by the Cock Inn in the village of Detling, where there are RAF war graves in the churchyard. All are reminders of the men and women who served at the now-silent Detling airfield.

'On Top of Detling Hill'

This poem appeared in the *Detling Bulletin*, which was published monthly at Detling from June 1939, and did much to boost the morale of servicemen and servicewomen in wartime.

Gods laughed when men made Detling, on top of Detling Hill,
A jewel on a jewelled mound.
The seasons work their will on canvas tent and mouldering wall
And every sea-born breeze brings misery to Detling men,
And droplets from the trees.

Huns laughed when we made Detling, on top of Detling Hill,
They said they'd send their Heinkels and drop their bombs at will
On canvas tent and mouldering wall
And every sea-born breeze would bring fresh waves of bombers
And force us to our knees.

We laughed when they said Detling, on top of Detling Hill,
We said the mist would hide us, the bombing would be nil
On canvas tent and mouldering wall, and every sea-born breeze,
Would bring fresh waves of dimness
As solid as Dutch cheese.

We're laughing on at Detling, on top of Detling Hill,
When the war is over, 'finds us laughing still'.
And canvas tent and mouldering wall will laugh at sea-born breeze,
While we the men at Detling, grope,
Searching midst the trees.

Detling airfield and surrounding area in 1945; the A249 borders the site. The site used in the First World War is seen in the lower part of the photograph, with the main RAF site at the top. Its Bellman hangar can be clearly seen.

CHAPTER 1

RNAS 1915–1916

The establishment of the airfield in 1915 – the Royal Naval Air Service – one of the earliest sound detector experiments takes place

The choice of a particular site for use by the RNAS and RFC for an airfield was often left to a group of officers. They were told roughly where the site was required, and when a suitable location was found the standard Training Depot Station layout was drawn on an Ordnance Survey map before a more detailed investigation was carried out. Sometimes sites were abandoned for various reasons, such as poor drainage.

Following the selection of Detling by the Directorate of Works in early 1915, it was not long before a detachment of American-built Curtis aircraft arrived. In fact, one of the first pilots to operate from the new site was Flt Lt A. F. Buck in Curtis 3393, which is recorded as being detached to Detling on 31 December 1915. It would appear from his logbook that he was test-flying this machine on 16 March 1916 and was not too impressed with the aircraft's performance:

> When going over the trees, it felt rather like riding on a large leaf in a gale force wind. The aileron wires were slack – but the machine answers quickly when they do catch. The landing was poor and too slow.

Over the following two days, Flt Lt Buck test-flew Avro 504c (Scout) 8574 at an altitude of 2,000 feet. He recorded that the engine was not running well and that the control surfaces were stiff. Other aircraft he flew between Detling and Eastchurch were BE2c, serial no. 986, and BE2c 8295 for the RFC. At the beginning of May he flew in RE8- 8458 with Flt Lt H. Lee Wood on photo-reconnaissance flights.

It is likely that most people in Kent, particularly those of Romney Marsh, are familiar with the strange-looking concrete mirrors and dishes that have become part of the landscape. Visitors are always intrigued by these structures and Richard Scarth has written two books on the subject,

Acoustic Mirrors and *Kent's Listening Ears*. He also conducts guided tours on Denge Marsh for those who wish to see them at close quarters.

Scarth's books describe in great detail what these structures were devised for and how they were intended to form part of the Home Defence System. Suffice to say that as early as 1915, experiments were conducted with early-warning devices, in order to detect the approach of Zeppelins and (later) aircraft from France. Constructed along the east coast, they are a reminder of the efforts made to defend Britain from aerial attack. However, one of the smaller mirrors, its location not so well known, was situated close to Detling airfield near Binbury Manor. This concave, 16-foot-diameter sound mirror was cut into the chalk face under the direction of Professor Mather FRS of City & Guilds (Engineering) College in London. Trials with an aircraft took place, as described by an officer of the Royal Flying Corps on 15 July 1915:

> About the experiment at Binbury with concave mirror for detection of approaching aircraft – I sent an aeroplane over yesterday but it did not come within the radius of action of the mirror. I paid a visit to the place myself on Sunday, and I suggest that either I send a pilot and observer, with lamp or a lamp ground station for a fortnight or so to the naval aerodrome at Detling, or that the Navy carry out the experiments altogether. As you know I can little spare the pilot necessary but I am

A Nieuport 10, serial no. 3964, flown by Flt Lt R. J. Bone from Detling in 1916. It was one of the earliest aircraft to operate from the airfield.

sure that unless the experiments are carried out methodically, no useful data will be obtainable.

Experiments by Mather at Binbury led to the construction of a smaller type, mounted on a stand and capable of movement. These early experiments at Binbury and the larger discs and mirrors along the east coast undoubtedly led to the invention of radar, which arguably saved our skins in the Battle of Britain. This is certainly worth considering as part of the history of Detling.

In 1916, No. 3 (Naval) Wing RNAS was formed. It was to be the second formation of the wing, as the first had been disbanded in December 1915, following service in the Dardanelles under the leadership of Cdr C. R. Samson RN. The original purpose of the wing was to bomb targets in Germany in retaliation for the Zeppelin raids on England. Early in the war, the RNAS had already carried out a few raids against strategic targets in occupied Belgium.

Following several meetings between the Admiralty and the French, it was proposed that a new Allied squadron should be formed to attack German munitions factories. The French wanted the squadron's base to be located behind French lines and operated under French control. However, the RNAS was unable to provide pilots or aircraft for such an undertaking at the time, and so the plan was abandoned. Forced to act quickly as a

The airfield as it was on 10 August 1916 before larger hangars were erected. The arrow is pointing in the direction of Stockbury; the road is the A249. This area is visible on the aerial photograph taken in 1945 (see page 12).

result of the continued Zeppelin raids, the Admiralty reformed 3 Wing in February 1916. It was the first British air wing formed to carry out specific long-range strategic bombing.

A squadron of Sopwith 11/2 Strutters was formed and dispatched to the chosen site at Detling, which had been originally designated as a satellite airfield for RNAS Eastchurch. Under the command of Sqn Cdr Reggie Marix, the plan was to bomb the industrial area of Essen and Düsseldorf from Detling. The Sopwith aircraft had been fitted with extra fuel tanks and could remain airborne for seven hours, which did not offer much reserve for the hazardous return from the heart of the Ruhr. Again the idea was dropped, as the squadron needed to fly over neutral Holland – the shortest route – and the Admiralty was concerned this may have caused complications.

The newly formed squadron at Detling was therefore without employment, and the original French proposal was resurrected at the beginning of May 1916. A naval officer was sent to Paris to establish if the French still wanted to proceed with their scheme.

The officer sent was William L. Elder, who in 1915 had established the successful RNAS recruiting scheme in Canada. Much to the Admiralty's relief, Elder was welcomed by the French, who were still keen to adopt the idea. An official proposal was sent to the Admiralty for the RNAS to co-operate with the French. To enable the squadron to join forces with the

An RNAS Be2c, serial no. 8408, is being dragged out of the heavy snow, causing problems for pilots and groundcrew alike.

French, it was decided to move the newly formed wing to Manston using the small squadron as its nucleus.

On 7 February 1917, a BE2c that had been delivered to Detling from Eastchurch on 21 November 1916 ploughed into fields near Stockbury. The crew, Flt Sub-Lt A. F. Buck and Flt Sub-Lt R. H. Horniman, were uninjured, but the aircraft had to be repaired in the field and was subsequently sent to the War School at Manston on 31 March 1917. Curtis JN3, serial no. 3420 – flown by Flt Sub-Lt J. A. Harman and AC2 B. R. Carter on 31 August 1916 while on a routine flight – hit tree tops and crashed. Both men were injured and their aircraft was written off on 11 September 1916.

Lt L. H. Rochford DSC DFC was transferred from RNAS Eastchurch to Detling in 1917. His previous CO, Cdr E. H. Dunning, the first pilot to make a successful deck landing (on 2 August on HMS *Furious*), was killed two days later in a similar attempt. Flt Lt-Cdr A. F. Bettington, who had only been with the War Flight at Eastchurch for a short while, had replaced the unfortunate Dunning, and was also despatched to Detling:

I arrived at Detling about a week before Christmas having flown there in Bristol Scout – 8969. Lt Lockyer RNAS, who was not a pilot, commanded the aerodrome on the North Downs and about four miles from Maidstone. Besides myself, there were flight sub-lieutenants

Lt W. J. S. Lockyer RNAS seated the station's Lanchester car outside one of the newly constructed hangars at Detling in 1917. Note that 'RN Detling' has been painted onto the car's windscreen. In the hangar is a Sopwith 1½ Strutter. Lockyer, the CO at Detling, had a distinguished career in the RNAS.

The wreckage of Harman's Curtis JN3; the aircraft's number is just visible. Both pilot and passenger had a narrow escape. The aircraft was scrapped on 11 September 1916.

Horniman, Ireland, Elliot, Bennett and Thomas. We were equipped with Bristol Scouts and BE2cs, the former for attacking enemy aircraft by day, the latter for shooting down Zeppelins at night. During the morning of 23 December, Lockyer drove me into Maidstone in the official station motor car, a Lanchester with tiller steering.

We left Detling, on the downs, in brilliant sunshine but halfway down the hill we ran into dense fog, which we drove through all the way to Maidstone. There we did shopping and called at the Royal Star Hotel for a drink before returning to Detling, the fog gradually clearing on our way home. In the afternoon of the following day, my brother Raymond, a 2nd Lieutenant in the RFC, telephoned me to say that he, my sister Lucy and my brother Clem, an Army cadet, had motored down to Maidstone and were staying at the Royal Star Hotel. The following day they called for me at Detling and we had lunch at the hotel.

Afterwards we all returned to Detling and I took each of my brothers up for flights in a BE2c followed by tea in the wardroom before they returned to Maidstone.

On Christmas Day the wardroom looked very gay with the Christmas decorations. In the evening we had a dinner party at which our guests were three young ladies who were friends of Lockyer, Fred Murray, a local farmer who often visited the mess to have a drink with us, and Fred's

Flt Sub-Lt Harman poses nonchalantly against a telescope following a flying accident in a Curtis JN3, serial no. 3420. Both he and AC2 B. R. Carter were injured when they hit treetops and nose-dived into a field near Detling on 31 August 1916.

Pilots of 3 Squadron RNAS at Detling in 1916. The aircraft behind them is a Sopwith 1 1/2 Strutter.

wife Ida. After a very nice meal with plenty of drink we played some party games. The favourite was a high-kicking competition in which a ball was suspended from the central electric light fitting and which each competitor had to try to kick. Those who failed were eliminated and the ball was raised higher. Eventually Ida Murray was the highest kicker and winner. She was a very tall girl.

On Boxing Day I took up 100 hp Mono-Gnome engine Avro for half an hour and two days later I flew to Manston in a Bristol to visit friends whom I had known at Cranwell and Chingford. The weather deteriorated so I stayed at Manston and the following night. Eventually on 30 December I returned to base in a 50 mph gale. This was my last flight at Detling for on New Year's Day the Deputy Controller Air Services, Wg Cdr Smythe-Osbourne, visited us in the afternoon and told Bennett's [sic], Thomas, Elliot and myself that we were to proceed to RNAS Dover on 10 January for a short course before going to Dunkirk on active service. We were given seven days' leave during which we were to get our overseas kit and khaki uniforms.

Returning from Dunkirk in 1915, Flt Cdr Reginald John Bone CB CBE DSO was given command of a detachment of 3 Wing RNAS at Detling. At the time, German aircraft were making frequent daylight bombing attacks on east-coast towns. These attacks killed many civilians (with no loss to the enemy) as there was no way of detecting the approach of the aircraft. They disappeared quickly out to sea before they could be intercepted.

Above: Detling covered in snow during the winter of 1917. The airfield later became infamous for its poor weather. In the background is one of the Bessonneau-type hangars and, to the left, wooden mess huts or workshops. The identity of the dog is unknown.

Right: An unusual visitor to Detling airfield in 1917 was this Short Bomber, serial no. 9315, powered by a Rolls-Royce engine. The aircraft was built at Eastchurch, Isle of Sheppey. It is interesting to note that this bomber had folding wings, an innovation at the time.

One memorable Sunday, Bone put some sandwiches and coffee into his Nieuport aircraft and set off for the RNAS base at Westgate. There he put his aircraft on the airfield in position for take-off, and settled down to eat his lunch. As he had expected, German aircraft arrived over the area at about midday and bombed Margate, killing civilians. He took off after one of the German aircraft and once at the same altitude the Nieuport had superior performance. After a long pursuit in the direction of Zeebrugge, he finally drew close and opened fire. In his own words in an official combat report dated 19 March 1916, Flt Cdr Bone recalled the event:

I left Westgate with the enemy machine in sight to Northward of aerodrome at 2.12 p.m. and made no attempt to climb my machine (Nieuport 3964) steep but concentrated attention on keeping German machine in sight. The German machine, after proceeding about 15 miles North East came round to East South East and steadied on that course. After pursuing for sometime the superior climb of my machine enabled me to attain a position at 9,000 feet, 2,000 feet above the enemy. From this position by flying level, or slightly nose down I rapidly overhauled and finally intercepted the enemy. I first endeavoured to make a vertical dive on to him, but was alarmed at the speed necessary to keep the sights on. As I closed him, firing bursts, he opened fire vigorously and fired a white light.

Abandoning this attack I manoeuvred to get ahead of him and on his level and, having succeeded, I steered straight at him, diving so as to pass below him. I turned with a vertical right hand bank almost immediately under him. He turned away a little to his left just before we met and my turn occurred just under his right wing. He did not open fire and the Observer was visible hanging over the right hand side of the fuselage, apparently dead or severely wounded. The gun was cocked up at 45 degrees to the vertical. My position for tail attack happened to be ideal and, in spite of throttling down, my speed carried me up to within 15 to 20 feet of the enemy machine. I fired the gun so as to train it upwards, and had no difficulty in keeping my sights on, firing 4 or 5 bursts of about 6 rounds into him; he dived steeply with smoke pouring out of his engine. I had to avoid him.

The enemy machine was, however, under control and fired a red Very light before landing on the sea. The propeller stopped vertical shortly after the machine dived and I am sure the engine was no further use on account of this and smoke that poured out. At the same time as the machine was landing another German machine, which I had not seen before, landed beside it. That I had not seen it I attribute to the fact that my attention had been concentrated entirely on the machine I was fighting. The first was

Football was very popular with servicemen. Here, the RNAS team pose with their coaches for a photograph outside one of the mess huts in 1916. The leather football could get extremely heavy when wet and muddy – conditions pilots and groundcrew would have to get used to at Detling airfield.

over at 2.50 p.m. and I was powerless to do anything to them on the water. I returned to get Seaplanes sent out to bomb them.

I endeavoured to signal to a destroyer flotilla proceeding southerly just south of the Kentish Knock light vessel but failed to make them understand. I landed at 3.30 p.m. at Westgate and Seaplanes were dispatched. The reason I didn't wait over the seaplanes on the sea was that my engine was not giving full power and was cutting out occasionally. This was due to the spring contact of the high tension lead having become disconnected. Contact was maintained due to the parts being held in place by wiring – a precautionary measure. The cause of the cutting out was not discovered until Petty Officer Marden went over the machine at Eastchurch.

It was for this brave action that Flt Cdr Bone received the DSO; the appointment was announced in the *London Gazette* in April 1916.

After recovering from a hernia operation, Ivan de Burgh Daly joined the RNAS in August 1915. Following a navigational training course at Portsmouth, he commenced instruction at the Naval Flying School at Eastchurch. On the second day he made his first solo flight, qualifying for the Aeronaut's Certificate of the Royal Flying Club of the United Kingdom in his second week. In his fifth week he passed into 4 Squadron, and remained at Eastchurch for advanced training as a fighter pilot. An interesting passage in his log book reads as follows:

> Solo: got into cloud – got to 1,100 feet – stalled, dropped 3,000 feet; had great difficulty in bringing the machine up again – lost for some time and eventually picked up south coast of Essex at 5,000 feet: managed to get back to Sheppey at 11.11 a.m.

On another occasion:

> Engine failed, petrol supply – landed at Eastwell near Ashford, uphill very bumpy landing. Found the throttle had stuck at shut position as spring was not strong enough. Got off with the engine misfiring and choking I came down on the aerodrome after missing 40 feet of ground; cleared sheds by 10 feet.

In a letter to his parents he wrote:

> I went for a cross country journey in a Bleriot – the idea being to fly Canterbury across Ashford and on to Detling, later returning to Eastchurch, making a circuit of it – but again engine trouble made me do a forced landing at Eastwell Park where Lady Northcote is. She gave me lunch the Dowager Lady Jersey was there so it was quite good fun.

A 'one pipe' job. Two RNAS officers are extracting an incendiary core from a site near the airfield. It may have been dropped by one of them during an exercise. Hopefully they both knew what they were doing.

Eventually got off to try and land at Detling near Maidstone but it was so foggy that I lost my way, and after flying around for 1½ hours, I managed to find Gravesend and land there. I flew over the main magazine at Chatham at a height of 500 feet as they could open fire at you if you were too high. The Admiralty heard of my flight and phoned Eastchurch before I arrived; they were quite keen to know my path in case I was a German aircraft.

On a similar occasion, just getting dusk, I managed to get over the trees downwind and picked up Maidstone lights by which time it was quite dark and ground invisible at 2,000 feet. Climbed to 3,000 feet and one torch gave out – held the other over the compass and steered about 5 points north of west. Picked up Detling where they had struck out flares – went on and eventually saw the sea and guessed it was Herne Bay – came West to the aerodrome – saw flares put out and made a fair landing a little short of flare my first night flying.

Daly was later responsible for inventing the cross-wire lights. In his own album there is a photograph with the caption, 'Bristol fitted with 110 Le Rhône engine and Daly Cowl, Eastchurch 1915.'

On 26 May 1916, Flt Sub-Lt Douglas Alexander Hardy Nelles RNAS struck a hedge and crashed into a field near to Redcar airfield while the pilot was attempting a forced landing after the aircraft's engine had failed and could not be restarted. The pilot attempted a gliding approach to Redcar, but struck the hedge. The aircraft, bought from Caudron at Le Crotoy, was on its delivery flight from Detling and was delivered to the Central Supply Depot at Wormwood Scrubs in June 1915. It was then dispatched to RNAS Chingford for erection, testing and acceptance on 19 June 1915. It suffered a major accident at Hendon on 3 July 1915 when it collided with a fence (the pilot being Flt Sub-Lt B. Travers RNAS).

Later that day it was dismantled; it returned to Chingford the next day. It was re-erected, tested and finally accepted on 24 September 1915. It was later transferred to RNAS Dover on 10 February 1916, and on 18 March it was slightly damaged in a forced landing (the pilot was Flt Sub-Lt I. N. C. Clarke RNAS). Following repair, it was sent to Detling and soon after to Redcar on 23 May 1916. It reached Cranwell by 24 May and arrived in Redcar on 26 May 1916. The aircraft was deleted on 15 July 1916, although certain records do not mention that this was due to a flying accident. By the end of May that year, Detling was reduced to Care and Maintenance. 3 Wing RNAS was moved to Manston.

CHAPTER 2

RFC 1917–1919

The Royal Flying Corps moves to Detling – operations undertaken – the airfield placed in Care and Maintenance

On the night of 19/20 October 1917, eleven Zeppelins passed over the Channel to attack targets in England – the first occasion on which Detling was targeted. Winds were minimal over England and the North Sea at ground level, but north-westerly winds prevailed at around 10,000 feet, and above that height the wind suddenly increased to some 40 mph and progressively climbed, so that at 20,000 feet, the only safe height for these airships, it was blowing a gale from the north and north-west. It seems the airships made landfall at various places – the Humber, Lincolnshire, the Wash and the northern coast of Norfolk. Many were forced to the South East. Zeppelin L54 went directly home over the North Sea. Three returned along the Dutch coast or across Holland. Three flew over the north of France and crossed Allied lines between Ypres and Luneville.

The remaining four – L44, L45, L49 and L50 – seem to have been driven further southwards while trying to head east. Commanded by Kapitänleutnant F. Stabbert, L44 entered the Wash at around 7.30 p.m., rounded Boston, and followed the Great Northern Railway to Bedford. It dropped bombs between Elstow and Kempston, then went west to Wolverton, where it turned south-east. L44 then dropped ten bombs near Leighton Buzzard, and passed over Luton to Maidstone. It is believed that Stabbert was attracted to Detling by flares on the airfield. Zeppelin L44 later went out to sea between Folkestone and Dover at 11.30 p.m. Twenty minutes later it was at Boulogne, travelling south-east. At 1.15 a.m. it was at Montdidier, and it continued over Reims, Bar le Duc and Lunéville. Near Vathimenil at 11,000 feet, L44 was shot at by AA guns and tried to rise but was hit at 19,000 feet and caught fire immediately. It crashed at Chenevières, killing all of her crew.

Two of the night's bombs fell on Detling aerodrome. These caused no damage, but another, which cratered an adjacent field, caused a minor

This SE5A of 143 Squadron – seen here at Detling *c*. April 1918 – is C1805. It is believed that this was flown by 2Lt W. R. Oulton, who may be standing by the aircraft.

incident. Lt C. Ossenton of 143 Squadron put down in this field with an ailing engine that just failed to carry him to the flare path, and some uncanny magnetism drew his SE5a to the crater, where it nosed over and received fire damage when the Holt flares, used for night-flying, inadvertently ignited. Discussions about RNAS assistance of the Home Defence Wing escalated to the Home Forces' Admiralty level, and the eventual outcome was that the RFC, with twenty-four BE12s and BE12as, was made available for daylight patrols, and was considered able to deal with day-raiders over South East England, except in the immediate vicinity of Dover.

It was agreed that the RFC should maintain responsibility for the defence of Sheerness and Chatham, and it took over the RNAS airfield at Detling from 3 April 1917. RNAS Manston was nominated to patrol between Herne Bay and Deal, while the RNAS at Grain covered the Sheerness–Foulness line. The RNAS had discretion to mount 'ad hoc' night defence sorties. In December 1917, the raising of two additional fighter squadrons to augment the London Air Defence Area was sanctioned. These squadrons were to be 141, formed from a cadre of 61 Squadron, and 143 Squadron RFC, comprising a cadre drawn from 112 Squadron. 143 Squadron RFC was actually formed at Throwley on 1 February 1918.

Initial equipment was the Armstrong Whitworth FK8, which may have seemed an unlikely choice as an air-defence fighter, although the type had been used in this role in small numbers since 1916, albeit against Zeppelins.

It seems that the FK8 was a stopgap measure, as the original intention had been to equip 143 Squadron with Sopwith Dolphins. 141 Squadron did receive a few Dolphins, but the report submitted by 141's commanding officer, Maj. P. Babington, on 17 March 1918 made it quite clear that the Dolphin was not suitable for night-flying.

The first FK8 arrived in February; the squadron moved to Detling on 14 February. On the same day, Maj. F. Sowrey DSO MC, the famous 'Zepp-Killer', was posted in as commanding officer. There 143 joined 50 and 112 Squadrons as part of 53 Wing, which had been officially formed on 8 February. No. 53 Wing was part of 6 Brigade. The headquarters for 53 Wing was at Harrietsham in Kent. The squadron was operational on the night of 16/17 February, when five German Giants raided Britain, although only four actually bombed. FK8 B3316, piloted by Capt. Cyril J. Truran with Lt T. E. Garside as gunner, took off and returned shortly after an uneventful patrol. Truran reported that he had seen 'Brock flares lit near Dover – quite useless'. Lt F. V. Bryant and 2Lt V. H. Newton took off in FK8 B223 and landed at midnight after a similarly fruitless patrol.

The following night, another Giant attempted to bomb London and this time 143 Squadron put up four patrol aircraft. These were: B223, again crewed by Bryant and Newton; B3316, crewed by Truran and Garside; B224, crewed by 2Lt W. R. Oulton and Lt J. Tennant; B220, crewed by 2Lt N. F. Perris and 2Lt R. C. Cowl. No interceptions were made. The last operational sortie with the FK8s was another raid against London by six Giants, five of which reached the target. It is interesting that only the pilots' names were recorded for this sortie, perhaps suggesting that the FK8s were flown as single-seaters in an attempt to improve performance. Lt Ossenton took off in B4017, 2Lt W. R. Oulton in B224. 2Lt F. V. Bryant joined them in B3316, but once again no interceptions were made.

In March 1918, re-equipment with Wolesley Viper SE5a scouts began. These were in normal night-fighter finish, with the white parts of the national colours of the roundels and rudder stripes over-marked with 'PC10'. Flight markings consisted of coloured bands, outlined in white, aft of the fuselage cockades. Both red and blue stripes are known, but it is unclear which flight these denoted. Aircraft numbers, in the form of a white numeral, were superimposed on the fuselage banding. Wheel disc covers were decorated with French-style cockades.

The first known operational patrol by 143 Squadron SE5a scouts was on the night of 19/20 May 1918, against raiding bombers. Thirty-eight Gothas took off, of which twenty-eight reached the target area, together with three Giants. Four aircraft of 143 Squadron took off just after 11.00 p. m. The first of these was Capt. J. Potter in C1879, who returned forty minutes later, followed by 2Lt N. F. Perris in C1809, Capt. C. J. Truran

143 (Home Defence) Squadron was the first RFC unit based at the airfield. William Harbrow Ltd, a company based in St Mary Gray, was contracted to supply and erect various buildings at Detling, including hangars. The company provided such buildings on many Kent airfields such as Bekesbourne, and earlier for the Royal Aeroclub at Shellbeach and for Eastchurch on the Isle of Sheppey.

flying C1803, and Lt W. R. Oulton in C1805. No interceptions were made. The first to land was Truran, who was forced to return because of engine trouble. Oulton and Perris returned safely without incident.

Meanwhile, the commanding officer, Maj. F. Sowrey, had taken off in B1804 at 11.30 p.m. Sowrey saw a Gotha north-east of Maidstone at 11.45 p.m. and closed in on it. Positioning B1804 underneath the Gotha, Sowrey emptied an entire drum of ammunition from his top wing-mounted Lewis gun. Seemingly, this had no effect on the Gotha, which failed to retaliate. Unfortunately, as Sowrey attempted to change the drum he dropped the empty drum into the cockpit. Fearing that the drum might foul the controls, Sowrey broke off the action as he sought to retrieve it.

Sowrey encountered another Gotha in approximately the same place, but this time as he was heading home after bombing. Again he chose to attack from underneath, and this time he got off two drums from his Lewis gun. The Gotha fired back this time, with the rear gunner making full use of the 'tunnel' cutaway in the lower fuselage of the German bomber. The bullets passed over the fin of the SE5, but, as Sowrey tried to fire again, possibly with the fuselage-mounted Vickers gun, he stalled his aircraft, which fell away in a spin. He recovered from this, but he failed to relocate the target.

Pilots and trainees of 50 Squadron pose for the camera after inspecting an aircraft that nose-dived on the airfield at Detling during 1917. The pilot's fate is unknown, but as fellow airmen appear cheerful, he may have survived with minor injuries.

As a Gotha crashed near Frinsted landing ground in the early morning, 6th Brigade initially credited this to Sowrey. However, it seems that the same Gotha (GV 979/16) was engaged a second time by a 141 Squadron Bristol F2b fighter over South Ash. The front gunner, Uttz Hermann Tasche, survived the crash and confirmed that the Gotha had been attacked twice. Credit was then awarded to the 141 Squadron crew. It seems that Sowrey may well have wounded the pilot, Vizefeldwebel Albrecht Sachtler, and that 53 Wing HQ was not prepared to share the claim between the two squadrons.

A further four 143 Squadron aircraft were in the air that night, all of which took off after midnight. These were: Lt D. d'A. Northwood, in C1118; Lt Jones, in C1802; Lt C. Ossenton, in C1873; Lt W. C. M. Harbottle, in C1808. Harbottle landed first, followed by Ossenton, who managed to taxi into a crater caused by one of two German bombs that had landed on Detling. C1873 nosed over, and was further damaged by fire when the Holt flares ignited. Northwood and Jones landed together. According to the 53 Wing summary of the response to the raid of 19/20 May 1918, a number of the aircraft operated by 143 Squadron had been fitted with R/T receivers. If this was indeed the case, they seem to have been of no real practical assistance during the raid.

So far, 143 Squadron had escaped any fatalities as a result of the dangers of flying at night. This changed on 20 April 1918 when Lt N. F. Perris, in C1809, collided in mid-air with SE5a C1831, flown by 2Lt T. Wright. Both

A four-bladed Bristol Fighter F2b was used for night-fighting at Detling. To its left stands an SE5A, possibly of 143 Squadron.

pilots were killed. Noel Felix Perris had been commissioned in the 2nd Battalion of the London Regiment, a Territorial Force battalion. He was aged twenty-four, and was the son of Mary Annie Perris, of Wellington House, Eton Road, Hampstead, and the late George Herbert Perris. Perris was buried in St Martin's churchyard at Detling. Thomas Wright was the twenty-year-old son of William Thomas and Grace Wright, of North Church Street, Fleetwood. His body was returned to Fleetwood for burial in the borough cemetery.

A third 143 Squadron pilot was to be fatally injured while flying at night. This was 2Lt David Wilson, who was on an anti-Gotha patrol in SE5a C1799, which stalled on a turn and spun in on 20 July 1918. He died of his injuries the following day. Wilson was then aged twenty, and was the son of Duncan and Christina Wilson of Tenino, Bishopbriggs, Glasgow. He had been commissioned in the 5th (Territorial) Battalion of the Prince of Wales' Volunteers (South Lancashire Regiment) before being attached to the RAF. Wilson's body was returned to Scotland and buried at Calder in Lanarkshire.

In July 1918, information from a prisoner indicated that a new Gotha was being developed that would be capable of operating in formation at 15,800 feet, with the possibility of single aircraft flying at up to 25,000 feet. At such altitudes, the air-cooled rotary engines of the Sopwith Camels were thought to be effective, but not the water-cooled engines of the SE5a scouts. The need to re-equip had already been recognised, however, and a decision had been made to replace the SE5as in 50, 61 and 143 Squadrons with Camels. There is evidence that 143 Squadron began to receive Camels as early as June 1918, but the majority of aircraft operated were still in SE5as in August. That month, Sopwith F1 Camel F2175 arrived. From June 1919, Sopwith 7F1 Snipes began to arrive to augment the Camels, the former including E6843. These aircraft continued to be operated by the squadron until its disbandment on 31 October 1919.

Two other ranks died while serving in 143 Squadron. AM1 Maurice Lea Newman, aged twenty-three, died on 7 November 1918 of influenza. He was the son of Benjamin and Mary Newman, of Walsall, Staffordshire, and is buried at Maidstone. AM1 Harold Weston died on 1 November 1918 and is buried at Detling. It is assumed that Weston died of natural causes, possibly influenza.

143 Squadron RFC was formed from a nucleus drawn from 112 Squadron at Throwley on 1 February 1918. Initial equipment was the Armstrong Whitworth FK8, although it is unclear whether this constituted full equipment or a stopgap for training purposes. The squadron moved to Detling on 14 February 1918, and began receiving SE5a fighters in March. 143 Squadron then formed part of 53 Wing in 6th Brigade.

The SE5a was retained until June or August (sources differ); but by August, Camels had arrived. From June 1919, Snipes supplemented the Camels, and both types were on charge when the squadron disbanded in October 1919. Maj. F. Sowrey DSO MC commanded 143 Squadron from 14 March 1918 until the Armistice.

When the war came in 1914, Stanley Burdett was an apprentice at a garage and engineering works in Northampton where his father was the manager. He very quickly gained skills working on a lathe, turning shell cases. Although he was exempt from military service, he was keen to join the RFC, as many of his friends had already enlisted. Following his application and medical, he was at last recruited. He found himself sent to Farnborough. Dressed in his best blue suit, he was soon issued with a service number and essential equipment such as a knife, fork and a spoon. He was also issued with an RFC overcoat for which he was very grateful, as the weather was cold at the time. He and his fellow recruits were billeted in tents close to the camp. It was not long before his smart blue suit was soiled by potato peel – on top of which, he lost his new overcoat.

Following basic training, Burdett was posted as far afield as Halifax, and on return to England he was posted to No. 11 Training Squadron RFC at Spittlegate, Scampton and North Weald. It was not long before he was transferred to 143 Squadron at Detling. By 1918, the squadron was still operational and carrying out patrols. It was equipped with Sopwith

A War Office Class 'A' Type 5000 Mobile Workshop manufactured by Leyland. It is similar to that used by fitters/mechanics of the RFC at Detling airfield in 1917–19. The cross-shaped container fitted to the side of the vehicle was used to store a four-laded propeller. The vehicle contained work benches, drills and other engineering equipment required for its purpose.

Snipes, but by the time Burdett joined 143 Squadron, the war was almost over. He was pleased that he was a fitter and not an armourer, as he had been at previous postings. He was put in charge of a mobile workshop, which was equipped with blacksmith's forge and essential tools, and an AC2 was assigned to assist him. The pair soon found themselves making and repairing aircraft parts and fittings:

> Detling could be a bleak place, situated on a hill just outside Maidstone, very high, and on a clear day one could see right over to Sheerness. At the time the fruit trees were in bloom and later, full of fruit. Everyone was friendly, and the huts were similar to those at Scampton – even to the earwigs. Yet even here, the 'run down' was beginning to show, for when things were easy, we began to be sent to other dromes in the area to remove and pack machinery and equipment from their workshops, and it seemed that many of these units were closing down, at least for the time being.
>
> It seemed that there had also been a Concert Party at Detling, for we came across odd costumes and programmes referring to the 'Very Lights' and an effort was made to revive the party. We did give one performance, but the summer weather was not conducive to indoor entertainment,

and the general malaise seemed to persist. I think this is reflected in a parody that I wrote for the one show.

> It's the same old RFC though we're now in 143,
> It's the same old Detling, where I'm settling.
> Down for 'Four and Four'
> And when I'm on leave, I just pine and grieve,
> Lord how I sigh,
> Just to get back here. I can't think why.
> We've got the neatest, smartest Squadron here 'n' everything,
> We've got a distant view of Sheerness Pier, 'n' everything,
> We've no YMCA, the Canteen's closed all day,
> For hours and hours, we tend the flowers,
> Cut the lawns 'n' everything.
> We've got a brand new cut of tunic now 'n' everything,
> And a lovely bright RAF badge to show, 'n' everything,
> But when I've done my 'Four and Four',
> I'll serve no more,
> I've done with war and strife; I've done with Army life
> 'N' everything.

Then I went solo on the Avro for a good many hours and I still have a mental air picture of the county of Kent. Twice I landed at Bekesbourne, not easy because there was a deep railway cutting at the side of the airfield. It was pleasant enough at Detling, but all the time there was a little less work being done, and a little more 'Bull' creeping in. With the reversion to Peacetime routine, stones were being white-washed around the Camp roads, white lines painted where the planes stood, and Riggers spent hours shinning up the flying wires with emery cloth, it was so futile.

Maidstone itself provided a welcome release. One could walk among the hop fields and fruit trees of Kent, or on Sunday one could row down the river, to find pretty little back-waters, and sometimes, unexpectedly, a family of Hop Pickers from London, bathing in the nude: 'It's alright ducky, we're all married.' All at once, everyone seemed carefree. And so it went on, until November, when once again, some of us were moved on, all on the spur of the moment it seemed, so quickly in fact, that I went away without handing back my Mobile Workshop, out at last, but not quite. When we turned up in the morning, we found that, through some error in the Orderly Room, the whole thing had been cancelled. It was not until 23 March 1919 that it was finally confirmed, and I was discharged with many others as 'surplus to requirements'.

Sgt R. A. Brooks RFC was transferred from Newmarket in 1918 to Throwley airfield near Faversham to continue his pilot's instruction:

In addition to our training squadron under a Maj. Cook there was a Service Squadron of Sopwith Camels [112 Squadron] on Night Flying in Defence of London against Air Raids. Here I started with an Instructor and dual control again but this time on the Avro 504, fitted with 110 hp Le Rhône engine – liable to cause a nasty bump.

Here was another squadron of Night Flying Camels, belonging to the same wing as the squadrons at Throwley and Detling. After that I went onto Camels, a single-seat plane demanding great concentration. The next thing was night-flying to be started on Avros and graduating onto Camels at night. To maintain position on moonlight nights one could see the Thames but otherwise you were dependent on the light shining upwards and sending periodically in Morse code, 'B' for Bekesbourne, 'T' for Throwley and 'D' for Detling from the three aerodromes in the wing. Take-off and landing had to be done in the beam of light from two searchlights, no runway of course, just a fairly level field.

In midsummer I got my wings, as did my roommate Eric Bennett of the Gordon Highlanders. We were both then posted to 143 Squadron RAF stationed at RAF Detling on the North Downs and about 3 miles from Maidstone. In command was Maj. Fred Sowrey DSC DFC AFC, a younger brother of Maj. Bill Sowrey who was at Newmarket. The Camels we flew at 143 Squadron were fitted with 110 hp Rotary engines, the same as both the Avros and Camels at Throwley. These were also Le Rhônes, although some Camels had 130 hp Clerget engines and just a few had a 150 hp Bentleys. We continued regular flying, both by day and night, and also went on to formation flying and later firing our two Vickers machine guns at a ground targets.

We had no formal Church parade, but a number of us went to morning service at 11.00 a.m., in Detling village church. The elderly vicar read Matins, preached the sermon and played the organ, and his daughters were the sidemen.

In the autumn I was sent for a course in Wireless Telephony to Penshurst, Kent. After the apparatus had been explained to us they arranged us in pairs to take up a DH6 plane with dual control, one man to be pilot and the other to operate the wireless. My partner was Canadian but we had both flown DH6s and thought we should be alright. He acted as pilot first and did a circle whilst I prepared the wireless and had a satisfactory talk with ground operator. Then I was told that I should fly the plane and get the other man talking. I managed to make him understand; he let go of the joystick and rudder bar and

On 20 July 1918, a mid-air collision over Detling cost two young pilots their lives. SE5a C1802 was flown by 2Lt N. F. Perris, and SE5a C1831 was flown by 2Lt C. T. Wright. Both pilots and aircraft were of 143 Squadron. Perris was buried at Detling cemetery. The unusual camouflage pattern of the SE5a indicates that this aircraft once served with 61 Squadron.

Flying in open-cockpit aircraft of the First World War could be cold, and this pilot appears to be prepared in his warm flying coat. He is seated in a BE12 of 50 Squadron.

I attempted to take over but immediately I did so I realised the dual controls had not been connected by the ground staff.

My partner could not hear my warning for the noise of the engine and we were already in a steep dive, so he took over and just managed to zoom over a massive oak tree. I wound up what was left of the trailing aerial but on landing we found that the lead weight had been caught up in the tree. For a change my Canadian and I walked to Penshurst Place, and knocked on the door to be told by the housekeeper that the house was not open to the public. During the war, however, she let us in and showed us the Great Hall and other items of interest. Back at Detling we soon had a telephony set, so we all had turns tuning in to a man at Biggin Hill reading Dickens.

In October 1918 there was widespread illness throughout the country due to the epidemic of so-called Spanish Influenza. One of our pilots died and we understood that he was to be buried at Chingford, near to his parents' home. Another victim of the epidemic was Lt W. Leefe Robinson who had been the first pilot to shoot down a German airship over England on the night of 2/3 September 1916; I think it was a Schutte-Lanz (SL11). He was a friend of our CO, Maj. Fred Sowrey, who brought down a Zeppelin on 23 September 1916 – either a Billericay, Essex or L33 – at Wigborough, Essex, and both Zeppelins brought down the same night. Leefe Robinson was awarded the VC and Fred Sowrey the DSC.

About 9 November Maj. Sowrey had a talk with Bennett and me saying he had just returned from the Robinson funeral and that he had agreed to go to the funeral of our own pilot, Lt J. E. Child, on 12 November 1918. He felt he could not face another funeral so soon and asked us to go together to represent the squadron in his place. We agreed and made an early start and went to the child home in Chingford. Mr and Mrs Child welcomed us and were very composed in the face of the great loss they had suffered. Their other son had also been a pilot in the RFC, but on leave had been killed in a motorcar accident. RAF transport took us all to the cemetery where Eric Bennett and I acted as bearers of the coffin together with four of the RAF officers. The burial was thirteen days after death and at the cemetery there were several large stacks of coffins waiting for graves to be dug.

It was the day after the Armistice, which was signed on 11 November 1918, Maj. Sowrey had told us that as we had to make a very early start we could stay overnight in London. In the evening we went along to the Mall to join the huge crowd at Buckingham Palace and there we saw King George V, Queen Mary and family come out onto the balcony. Then on to Trafalgar Square packed with people and a large bonfire with a London cab blazing away. Bennett was a member of the Royal Automobile Club and they gave us camp beds in a corridor for the night. After the Armistice we continued flying but on a reduced scale. We could go into Maidstone occasionally to visit the cinema or have an excellent dinner at the Star Hotel for about three shillings. On Boxing Day a few of us went beagling at the invitation of Capt. Cornwallis, Grenadier Guards – later to become Lord Cornwallis.

At the end of January 1918 we heard that our Sopwith Camels were to be replaced with Sopwith Snipes, a single-seater, larger and more powerful. Our Camels were to be allocated to a squadron at Elmswell, near Thetford, Norfolk. I was ordered to take a Camel there and hand it over. On the way, passing over the Orwell, I had a good view of the dozens of surrendered German submarines. It was a clear day and I was glad to make a landing. Back at Detling by train and then orders to take another Camel to Elmswell. On the appointed morning there was a moderate mist, but it was thought likely to clear so I took off hopefully.

Over the Thames Estuary the fog was dense, with no land in sight. I groped about with little help from the compass, which was spinning around. Then I saw land and recognised Herne Bay, so I was back on the South Bank. I decided to turn west and continued until I could see both banks of the Thames. Crossing the river and turning east, the fog persisted so I landed at Rochford Aerodrome near South-on-Sea. They telephoned my position both to Detling and Elmswell, also kindly gave me lunch. By mid-afternoon the fog cleared so I started off again and handed over my second Camel at Elmswell. They took me to Thetford and I set off by train for Detling.

A while later in February, although I had been in normal health throughout my year of flying, I suddenly had acute abdominal pain one evening. We were not a large enough unit to have our own doctor and the Area Medical Officer was already out on an emergency case at Linton, six miles on the other side of Maidstone. Throughout the night I was very ill, but Eric Bennett looked after me and the doctor arrived at 3.00 p.m. the following day. He at once sent me in our own squadron ambulance, a bouncing Ford Model T, on the 11 mile journey to Fort Pitt Military Hospital at Chatham.

There, within an hour or two, I had my appendix removed together with a large abscess. The man in the next bed offered to bring me a book from the library and suggested *Pickwick Paper* [*sic*]. After a month I was sent to Osborne House on the Isle of Wight, which had been given to the services in 1904 by Edward VII to be used as a hospital. I eventually returned home to my parents at Harrogate. Of the three

Front row centre is Captain J. S. Shaw, 50 Squadron 'C' Flight commander. The other pilots, apart from 2Lt L. Lucas (seated right), cannot be identified. Note the varied style of uniforms. The aircraft in the background is a BE2c.

close friends I enlisted with in 1914, two had been killed on the Somme in July 1916.

The origins of 50 Squadron can be traced to the outbreak of the First World War, prior to the formation of the Royal Air Force. The squadron was formed from the nucleus of 20 Reserve Squadron on 15 May 1916 at Swingate Down and was designated 50 Squadron, Royal Flying Corps. At that time it was one of only twenty-five or so squadrons in existence within the Royal Flying Corps. It was classified as a Home Defence Unit and initially equipped with the Royal Aircraft Factory's single-engine, two-seat biplane fighters: the BE2c and BE12. The squadron, like all others of this time period, fell under the control of the British Army.

By June 1916, the squadron began the first of what was to become a common occurrence throughout its history – the conversion from one aircraft type to another. In this case the BE2cs and BE12s were exchanged for Vickers ES1s. Designed under the direction of Harold Barnwell, this single-engine, single-seat biplane was considered a tractor scout aircraft and was nicknamed 'The Barnwell Bullet'. With a top speed of only 114 mph at 5,000 feet, the aircraft was only a slight improvement on the (roughly) 100 mph at 3,100 feet of the BE2cs and BE12s. With the conversion period complete, the squadron appears to have settled into a regular routine of training and operational sorties.

By October, the squadron was uprooted from its base at Swingate Down and relocated to Harrietsham. However, flying detachments were soon dispatched to Detling, Bekesbourne and Throwley – all in the county of Kent. It is unclear precisely how long these detachments were away from Harrietsham, or for that matter if they occurred at the same time or individually. Christmas 1916 appears to have come early, as new Royal Aircraft Factory single-engine, two-seat BE12a and BE2a biplanes began to arrive in December. Once again, the squadron converted to a new aircraft type. However, with both types proving to be a disappointment, a mere three months were to pass before the entire conversion process was again undertaken.

By March 1917, orders to begin conversion to the single-engine, single-seat Bristol M1b monoplane fighter had arrived. With the coming of May, less than two months after conversion to the Bristol M1b, new orders were once again received to convert to two new types of aircraft, the Armstrong Whitworth FK8 and the Royal Aircraft Factory RE8. Both types were single-engined, two-seat biplanes designed for reconnaissance and bombing duties.

Following the detachment of 50 Squadron's 'C' Flight to Detling, it was not long before they were involved in operations against the German Navy Zeppelins targeting London. On the night of 23/24 May 1917, aircraft from RNAS bases at Felixstowe, Killingholme, Manston, Westgate, Yarmouth, Burgh Castle, Covehithe and Holt, together with various aircraft of 37, 39 and 51 squadrons, plus 'A' Flight 50 Squadron, Bekesbourne, and 'B' Flight 50 Squadron, Throwley, took off to locate the incoming raiders.

Due to the poor weather conditions, 2Lt C. C. White, flying a BE12 (6183), returned to Detling at 2.50 a.m., having taken off only twenty minutes earlier. On this occasion, both fighters and Zeppelins were hindered by the weather, and the German force suffered no losses. This unsuccessful raid was quickly followed by a daylight attack on Folkestone by a force of twenty-three twin-engine Gotha biplanes on 25 May 1917. Later, 2Lt. C. C. White took off at 5.38 p.m., but returned to Detling, as did 2Lt W. R. Oulton. Neither pilot saw the enemy.

This combined RNAS–RFC operation involved no fewer than seventy-seven sorties. The Germans admitted one loss, when two airships had in fact been destroyed. One was shot down into the sea, the other on land. Oulton and White joined forces again on 5 June to attack twenty-two Gotha bombers, but they returned to Detling disappointed.

On 13 June, flying BE2c 2711, 2Lt W. R. Oulton, during another Gotha raid, was forced to land at Kingsnorth airship base due to engine problems. The first victory of 50 Squadron was claimed by second lieutenants F. A. D. Grace and G. Murray in their Armstrong Whitworth FK8 B247. They shot down a Gotha during a daylight raid on 7 July. They were on detachment with 'B' Flight, Throwley. By 22 July 1917, the squadron's 'A' Flight had taken charge of five Sopwith Pup aircraft. It was these that soared into the air in the morning mist at 8.28 a.m. to track down a force of twenty-three Gothas en route to Harwich and Felixstowe. That day, 'A' Flight flew five sorties, only sighting the enemy. Aircraft of 'B' Flight were dispatched from Throwley to Detling in August 1917. The Sopwith Pup aircraft had been removed from 50 Squadron and were now flying Armstrong Whitworth FK8s. The Pups were flown from Detling to Throwley to form the new 112 Squadron.

On 12 August, 'B' Flight was searching for Gothas when 2Lt F. A. D. Grace in his FK8 B247 had to return to Detling with a loose cowling. During a daylight raid to Northern England by eight Navy Zeppelins on 22 August, Capt. C. J. Truran diverted south of his official patrol line from Detling and gave chase to the departing enemy aircraft, despite being 2 miles behind as they passed North Foreland. Firing a few bursts, he then began a long chase over the sea, eventually reaching the bombers' height of 15,000 feet, and in sight of the Belgian coast. 2Lt F. V. Bryant had kept pace with Truran in his B225, and he fired a long burst at the Gotha from 1,000 yards, but the bomber escaped. Another of the squadron's pilots, 2Lt L. Lucas, made history in his BE12 'Tracker' by transmitting the first air-to-ground wireless telegraph message. He had seen raiders close to Dover and signalled that nine hostile aircraft were flying north-east. He made the mistake, however, of miscounting the number of hostile machines, for the numbers had been reduced to eight.

No sooner had May turned into June than orders were received for the squadron to convert yet again, this time to Sopwith's single-engine, single-seat biplane fighter, the Sopwith Pup. With conversion to the Pup complete and with the return to regular flying, some stability appears to have been re-established. No further conversions or movements appear to have graced the squadron for the remainder of the year. January 1918 dawned and the squadron entered what was to be the final year of the war. Orders were once again received to convert to a new aircraft – the Pups were to be exchanged for the Royal Aircraft Factory's single-engine, two-seat BE12b biplane fighter.

On 5 March 1918, new orders again came through, this time ordering the squadron to relocate to Bekesbourne, Kent, an airfield at which the squadron had previously had a detachment of aircraft, in late 1916. With the move complete and the resumption of regular flying, May soon arrived and with it yet another set of orders to begin conversion to the Royal Aircraft Factory's single-engine, single-seat SE5a biplane fighter. As spring gave way to summer, it seemed only fitting that orders be received for the squadron to once again convert to a new aircraft type. In July, the SE5as were exchanged for Sopwith's single-engine, single-seat Camel F1 biplane fighter. Unknown to the squadron at this time was the fact that this, the eighth conversion in three years, was to be the last during the First World War. The Camels would continue in squadron service until 13 June 1919, when orders for the disbandment of 50 Squadron RFC were issued.

CHAPTER 3

1920–1940

Flying activities – early gliding – the British Aircraft Company – accidents and celebrities

An unusual event took place in 1923 when Shorts, based at Rochester, transported the Short Springbok Mk I biplane J6974 by road to the almost-abandoned airfield for flight tests. This, the second machine of its type, had been returned to Rochester on 23 May following the discovery of a defect in both aircraft. The trailing-edge skin was splitting due to the vibration of the slipstream. At Rochester, the aircraft's wings were converted from metal skin to doped-fabric covering. Once the work was completed, John Parker, test pilot, flew the Springbok from Detling on 13 September 1923. Parker flew the aircraft onto Martlesham Heath, Norfolk, for further flight tests.

On Sunday 23 February 1930, many people made their way to Detling airfield to witness the first flight of a glider constructed by a British gliding club. Kent Gliding Club was founded on 4 January 1930 and documents show that is was the first British club of its kind to be formed. Founder member 'Jimmy' Lowe-Wylde not only gained Britain's first gliding certificate, he had also built the glider, which was registered by the BGA as a 'Primary Glider'. It was affectionately named *Columbus*. The glider had been constructed in a room behind the Nag's Head public house in Maidstone. Parts of the glider were carefully loaded onto a trailer under the watchful eye of Lowe-Wylde, and the vehicle set off for the airfield at Detling. The past five weeks had been hectic at the pub. The members of the new gliding club had worked hard to complete the glider in time for the test flight.

The design of *Columbus* was based on that of the Zögling primary glider. The prototype had been on display in the window of Messrs Haynes Brothers' showrooms with a poster advertising the date of the event due to take place on the Sunday. As the car and its trailer neared the airfield, the roads were packed with vehicles, cyclists and pedestrians. On reaching their destination, the club members unpacked their pride and joy as the impatient crowd looked on. Finally, the glider was ready and the long

Shorts, based at Rochester, transported the Short Springbok Mk I biplane J6974 by road to Detling for flight tests. John Parker Short's test pilot flew the Springbok from the airfield on 13 September 1923.

'Jimmy' Lowe-Wylde set up a workshop to construct his gliders behind the Nag's Head public house in Maidstone, and he established the British Aircraft Construction Company. An assembled *Columbus* can be seen here outside Isherwood, Foster & Stacey brewery, which was where Lowe-Wylde transferred BAC operations.

rubber bungee cords were prepared for the launching crew, who would pull Columbus into the air.

The machine was to be piloted by the designer, and once he was ready for the flight he gave the order to 'take up the slack'. The cords stretched out as the assistants gathered pace. At the critical moment, the pilot gave the order to let go. The glider sped across the grass but did not rise into the air – this test run was known as a 'slide'. After a further two runs, *Columbus* was launched and flew for 30 yards at a height of 10 feet.

The glider's performance was enough to satisfy Lowe-Wylde that his creation was airworthy. Following congratulations from the members of Kent and London gliding clubs present that day, *Columbus* was put back on the trailer. Unfortunately, the expectant crowds were rather annoyed that the glider had not been flown higher, but once they had been informed there would be no further flying that day, they drifted off home. Kent Gliding Club subsequently lost a certain amount of its popularity, and it took a while to recover.

The club flourished during the 1930s with gliding at a number of sites, mostly Lenham and Eastchurch. Lowe-Wylde transferred his operation from the Nag's Head to part of the Isherwood, Foster & Stacey brewery at Maidstone. He named his new business the British Aircraft Construction Company. Here he developed a new type of two-seat sailplane powered by a 600-cc Douglas motorcycle engine. The aircraft was called the Planette.

Between 1930 and 1933, he developed the aircraft until he was killed flying it at West Malling airfield on 13 March 1933. It was found that he was taken ill during the flight and was unable to control the machine.

A tragic aircraft accident occurred at Detling on Sunday 20 July 1930, when Mary G. Grace (daughter of Rear Admiral H. E. Grace of Alverstoke, Hampshire, and granddaughter of Dr W. G. Grace, the famous cricketer) and Lt S. E. H. Spencer of Staplegrove, near Taunton, were killed. Miss Grace was a qualified pilot recovering from a serious accident that had occurred in March, when she had flown a Tiger Moth at the Hampshire Flying Club. The aircraft spun into a creek at Bursledon on the River Hamble.

At an inquest, held at the Cock Inn, Detling, the following Wednesday, identification was given by Mary Grace's brother-in-law, paymaster Cdr Roger E. Worthington of Gillingham. He said that she and Lt S. E. H. Spencer RN had flown from Hamble airfield in Hampshire on the Sunday for lunch with his wife. It started to drizzle, and so he decided to leave. He saw the aircraft loop twice, but on the second it failed to recover and dived into the ground, catching fire. He remembered the pair saying that the altitude gauge was not working. He was sure they would not have looped had they known how low they were. Victor G. Love of Detling saw the aircraft rise and said it seemed as if the wind caught it. Recovering, the plane

Left: 'Jimmy' Lowe-Wylde, the intrepid glider designer and pilot who founded the Gliding Association. He attempted to fly his own glider, *Columbus*, at Detling on Sunday 23 February 1930.

Below: The wreckage of Lowe-Wylde's Planette light aircraft lies strewn over the grass at Kings Hill, West Malling. He lost his life here on 13 March 1933.

looped neatly at about 150 feet, but could not get back again. Chief Officer Dunk of the St John Ambulance Brigade, Maidstone, said both victims had fractured skulls and severe injuries. Police sergeant W. Groombridge of Bearsted also gave evidence and a verdict of accidental death was given.

Spencer's aircraft, a DH 60x Moth G-EBUR, built by De Havilland Aircraft Co. Ltd in the autumn of 1927, had been purchased second-hand from Brooklands School of Flying in April and had recently been granted its Certificate of Airworthiness. Unfortunately, due to the ensuing fire, the logbooks were destroyed, so there is no record of its flying time. The official accident report states that

the aircraft arrived over Detling at 500 feet and the sky was completely overcast, it was raining and visibility was poor, with the wind gusting. The DH Moth arrived at the airfield at 1.00 p.m. on 20 July 1930, with the pilot in the rear cockpit and both occupants strapped into their seats, took off in a normal manner, heading into wind and climbed to about 300 feet whilst circling the airfield.

The pilot then executed a half roll to the right. This manoeuvre was followed, as soon as the aircraft had recovered from the loss of height and was again heading up wind, by a loop which was made with a very low margin of speed and from which the machine levelled-up little more than 50 feet from the ground. Almost immediately on completing the loop and assuming a slightly climbing attitude, [it] fell over and nose-dived into the ground. No part of the machine or structure was defect[ive], evidence suggests the aircraft stalled. The conclusion being that the accident was caused by an error of judgement by the pilot.

On a Sunday evening in October 1930, Albert Bull, a gamekeeper at East Sutton Park, close to Detling, was surprised to hear the approach of a low-flying aircraft. A Westland Widgeon, a high-wing monoplane, was losing altitude fast. The pilot was making for a field in front of some woods. Suddenly, the engine noise increased and the machine reared up, trying to gain height. Mistakenly, the pilot had thought the field he had chosen was flat, but it was ploughed and the aircraft caught the rough ground and flipped over. It barrelled between trees, which ripped off the wings. The fuselage continued, ending up in a clearing. By then, Sub-Lt George Fowler RN joined Bull and they rushed to the wreckage. The aircraft was upside down.

The pilot was badly injured and his passenger, a young lady, was dead. With a serious head wound, the pilot was placed on a stretcher and taken by ambulance to West Kent Hospital. He later died as result of a fractured skull. Dr E. D. Whitehead-Reid was the son of Dr Thomas Whitehead-

Doctor Whitehead-Reid, who died of his injuries following a crash in October 1930. It is thought he was trying to land at Detling aerodrome during poor weather.

Reid. Edward was born at St George's House, Bridge Street, Canterbury, in 1883. He was educated at Tonbridge School and later studied at Cambridge. He became keen on shooting and other sports and was an aviation enthusiast.

When war came in 1914, he became an acting captain in the RAMC. While in Cairo, he managed to learn to fly with the RFC. On return to Canterbury Hospital, he joined the flying club at Bekesbourne, and had various aircraft – a DH6 Trainer, an Avro 548, and later two SE5as. His last purchase was the Westland Widgeon, a particularly small aircraft, in which he attended many aviation events at the Cinque Ports Flying Club at Lympne (of which he was a founder member).

This aircraft was built by the Westland Aircraft Works in the autumn of 1924 and was used by them as a demonstration machine for three years. Up until the time of the accident, the total flying time of the Widgeon was 230 hours, of which about forty-six were subsequent to the last overhaul and inspection for renewal of a Certificate of Airworthiness. The engine had run for about ninety-six hours since top-overhaul.

Whitehead-Reid later joined 601 (County of London) Squadron RAuxAF and was president of Kent Gliding Club, which used Detling airfield in the 1930s and again in the 1950s. On the day of the fatal crash, he had flown to Ditchling Beacon, Sussex, for a meeting of the Southdown Gliding Club to take his glider pilot's 'A' licence. He had offered a flight

Doctor Whitehead-Reid stands by his Westland Widgeon Mk I G-EBJT, which he owned and died in. The aircraft behind is a DH 60 Cirrus Moth; the company logo is painted on the fuselage.

to Miss Annie Burnside, who was the daughter of Canon Burnside, the principal of St Edmund's School, Canterbury. With the weather closing in, he decided to leave early to return home, and it was because of the poor weather that he decided to land, flying onto Bekesbourne when the clouds lifted. He was accompanied by a service pilot in another Widgeon, which eventually landed some miles south of Tunbridge Wells.

The funeral took place at Canterbury Cathedral on 24 October 1930 and was attended by many people. A procession was led by 601 Squadron (i.e. the guard of honour) through the crowded streets of Canterbury. His brother, Lt-Col. T. D. Whitehead-Reid, said that he was a careful pilot and had never had any previous crashes since learning to fly. Cinque Ports Flying Club was represented by Mr T. A. M. S. Lewis. Dr Whitehead-Reid had fallen victim to the poor weather conditions that plagued Detling airfield – it was felt at the time that he was indeed trying to land at the disused airfield.

One happier event took place at Detling airfield in June 1931, when the first aircraft-towed passenger-carrying glider was christened the *Barbara Cartland* by the eponymous authore. The aircraft, a BAC 7 constructed by British Aircraft Ltd, Maidstone, was a new type of glider. The famous writer was wearing red and white, the same colours as the new glider. The wife and one-year-old son of Mr K. B. Green, managing director of British Aircraft Ltd, presented Barbara with a red and white bouquet.

She was introduced to the crowd at Detling by Ian Davison, the organiser of the so-called Barbara Cartland Air Train. He said that the glider had been named after her because she had generously offered to finance the enterprise in the interest of British trade; it was thought its launch could help British aviation in the future.

At this point, the flamboyant lady addressed the spectators, as reported by the *Kent Messenger*:

> I think progression must always be animated by vision and a certain amount of imagination, so when I say that I believe this experiment may develop into something of national importance, I am speaking sincerely and I hope prophetically. We who are concerned have set our hearts on successful achievement and believe that the 'Barbara Cartland' will carry British aircraft one step further towards a glorious future.

Also present on the day were Admiral Snagg, Commodore of Chatham, Maj. Surtees, Assistant Chief Constable of Kent, Lt-Cdr Geoffrey Rod RN, and E. L. Mole RAF, who was to pilot the glider on its maiden flight, scheduled for the following day. The glider was towed by a Tiger Moth flown by E. O. Wanliss, who had landed at Detling earlier, entertaining the

The well-known author and socialite Barbara Cartland (far right) visited Detling airfield in 1931. Barbara was an enthusiastic supporter of British aviation and helped to finance gliders constructed by the newly formed British Aircraft Company, which was based in Maidstone. The BAC glider was named after her and in 1984 she won the Bishop Wright Air Industry Award. This photograph was taken at Brooklands.

crowd with an impressive display of low flying. Following the introductions and speeches, Cartland christened the glider with champagne to the delight of the gathered onlookers. The maiden flight took place the following day. A Tiger Moth took off from Detling and towed the glider to France, with Cartland a willing passenger. Her passion for aviation was lifelong, and in 1984 she received the Bishop Wright Air Industry Award at JFK Airport for her contribution to the development of aviation.

The aero tow was developed to give them 10,000 feet for gliding flights across the English Channel. Later Geoffrey Tyson, who towed the BAC 7 up from London with a pit stop at Birmingham, flew a DH Cirrus Moth. He landed by mistake at Squires Gate, took off again for Stanley Park, and released the glider. The trailing rope then struck the wing of a parked aircraft while the Moth was approaching to land.

The Coast Defence Co-operation Flight was formed at RAF Eastchurch as early as 1 December 1924 for the purpose of working with the Coast Artillery School, Shoeburyness, and the flight was transferred from No. 22 Group to Coastal Command in 1933. In 1934, two more flights were added and the unit became the Coast Defence Development Unit. No. 1, the original flight, remained primarily employed in co-operation with the Coast Artillery School. In October 1935, No. 1 Flight was sent to Malta, returned to Gosport in August 1936, and rejoined the Coast Artillery Co-operation Flight, where its role involved the training of personnel and the formation of Coast Artillery units in emergencies. By the outbreak of war in September 1939, No. 1 Flight was still at Gosport, equipped with Anson aircraft. A detachment of No. 1 CACF was moved to Detling on 2 September to assist the Thames and Medway fixed defences.

In May 1940, the detachment at Detling was formed into No. 1 Coast Artillery Co-operation Flight, with permanent headquarters at Detling. It was to co-operate with the Thames, Medway and Dover gunnery defences. The unit provided two Ansons at readiness on short notice from dawn to dusk. During the Battle of Britain, No. 1 CACF provided spotting for the Royal Marine Siege Regiment at Dover, whose 14-inch guns bombarded the French coast.

During the period between 23 August and 23 September 1940, the flight carried out ten sorties, in the Cape Gris Nez and Calais Harbour areas. German aircraft harassed them during these operations, and the final sortie resulted in an Anson force landing at Dover. The air gunner was killed and the remainder of the crew injured. The pilot was awarded the DFC. In November 1940, Blenheim aircraft replaced the slow Ansons. Later, in April 1941, Blackburn Defiant aircraft were added to the establishment at Detling. The unit was to remain at Detling airfield throughout the Second World War.

CHAPTER 4

1938–1941

No. 500 (County of Kent) Royal Auxiliary Air Force Squadron moves to Detling – war is declared – the airfield reopens – operations against German E-boats commence

In May 1938, the CO of 500 Squadron, Sqn Ldr C. G. Hohler, received orders that his squadron was to move from RAF Manston to Detling. Once a headquarters had been established, Flt Lt A. C. Bolton was tasked with taking an advance party to the grass airfield on 14 September 1938 to prepare for the squadron's full complement to arrive. After years in the doldrums, the airfield had been reactivated because of its location, which had excellent views over the Medway towns and the Thames Estuary, although it was prone to fog. With hangars prepared for use, it was not long before the airfield was ready for action. It was little wonder that Kent's Own had been moved earlier than anticipated – due to the worsening situation in Europe and the threat of war. At the time, the squadron was operating the Hawker Hind, and in October it took part in an air-raid precaution demonstration at Faversham. Shortly afterwards, a few semi-permanent officers arrived at Detling, including the Reverend N. R. Carmichael, who had been appointed as chaplain.

The winter of 1938 was severe with heavy snow, which, although ideal for Christmas, did not impress airmen sent to RAF Detling, set high on the downs. The conditions were very similar to those experienced by the RNAS during the winter of 1915. By the beginning of 1939, there were some 250 officers and airmen based on the site, and the squadron was preparing for the inevitable. The squadron's role was now that of reconnaissance, and there were rumours that it would shortly be equipped with new aircraft. On 19 March, the squadron started to take delivery of the Avro Anson Mk I, the unit's first twin-engine monoplane. This aircraft, with a crew of four, was armed with machine guns and was able to carry a small bomb load.

On 30 May 1940, an Anson of 48 Squadron was assisting aircraft from Detling in a parallel-track search for enemy motor torpedo boats while four others carried out patrol. One of the aircraft was fired on by an armed

Members of 500 (County of Kent) Squadron RAuxAF in front of one the unit's Avro Ansons. Some of the squadron's personnel were local lads who joined the unit shortly before the war.

An Avro Anson of 500 Squadron stands outside the Bellman hangar, no doubt awaiting urgent repairs to its damaged wing. Just visible inside is another aircraft of the same type. The hangar is still in use today, although not as was originally intended.

Allied trawler in spite of the required signal being flashed. Eventually it was forced to ditch in the sea; one crew member was injured in the foot.

By 14 August 1939, a detachment from 48 Squadron had moved with seventeen Avro Ansons to Detling from RAF Eastchurch to take part in a large-scale exercise – searching for enemy shipping – on 15–20 August. Returning to Eastchurch, the detachment was placed on twelve hours' notice to move to its war station. In fact, this squadron would operate from the airfield until January 1940. The next few weeks were hectic, not only with intensive flying training, but also instruction on servicing the new type. It was at this time that a radio mast was eventually erected; on the first attempt to raise the new mast, it had collapsed, narrowly missing fleeing airmen. In May, 500 Squadron came under the control of No. 16 (General Reconnaissance) Group, Coastal Command, and the squadron was given the freedom of the Maidstone. It celebrated with a march through the town.

One of the earliest recruits to join the squadron was F/O J. F. Spanton, who at the time was a flying instructor with No. 20 Elementary Reserve Flying Training School, based at Gravesend Airport, not far from Detling airfield. Sadly, his untimely death on 12 May 1939 deprived the squadron of an exceptional pilot. Tiger Moth N5487, piloted by Spanton with Mid. C. G. Hodgkinson in the rear seat, collided with N6451, piloted by

An important day for the RAF at Detling. HRH The Duke of Kent visited the airfield and met members of 500 Squadron and other personnel. The Duke is seated in the centre of the second row and P/O J. D. Ready, who was later killed while flying from the airfield, is seated in the front row, second from the left.

F/O F. R. Mathews with Mid. A. Taylor. Spanton's aircraft hit the tail section of Mathews' machine; both crashed in Claylane Woods, Gravesend.

Tragically, F/O Spanton was killed. The other three survived, but Hodgkinson lost his legs. He later became a successful fighter pilot, and acquired the name 'Hoppy' Hodgkinson. According to the Court of Enquiry, the crew of N5487 failed to keep a proper lookout for other aircraft. F/O Spanton had recently been involved in a car accident and a young women had been killed, so it was thought that maybe he was still suffering the effects of the accident.

In the previous year, Spanton had married the daughter of the rector in Great Chart, Ashford, and was buried there. The funeral was attended by many officers and airmen of 500 Squadron RAuxAF and the CO, Sqn Ldr H. Hohler. The young pilot's coffin was draped with a flag and the service was conducted by his father in-law, the Reverend W. R. Powell. Their unusual specification did not comply with official records and to this day no files exist.

Empire Day, which took place on 20 May 1939, was an opportunity for the RAF to show the public its latest aircraft. It was to be the last peacetime display. Supporting the show were Hurricanes from RAF Biggin Hill, and Sunderland and Stranraers flying boats, which were based at

F/O J. F. Spanton, who joined 500 (County of Kent) Squadron in 1938, is seated in the front row, fourth from the left. Seated third from the left is F/O Mathews. Both were killed in a mid-air collision not far from Gravesend airport in May 1939.

Felixstowe. The Hawker Hinds of 500 Squadron took part and civilian aircraft provided the public with flights over the airfield and Maidstone. Flt Lt G. A. Garland gave the crowds a fine commentary throughout the day, and the show continued until early evening.

Following a summer camp at Warmwell, 500 Squadron returned to Detling on 13 August. Active service with the RAF began on 25 August; at this point the unit had fourteen Ansons, three Avro Tutors, and a Hawker Hind. With German troops preparing to invade Poland, the first units to be called up were anti-aircraft units. Roy Foster arrived at Detling in early August 1939, from Wittering, and recalls his time at the airfield with 500 Squadron:

> After the 'regular' posts I had been on before, I found it extremely relaxed and a trifle dégagé. It being an auxiliary squadron, everyone was very 'matey', and there was a lack of 'bull', which I found gratifying. I was only an AC [aircraftsman] plonk GD [General Duties], although I had my application in for air gunner training, which never materialised, as events overtook me. I had some training in Lewis and Browning guns at Wittering, and when the war broke out in September, I along with others took my place on top of the water tower with a Lewis gun and old oil stove to keep me company. The other chaps there were really great, particularly one called Bill Bonfield, bald and middle-aged at the time,

The crew of a 500 Squadron Anson pose for the camera. The date is unknown, but most probably it is 1939–40.

with a pub or something in Chatham. He was good for a laugh at all times. So were all the other blokes, I only wish I could remember their names.

I don't think, before or since, I have ever found myself in such congenial company. I wonder what happened to them all. My first impression on being posted to Detling was how small the set-up was. Also, how informal. The fact that we were all initially sleeping in tents was quite exciting and took me back to my scouting days. When the winter came it was quite a different matter, and we had a winter that year that broke all records for cold and snow. Of course, we were all out on the runway, shovelling snow. The Ansons were flying out over the Thames Estuary daily, ostensibly to find sea mines. This was from the beginning of the war.

We used to play cricket and football quite a lot. In fact, I had a few weeks away to go to Chatham Royal Naval Hospital to have a cartilage removed, but otherwise it was quite uneventful. The whole time I was there, I went home every weekend to Brighton, which was quite unusual, but as I said, it was a good posting. War was declared while I was in Chatham Hospital, and when I came out we were on a war footing. I stayed there until the late spring of 1940, when reluctantly I was posted to the BEF in France to be attached to No. 218 Battle Squadron, but that was a different story. I finally came out of the RAF in 1942 with a war disability pension.

Also preparing for hostilities was the Kent WAAF. Three girls were told to report to Detling and were eventually set to work in a telephone exchange. There were twenty-five WAAFs posted to the airfield and they were billeted at Binbury Cottages, located on the edge of the site. One of Detling's WAAFs later had a major role in an incident that occurred at the end of May 1940.

Following the declaration of war on 3 September 1939, the squadron was on full alert, and on 5 September an Avro Anson bombed a German U-boat caught on the surface of the English Channel. Anson N5052 crashed due to engine failure near Canterbury on 9 September. Another, N5233, suffered engine failure while approaching the runway at Detling. F/O D. G. Mabey bailed out his fellow crew members, but they were killed as the Anson dived to its end near Benenden. Avro Ansons were attacked by Me 109s at the beginning of January 1940, but they retaliated and destroyed two of the enemy aircraft.

Detling played host to many types of aircraft, not least a Fleet Air Arm Blackburn Skua of No. 2 Anti-Aircraft Co-operation Unit from Gosport, which was flown by P/O D. H. Clarke, who – having orders to patrol west of Dunkirk following the evacuation that had begun on 25 May – dropped flares to alert the Navy of any attempt by the Germans to harass

A mobile radar unit typical of the type seen on many airfields during the war. Just visible to the right is a Hawker Hurricane of 318 Squadron, which was formed at the airfield.

the evacuation under the cover of darkness. Clarke helped naval crews prepare fifty Swordfish aircraft, which were to patrol the beaches, the idea being that the Germans might think they were Gloster Gladiators. The ploy did not work. Several Blenheim bombers were on standby to deliver retaliatory poisoned gas, should the Germans use gas on the retreating army.

The Fleet Air Arm took off from Detling to patrol; the force comprised thirty-seven Skuas and Blackburn Rocs, of which only nine returned. Four of these were soon patched up and returned to the beaches. Clarke recalls the scene in his own words:

> One belly flopped and I went across to see what happened. The aircraft was a complete write-off. Bullets and cannon shells had ripped the fuselage from end to end; the cockpit was sprayed with blood. The instrument panel was shattered and on the floor was the remains of a foot.

The Fleet Air Arm based at Detling continued their patrols against gun sites at Cap Blanc Nez. 801 Squadron mainly undertook these duties. P/O Colin Gray was based with 54 Squadron at Hornchurch when they were chosen to escort Fleet Air Arm Swordfish from Detling on a bombing raid. A New Zealander, Colin was keen for action. He returned to Detling as CO later in the war:

Staff in the grounds of Thurnham vicarage in 1943 enjoy a drink during a party held to celebrate the promotion of one of the many WAAFs stationed on the airfield. Note the presence of Naval personnel.

Sqn Ldr D. C. Oliver, who was killed with other officers in the Operations Block during the notorious air raid on Detling of 13 August 1940. At the time of his death, Oliver was operations and signals officer with 53 Squadron. Eight of the unit's groundcrew were also killed.

We'd been sent on a mission to escort some Fairy Swordfish from Detling, across the Channel to dive-bomb Gravelines. Now this took quite some time, because they only cruised at about 90 mph and it took almost an hour before finishing the job.

The three Ansons droned low over the English Channel. They presented an easy target to the pilots of the Me 109s flying at an altitude of 2,000 feet above them. It was 1 June 1940, and, understandably, the Germans were full of confidence as they peeled off to attack the unsuspecting twin-engine reconnaissance aircraft. However, these were not ordinary Ansons, and at the end of the attack three of the German aircraft would be at the bottom of the Channel. The Ansons' unusual specification did not comply with official records and to this day no files exist giving exact details of these aircraft. The Ansons were of 500 (County of Kent) Squadron, based at RAF Detling, and had been modified so as to enable the slow reconnaissance aircraft to achieve an impressive score against the Luftwaffe, a score that compared well to that of any other squadron during, and in the two months prior to, the Battle of Britain.

A Fairey Swordfish of 825 Squadron Fleet Air Arm, based at Detling during the Dunkirk evacuation. L7675 – '5G' – is on patrol. The squadron was also based on HMS *Glorious*. *(IWM HUB7776)*

A fixed forward-firing machine gun in the nose and one moveable gun in the dorsal turret was the official armament of the Anson Mk I in 1940. It was the squadron's own inventiveness to double the firepower by fitting two additional .303 swivel guns to the fuselage sides. So it was on 1 June that the three Ansons – led by P/O Philip Peters – were carrying out a daylight patrol between Dunkirk and Ostend and were sighted by the enemy while flying at 50 feet above the sea. At precisely 10.40 a.m., LAC Smith, turret gunner in Peters' aircraft, reported the enemy to the skipper. Peters dropped to sea level and throttled back, almost to stalling speed. Sgt D. Spencer scrambled to a side gun, and the wireless operator, LAC Pepper, sent out his contact report to Detling. Peters lost sight of the aircraft as they turned to attack from astern, but Smith kept up a running commentary for his skipper's benefit.

The other two Ansons remained with Peters as he dived to the sea, but, now badly damaged, they broke formation. Leaving these two alone, the Germans pressed home their attack on P/O Peters. He did not see the Me 109s, but their gunfire streaked past his cockpit, and because he pulled up suddenly, the enemy underestimated his speed and height. Their gunfire passed over the Anson and into the sea about 100 yards ahead of Peter's aircraft. Suddenly the enemy roared past him and at that moment one of the side gunners hit his target. It did a stall turn in front and 300 feet above the Anson. Peters pulled back on the control column and fired the nose gun. The Me 109, hit again, flew into the sea. The enemy attacked again and made the same error. LAC Smith hit another German aircraft; it plunged into the sea.

On the third attack, as the 109's guns blazed astern at 800 feet, Peters jammed hard on the rudder. The Anson skidded around in a wide, flat turn through 180 degrees, giving the side gunners a chance to open fire. But although it had been hit, the aircraft did not crash into the sea. To the amazement of the Anson's crew, the remaining Me 109s manoeuvred into close formation and turned away. Peters later said:

> The whole engagement lasted no more than seven or eight minutes, which seemed like hours. We spent some time searching the area for the other Ansons, but did not see them or the Me 109s. We continued our patrol.

On inspection of the Anson back at Detling, despite the combined gunfire of nine enemy aircraft, only one bullet hole could be found.

Two months later, when Peters had his parachute repacked, he found that an armour-piercing bullet had ruined the pack, finally coming to rest against the metal frame. 'The chute had been stowed behind my seat during the attack,' said Peters, 'and I have always been grateful to silk as a consequence.' The deadly fire from the modified Anson had paid off. Two Me 109s were destroyed and one was damaged. P/O Peters was awarded the DFC for his role in the combat and retired as a squadron leader in 1953. He took up farming in Devon. The brains behind the idea of fitting additional guns were those of 500 Squadron's gunnery officer, F/O Harold Jones, a cheerful, popular character with many good ideas. The CO, Sqn Ldr Le May, approved the idea immediately, as it was the answer to a lot of problems he was facing in early 1940.

500 Squadron converted to the Anson a few days before the outbreak of war, and although generally pleased with the new aircraft, the pilots soon discovered its disadvantages. Without any fighter cover, they were expected to carry out long daylight patrols, taking them as far away as the Frisian Islands, where they were sitting ducks. However, Le May and his pilots soon worked out their tactics. They would make use of the Anson's manoeuvrability at low speed and get down as near to sea level as possible. Then they would perform low skid turns towards enemy aircraft, and continue this manoeuvre when flying at deck level. Thus they prevented attacks from underneath and enabled the Anson to turn well inside the turning circle of an enemy fighter, restricting the available time for a gun sight to be brought to bear on the Anson.

Blackburn Skua L2928 – 'S' – of 801 Squadron. The Fleet Air Arm travelled aboard HMS *Glorious* and HMS *Ark Royal* during the 1940 Norwegian Campaign. Flying from Detling, the aircraft took part in defending troops at Dunkirk in 1940.

These tactics saved many Ansons from attack. But the aircraft were being used in situations they were not designed for, and pilots wanted some method of hitting back. Le May and Jones joined forces to think of ways of mounting additional guns in the side of the fuselage – port and starboard. A prototype was soon developed in the squadron's workshop, consisting of a stout wooden block strapped between the 'V' struts below the windows. A metal mounting pin was sunk into the block to form a mounting for a Vickers 'G' gun. The early guns were found to work loose when fired and 'put the wind up' many fishing vessels by spraying the sea with shots when this happened.

A Maidstone engineering company, Tilling & Stevens, offered to manufacture the gun mountings. This was a gift to the squadron. The problem was solved. One gun was mounted on the port side, near the wing route, the starboard gun a section further down. Le May later recalled:

> There was thus a fairly restricted horizontal arc of fire between the leading edge of the tail plane and the trailing edge of the wing, nevertheless the guns were very effective. The ability of the Anson to skid turn at low speeds was its greatest tactical asset and the placing of the guns took full advantage of this.

The guns boosted morale. Without them, the second pilot and warrant officer could only look on when under attack; with them, they could also open fire on the enemy.

Le May himself tried these tactics in a mock battle with a Spitfire flown by a crack fighter pilot, but he could have shot down the fighter on several occasions. On landing, the pilot said at no time was he able to align his sights with the Anson. The work had been unofficial – there being no time to get guns through the 'usual channels' – and he was able to have two aircraft fitted before supply ran out. During a visit to Detling, AVM Sir Edgar Ludlow-Hewitt, Inspector General of the RAF, saw the modifications to the aircraft and was very enthusiastic about the idea and promised the pilots more guns. Within a week of his inspection, sufficient guns were delivered to the squadron to equip all the Ansons.

The squadron suffered a severe blow on 11 July 1940 – three Ansons were ordered off for night patrol when the weather was particularly bad. Two of the aircraft took off without any problems, but the third MK-F, piloted by Sgt Wilson, with sergeants Shier, O'Kelly and Worton, ran out of luck and crashed on take-off. The crew's bodies were not recovered until the following morning. Sqn Ldr C. D. Pain remembered the tragedy:

With regard to Sgt Wilson's crash in MK-F, I remember the occasion very well as I was orderly officer that night, and went to search, with others, for the wreckage and bodies. The woods in the area of the crash were covered in fuel, which kept igniting, and we could find no recognisable pieces of the aircraft, or the crew. The bombs had exploded on impact. Sgt Shier had been navigator from Dunkirk time until this very trip. The accident happened on a night take-off at about 11.45 p.m. The first two aircraft made it back to Detling. I can remember Sgt Wilson's BSA Scout four-wheeler sports car standing for a long period in dispersal before being removed.

It was a difficult month for the squadron. Anson MK-D was lost during a battle with nine Heinkels when they attacked the squadron on 12 July during convoy patrol, although MK-L claimed one destroyed. The same day, Sgt Barr was protecting a convoy heading south when, just after 11.00 a.m., four Me 110s were sighted attacking MVs in the convoy. Without hesitation, an Anson went into attack and the enemy turned on the lone aircraft. During this encounter, one of the Me 110s was hit; an engine burst into flames. It dived past the Anson and crashed into the sea. The others soon sheared off. By the end of the Battle of Britain, the squadron's score was five 109s destroyed (one probable), and one Me 110 destroyed (one damaged). In addition, a He 111, a Ju 88 and a He 126 were added to the impressive scoreboard.

Later, German E-boats became prey to 500 Squadron's Ansons. These fast vessels were heavily armed and many aircraft returned to Detling with large holes made by the E-boats' AA fire. Faced with this new threat, Le May, Jones and F/O Elgar approached the British Cannon Manufacturing Company with an idea of having a cannon mounted on a trunnion and gimbal, firing downwards from the Anson. This was designed and manufactured by the BCMC and presented to the squadron by the company. The installation entailed cutting a large hole in the floor between the two main spars, the mounting itself being secured by steel plates on the main spars, which had to be drilled for this purpose.

The E-boats disappeared before the new weapon could be used against them. The Anson was the first aircraft in the world to fly with a free-mounted cannon, but although they could be swung around to face rearwards, they were not very accurate. When under attack, it most probably surprised the German pilot to see a stream of fiery red balls hurtling towards him from the defenceless Anson. The recoil of a fired cannon was reputed to add five knots to an aircraft's speed. By the end of 1940, many old members of 500 Squadron were posted and Le May was among them.

In 1957, the squadron, then stationed at West Malling, celebrated its twenty-fifth anniversary and the winning of the Esher Trophy. At the celebration dinner, the A. V. Roe Company presented a silver model of an Avro Anson to the squadron. It was modelled after a squadron Anson and carried the famous side guns. The pilots of 500 Squadron proved that the 'plodding' old Annie could be adapted and used in other roles than those for which it was originally designed.

P/O Chaffey and P/O Mallalieu were both killed on 8 November 1940 while flying one of the squadron's communications aircraft. A Miles Magister Mk I (serial no. R1917) crashed when the pilot had to make a forced landing while returning to Detling. The aircraft came down at Wrotham, near Ightham, but the cause of the tragedy is not known. The same day, Sgt Kosarz, a Polish pilot of 302 Squadron flying Hurricane Mk I P3538 force-landed at the airfield following combat with Me 109s. Shortly afterwards, Kosarz was dismayed to see his comrade F/O Wezelik forced down at Detling while flying Hurricane Mk I V6860. Fortunately, both pilots, who were based with their squadron at Northolt, were not injured. When war broke out in 1939, Vashon Wheeler was flying for an Egyptian airline, but he returned at once to England. Despite his forty-one years, he wanted to join the RAF and become a pilot. After some 'wangling' and certainly after understating his age – in contrast to 1915, when he had overstated it – he was granted a commission in the RAF Volunteer Reserve in January 1940.

He discreetly ceased claiming his First World War disability pension at the same time. For the next four months, P/O V. J. Wheeler spent his time as a staff pilot at a bombing and gunnery school in Wales, thus relieving a younger pilot for more important work. Target towing was not satisfying enough, and, at the end of April 1940, Wheeler managed to obtain a posting to one of the RAF's few transport squadrons, 271 Squadron at Doncaster. The aircraft used here was the old Bristol Bombay. The move came at an opportune time because, one month later, the Blitzkrieg in Western Europe began. In the following weeks, the squadron had to make some interesting flights to France, carrying important passengers and stores and, ultimately, helping in the evacuation.

Wheeler carried out twelve such flights without any accident or serious incident. In July came another operational posting, to 500 Squadron at Detling, and for the next four months he flew Ansons on convoy escort and anti-U-boat patrols in the Channel and the North Sea. He carried out twenty-two such patrols and had at least two encounters with German aircraft. On the first of these, he chased a Ju 88 away from the convoy, but on the second occasion, he was attacked by several Me 110s and was lucky to escape.

By 18 April 1941, the squadron was being re-equipped with the new Blenheim Mk IV, which replaced the ageing Avro Ansons. The crew of Blenheim Z6050 were shortly to meet their sudden deaths. P/O J. D. Ready (Canada), P/O Johnson, F/O Jones and Sgt Shepherson were taking off from Detling when one of the engines cut out. The ill-fated aircraft rolled and crashed onto the road outside the airfield, bursting into an all-consuming ball of flame that killed its young crew. P/O Ready wrote the following letter to be given to his family in the event of his death, and it is reproduced here with kind permission of his family:

Detling, April 1941

Dear Mary, Arthur and Kathleen,

By the time you receive this I'll have been on my last flight and arrived at the end of the trail. I know it will be a great comfort to you to know that I was prepared to face our Lord and that even as you read this I will be close by in spirit praying for you all. Ever since I started flying in Canada I've thought that this was likely to happen suddenly at anytime and ever since war started, so far I never left the ground without being prepared. Knowing this I'm sure you won't feel too badly about it all as the best any person would wish another is that they arrive safely. I realise

Groundcrew and airmen of No. 2 Anti-Aircraft Co-operation Unit outside their quarters at Detling in 1943. It was one of several units based at the airfield during the war.

I have been a great worry to you most of the time, and I want to thank you all for being so patient with all my faults and drawbacks during our time together. I realise also that it was a great sacrifice to you to finance my way through college and shoulder my hospital bills. I had hoped one day to be able to pay you back but it was just not to be so, and at any rate I want you to know that I've always appreciated it and always feel deeply grateful despite the fact that I might not have seemed so at time. I was not so nice dying so far from home and with comparative strangers but I thank God for the really great privilege of having such brother and sisters as you. Not everyone is so fortunate. Now it is time for a final goodbye – and knowing that you will all be leading good Christian lives, I'll be up there with Papa and Mama watching and waiting for you and praying for your success and happiness until the day when we shall all be once again reunited. May God bless you all.

Your loving brother,

Joe.

P/O Joseph Douglas Ready joined the RAF in July 1939 and was popular with all who knew him. Shortly after joining the RAF hockey team, he served with 500 Squadron, which later moved to RAF Detling. A Court of Inquiry was held and it was stated in the accident report that after being detailed to carry out local flying practice, P/O Ready took off towards the

P/O Joseph Douglas Ready (Canada) was killed on 18 April 1941 with his crew. His Blenheim Z6050 crashed at Detling on take-off.

guardhouse situated on the edge of the airfield. The aircraft was rather slow in becoming airborne and struck a flagpole, which caused it to crash. The inquiry concluded that the pilot, having only seven hours solo and ninety minutes dual in the Blenheim, should not have had passengers and took off in an unsuitable direction.

CHAPTER 5

1939–1940

*The evacuation of Dunkirk – the Battle of Britain –
anti-shipping and anti-submarine operations*

Among the Fleet Air Arm units temporarily based at Detling airfield was a detachment from No. 2 AACU, which operated from Roborough and Plymouth with single-engine Blackburn Shark Mk IIIs. These aircraft – L2366, L2375 and L2351 – moved to St Eval in April 1940 and two months later, during the Dunkirk evacuation, towed lighted flares from North Foreland across the Channel to the mouth of the Scheldt and back, to illuminate German E-boats in the vicinity.

On 31 May 1940, No. 2 ACCU, based at Gosport, experimented with towing a lighted flare. The pyrotechnic slid down a trailing towing cable and the abrupt stop at the end was sufficient to ignite it. The 20,000-candle-power flare that burned for about three minutes or so thus illuminated the area around and below it. Having proved that the proposal worked that evening, two of the AACU's target tugs – a Battle and a Skua – were sent to Detling.

The crews were briefed for Operation Flash, which involved patrolling off the enemy coast between Dunkirk and the Scheldt and illuminating the sea to enable other patrolling aircraft to attack any enemy warships that might try to make a night attack on the shipping conducting the evacuation from Dunkirk. The two crews were instructed to continue the task until lack of flares or fuel forced their return. This would also make the aircraft visible. Practice took place with RN Swordfish in conjunction with three fully bombed-up Ansons of 500 Squadron on 2/3 June. In perfect weather, P/O D. H. Clarke in Skua L2978 followed the Ansons, and eventually his winch operator, LAC Phelan, streamed the 6,000 feet of cable before letting the first flare slide down. After about half a minute, it ignited and illuminated all around – including the towing Skua – thus wrecking Clarke's night vision. For almost an hour the pair flew up and down the coast until the cable went limp as some unidentified aircraft sliced through it. Gratefully, the pair turned for home.

Lt Cdr A. M. 'Steady' Tuke FAA was based at RAF Detling for two days with 826 Squadron. Nicknamed 'Steady' due to the steady progress he made while training with No.4 Pilot Course at RAF Gravesend during 1938, he was one of the youngest recipients of the DSC during the Battle of Britain. Steady regularly supported squadron reunions after his retirement and was group secretary for the National Farmers Union. He died at the age of eighty-nine.

The Battle had also conducted a patrol. Later, the Ansons did claim to have attacked and sunk an E-boat. It was not the end of Clarke and Phelan's adventure, however, as they were illuminated and blinded by searchlights on the Kent coast and almost flew into the sea. The following morning, the small Anti-Aircraft Co-operation Unit detachment returned to Gosport after conducting one of the lesser-known actions of the Dunkirk evacuation; 'Nobby' Clarke was later Mentioned in Dispatches. Bad weather put a stop to this activity after only a few days. It was decided to move a detachment to Detling for the period between 11 June and 3 July. At the same time, Blackburn Roc aircraft were moved to Detling and were used in the vital role of searching for survivors of ships and aircraft in the Channel. They worked with Coastal Command in the Strait of Dover.

Capt. George Baldwin, who died in 2005, joined the Royal Navy to fly two years after the Inskip report of 1937, which returned the Fleet Air Arm to the Navy. He was sent to the RN College at Greenwich, but also took flying lessons in Tiger Moths at RAF Gravesend. Following successful deck landings on HMS *Argus*, he joined 801(FAA) Squadron, which joined the carrier HMS *Ark Royal*, and he flew Skua dive-bombers against the invading German forces. Baldwin continued operations against the Germans from Sumburgh and then, during the Blitzkrieg against the Low Countries and France, flew from Detling, where the squadron based from the end of May 1949 until late June. He was promoted to acting sub-lieutenant in July 1940 and awarded his first DSC the following year. He was reputed to have waxed his aircraft's wings with furniture polish, had shipwrights remove the exhaust manifolds and cut 9 inches from the propeller blades to make his aircraft fly faster. Whether these measures were undertaken at Detling is unclear, but it would be interesting to find out what effect these modifications had.

From May 1940 onwards into the succeeding months, Swordfish squadrons were loaned to RAF Coastal Command and conducted mine-laying operations and convoy patrols in the English Channel and the North Sea against German, Dutch, Belgian and French ports. The Blitzkrieg against the Low Countries and France forced the RAF and FAA to call on every resource they had to stave off complete disaster. In all, four squadrons of Swordfish were attached to RAF Coastal Command operating out of RAF Thorney Island, RAF North Coates, RAF Detling and RAF Manston. They were put to every task for which they were capable: mine-laying, bombing of naval and ground targets, spotting and reconnaissance (which often involved the pilot and observer flying unaccompanied throughout the night). With the threat of invasion from Europe, these four squadrons were called upon to bomb the build-up of invasion barges in enemy ports and to lay mines in the harbours. Their task went on into the Battle of Britain period, July–October 1940.

A Swordfish of 815 Squadron FAA attacked Waalhaven airfield on Sunday 12 May. Fortunately, Lt Downes and crew were unhurt after they were hit by flak and crash-landed at Herkingen, Overflakkee, at 10.10 a.m. During the same day, Avro Anson K8772 of 48 Squadron RAF was also hit by flak while attacking E-boats off the Dutch coast. It ditched in the sea off Texel at 7.00 p.m. The crew – Flt Lt Dodds, P/O B. S. Booth, LAC A. H. Gumbleton and LAC N. E. Jacobs – went missing and their aircraft, OY-G, was lost. With the German invasion of Norway in April 1940, the British Home Fleet was recalled. 825 Squadron disembarked HMS *Glorious* in Britain on 18 April to make way for a fighter squadron on the carrier.

On 20 May, the squadron moved to RAF Detling for operations with Coastal Command to help cover the Dunkirk evacuation. Operations included anti-submarine and anti-E-boat patrols, night reconnaissance, and hazardous daylight attacks on enemy troops and tanks surrounding the Calais area. Some of the squadron's Swordfish also spotted for the guns of HMS *Arethusa* when she bombarded the Calais area. During this hectic period of operations, the squadron lost eight aircraft, and the CO, Lt-Cdr Buckley, was made a prisoner of war. On Friday 24 May 1940, Swordfish of 825 Squadron FAA mounted an attack on a column of vehicles east of St Inglevert, Holland.

Two aircraft were shot down by AA fire and written off. Swordfish K5955 crashed near Pihen-les-Guines at 4.15 p.m., killing Lt M. R. North. His crewman LAM C. A. Chichester went missing. The other aircraft, K8380, was shot down while dive-bombing west of Gravelines and crashed near Oye Plage at 6.30 p.m. Both Lt R. Carmael and Lt K. P. Garr were killed. This period was particularly difficult for the aircrews. On 25 May 1940, Swordfish '5H' of 825 Squadron, flown by Sub-Lt J. B. Kiddle from Detling, was spotting with other Swordfish for HMS *Galatea* off Calais when it was attacked at 8,000 feet by two Bf 109s north-west of Sangatte. During the violent evading action of diving and turning at sea level, the observer, Lt G. N. Beaumont, was thrown out of the aircraft and killed. The aircraft returned safely.

Other Fleet Air Arm units at Detling, such as 819 Squadron, were detached for three days in May. The squadron's assignment was to hunt U-boats off the Belgian coast and carry out convoy patrols in Swordfish Mk Is. In August 1944, this unit returned to Kent and operated from the Advanced Landing Ground at Swingfield. 826 Squadron of the Fleet Air Arm moved from Ford in Sussex to join in the support of the Dunkirk evacuation on 31 May. It provided cover for the Army, bombed road and rail targets at Westende, and attacked E-boats off Zeebrugge.

One of these pilots, 'Steady' Tuke, later a lieutenant commander, was only nineteen years old. His squadron was the first to operate the Albacore biplane dive-bomber. Returning from mine-laying operations in June, he crash-landed at Waxham due to engine failure. He and his crew were uninjured, but the Albacore they were flying was write-off. His *Daily Telegraph* obituary, published on 14 September 2010, takes up the story:

> ... on September 11, at the height of the Battle of Britain, Tuke flew one of six Albacores, with an escort of six Blenheim fighters of the RAF's 235 Squadron, to attack a convoy of invasion barges off Calais. Descending from 10,000 ft he could see a cloud of Messerschmitt 109s rising to meet them, and an aerial battle involving at least two dozen aircraft quickly became a mêlée. The Messerschmitts, armed with cannons, attacked the much slower Albacores, which the Blenheims attempted to defend.
>
> Tuke jinked and slowed to outmanoeuvre the faster German aircraft, while Naval Airman Robert Mathews stood in the rear of the cockpit to fire his single .303 in Vickers machine gun until wounded in the shoulder. The cockpit was riddled with bullets, the main spar shot away, the upper aileron jammed, and Tuke's observer, sub-lieutenant EG Brown, wounded in the head. Despite a holed petrol tank and both tyres being punctured, Tuke nursed his aircraft back to Bircham Newton and landed safely.
>
> Two Blenheims and an Albacore were shot down and two more Albacores badly damaged, while the Albacores claimed one or two

Pilots and other ranks of 819 Squadron Fleet Air Arm flew Swordfish Mk Is from Detling on 21–23 May 1940 on anti-U-boat patrols.

Messerschmitts. All told 826 Squadron lost eleven aircrew and thirteen aircraft on these operations.

On Saturday 25 May, during an anti-shipping raid off the Dutch coast, Avro Anson N9731 (which was working alongside the FAA squadrons based at Detling) was hit in the port engine by return fire. It attacked E-boats and crashed in the sea off Texel at 7.12 p.m. P/O Grisenthwaite, P/O McLundie, LAC Bowers, and AC2 H. C. R. Hopwood were all uninjured. Later, HMS *Javelin* rescued the crew, although Anson MK-U of 500 Squadron sank.

On Tuesday 28 May 1940, four Blenheim IVF aircraft of 254 Squadron 'A' Flight, based at RAF Sumburgh in the Shetland Islands, were detached to Detling to operate with 248 Squadron on sea patrols covering the Dunkirk evacuation. These aircraft completed their first three-hour patrol of the North Foreland–Calais–Dunkirk circuit on 29 May, and this was repeated on 30 May, after their first attempt was aborted due to fog over the Channel. What follows is the story of the last patrol made by the Blenheim fighter aircraft, in particular that of L9481 (later the subject of a painting).

It is told by the only survivor from the 254 Squadron aircraft, the observer, P/O G. W. Spiers. At 4.50 p.m. on Saturday 1 June 1940, two Blenheims of 254 Squadron and two of 248 Squadron took off from Detling to make a three-hour shipping-cover patrol of the Dunkirk evacuation route. The patrol was commanded by F/O J. W. Baird in Blenheim L9481 with his crew P/O Spiers (observer and wireless operator) and LAC R. Roskrow (air gunner). Soon after take-off, first one and then the other of the 248 Squadron Blenheims radioed that they were returning to Detling due to aircraft unserviceability. The two 254 Squadron aircraft commenced their patrol at about 5.00 a.m. and had made several circuits by 7.45 a.m. During two of these circuits, they engaged in unresolved encounters with first a Junkers 87 aircraft and later a Heinkel He 111.

At about 7.50 a.m., they started their last circuit before returning to Detling, and at 7.55 a.m. they were at 8,000 feet and approaching Dunkirk – two miles out to sea flying parallel to the shore – when they were attacked by eleven Me 109 aircraft diving on them from the south. They were spotted by Staffelkapitän Oberleutnant Framm and shot down at 8.05 a.m. F/O J. W. Baird was killed. Sgt R. Roskrow of 48 Squadron, assigned to this flight, was declared missing. Blenheim R3630 of 254 Squadron hit the sea after being raked with fire from FW Sawallisch of 2-JG27. Sgt R. A. Bate, Sgt J. C. Love and LAC W. T. Harrison were declared missing, their aircraft destroyed. P/O Spiers wrote his account of 254 Squadron for www.epibreren.com/ww2:

I was sitting in the seat on the right-hand side of the pilot. Looking out to my right I could see the sand beaches with numerous clusters of troops queuing to embark on small craft. As I looked up I saw recognisable Me 109 German aircraft diving in line astern towards our rear starboard quarter. I managed to count eleven 109s and as I looked downwards I saw our other Blenheim, who had been flying in line astern of us, pass beneath to starboard with both engines on fire.

As soon as I had seen the enemy, I had yelled to Baird, 'Fighter!' In the meantime he turned to port and headed for North Foreland, giving the engines full power. We were slowly picking up speed in a shallow dive but a cold feeling in the small of my back made me realise we were 'sitting ducks' for fighters. In temper and fear I shouted to Baird to manoeuvre the aircraft about, at the same time I made demonstrations by waving my hand in front of him. Whether or not he understood I never found out, as the cockpit suddenly filled with acrid smoke and flying fragments as the dashboard and instruments disintegrated in front of me, under a series of violent crashes and flashes. Suddenly it stopped. The smoke started to clear and I looked back through the armour plate to see what had happened to Roskrow the gunner. The fuselage down to the turret was a mass of bullet holes which were accentuated by the sun beams that shone through the smoke. All I could see of Roskrow was a bloody green flying suit slumped over the gun controls.

Turning to Baird I immediately realised he had been hit, although he still held the controls. His head was slumped forward on his chest and blood ran down his right cheek from a wound in the temple that showed through the side of his helmet. Another wound in his neck had covered him with blood and it had gushed all over my left shoulder. He looked very peaceful with his eyes shut; I was sure he was dead. It was miraculous that I had survived that burst of gunfire into the cockpit. The two-foot-square Perspex panel had many holes in it. The bullets had passed me and gone into Baird and the cockpit panel.

I was now in the unenviable position of any member of aircrew who is not a pilot, as I was flying on my own and it was now up to me to save myself. My immediate reaction was to bale out, so I went forward into the navigation compartment and attempted to lift the navigator's seat, which was on top of the bale-out hatch. The seat would not fold back and was locked solid in the down position, and after struggling to raise it, for what seemed minutes, I realised the aircraft was beginning to roll to port. I then clambered back to the pilot's cabin and viciously hit Baird's arms off the controls. Leaning over I pulled back the throttles as the engines were still at full power and were vibrating excessively.

Yellow flames from the port engine were beating against the front and side windows and standing at the side of Baird I was about to level the aircraft to prevent the vicious sideslip that was causing the flames to play on the cockpit, when suddenly the windscreen shattered. I felt a hot searing wind on my face and I felt my cheeks, nose, throat and mouth shrivelling under the heat, but have no recollection of any pain. As soon as the aircraft righted, the cockpit cleared of fire and smoke and a noticeable peace descended as the cut back engines purred and the wind gently whined through the shattered glass.

Some miles off to port I saw an armed trawler and as the aircraft was now at 5,000 feet, I thought I could glide to it without having to open up the engines. As I lost height the speed of the sea passing beneath magnified alarmingly, and although the thought of using the flaps and lowering the undercarriage to reduce speed occurred to me, I realised that I could not take my eyes off the sea for the impending ditching. The trawler was now only a quarter of a mile off and closing fast, and I was only slightly higher than mast-head height. The aircraft was easy to control from my awkward position leaning over the pilot. I concentrated to keep the wings parallel to the water as I realised the danger of dipping a wing tip. The ripples on the calm sea closed nearer and nearer until there was suddenly a most violent jolt.

Although the impact took only a fraction of a second it seemed like a slow-motion cine film to me. I can still visualise the water bounding in through the nose like a dam which had burst; I remember turning my back to the barrage and gently cushioning on it. The silent cockpit was now full of blood-coloured sea and I struggled to reach the normal entry sliding hatch above the pilot's head. My feet kept slipping on the floor and I could make no progress despite numerous attempts. As I held my breath many of those past happinesses which had occurred during my life passed through my mind as I realised I would not escape. I had never prayed to God with such agony or earnestness. I tried to suck water into my lungs to hasten the end but I was unsuccessful and only swallowed it. My lungs were bursting and my pulse pounded in my ear drums, brilliant flashes and yellow spots appeared in front of my eyes; I thought of the sea bed, its creatures and crabs. I had relaxed my efforts and I had started to sink downwards.

I had sufficient consciousness to realise my right leg was straight and not in contact with what I thought to be the floor of the aircraft. Thinking this may be a way out, I drew my left leg up to it and paddled my way down in fear that my parachute harness and helmet lead would be entangled. After I had descended several feet I slowly backed away and then swam to the surface and broke water about five yards away from the starboard side of the aircraft. To my surprise it was not lying horizontal below the surface of the water but the stub end of the fuselage was pointing upwards at 80 degrees with a jagged scar from which the turret and tail had been torn off. The steep angle was the reason why I could not reach the normal exit hatch.

Being an experienced swimmer I think that I had been trapped inside the fuselage for over three minutes. My parachute floated in front of me and this I quickly discarded. My face now started to sting and I carefully abandoned my flying helmet. During this time I could see the trawler steaming up towards me and they were starting to lower a boat. I blew up my Mae West and started to swim away from the aircraft towards the trawler. The seamen stretched out a pole, on the end of which was a fish net and this they passed down to me. I thrust my right fingers through the mesh and they started to pull me up, but my grip failed when I was just clear of the water.

I fell back into the sea; the next attempt was successful as I interlocked my fingers on either side of the mesh. I was pulled up over the side and stood on the deck with the helping hands of the seamen supporting me. One pointed to my blood-stained shoulder and asked if I had been wounded. I said I didn't think so and added that if they took my wet clothes off they would soon find out. They helped me to walk along the deck towards the galley, but as I made a step I realised I had injured my ankle. I found it was not very painful when I walked on the toes of that foot. In the warm galley they sat me in front of a hot stove but the cheery warmth of the fire was agony to my face. So they moved me away nearer the door where it was cooler.

They cut open the left sleeve of my tunic but soon realised I had not been wounded. After dressing my face with ointment they took off my wet clothes. My legs had several small lacerations and they found there were small particles of shrapnel and metal in my skin. This they quickly removed and bound up the small wounds. After dressing me in a seaman's clothing they took me below to the skipper's bunk and he came down and introduced himself, clutching a half-pint glass filled with rum. I remember drowning the rum in virtually one gulp and asked him for a cigarette. He soon returned with a tin of Woodbines and put them in a net that was above the bunk that I lay on.

Slow drags of the cigarette and rum soon put me into a dreamless sleep, I awoke up about ten o'clock by the sound of heavy gunfire and a crashing of feet running on the deck above when suddenly there was an ear-splitting explosion that shook the ship. I was thrown out of the bunk and the blanket I had placed over my sore face chafed the skin from my left cheek. A sailor came down into the bunk via the vertical iron steps and took me on his shoulder to the upper deck, where he told me there had been a bombing attack on the shipping lanes by many Ju 87 Stukas.

The skipper came over and said he had notified the Admiralty of my rescue and added he hoped the trawler would be ordered to Ramsgate to put me off. He said his crew were exhausted after a continuous week at Dunkirk and I might have been an excuse to get them back, however the Admiralty had refused this request so the skipper said he had called over a tug which was returning to Ramsgate. I noticed we were just offshore in about five feet of water when the tug came towards us.

[The skipper] offered back my Mae West for the voyage, remarking it was better than the Navy issue. I told him he could keep it as a present and he was delighted, adding that he could soon patch the bullet hole in the neck rest, which he demonstrated by inserting his finger. The tug, which I later found out hailed from the Portsmouth, came alongside. Waving goodbye to the trawler crew, I clambered aboard the tug, on whose decks squatted forty or fifty exhausted North African Moroccan troops, I think the tug's skipper was delighted to see me as he had no other crew and wanted to have a chat with someone in English. He soon let me know he didn't think we would reach Ramsgate. He cursed the fog and he cursed the dive-bombers, but what really seemed to disturb him was a horrible knock coming out of the engine and he was sure this would soon pack up.

I regret I cannot remember the name of the trawler, neither can I remember the name of the tug. We set off in the direction of England and after an hour or so ran into very thick fog and the sound of ships that were accompanying us soon disappeared and we found ourselves very much alone. The skipper had no chart aboard and the fog closed in to only fifty yards' visibility. After a time we could hear surf breaking but he consoled me by saying it was the Goodwin Sands and asked me to go forward and point in the direction of any deep channels that I could see on the sand bottom.

I seemed to spend several hours doing this apart from one or two breaks when the fog lifted. We saw no ships. Neither did we hear anything but the breaking of the surf.

Suddenly, at about eight o'clock in the evening, the fog lifted and we were not too far off Ramsgate. He sailed up to the pier and I was taken off and sat on the ground. Some of the injured from other vessels made a terrible sight, particularly one Frenchman who had a large chunk of shrapnel protruding from his forehead. I seemed to be the only airman, but there were many troops of various nationalities who looked unkempt, filthy and completely exhausted. The volunteer Red Cross workers were working among them making them as comfortable as they could. I was soon attended to when an attractive young auxiliary nurse came across and looked at my face.

She immediately burst into tears when she saw me and said how terrible it was the sailors had put grease on my face. She then started to clear the grease away with wadding and this was a most painful operation as all the skin was coming off leaving me in red raw patches. She then put a cooling salve on my face and I felt much more comfortable. I was then asked where I would like to go. They said I could go to Ramsgate Hospital, which was taking many of the casualties, but I said as we were near the RAF Station at Manston I would sooner be with my colleagues. A car soon arrived and I was taken to the Station Sick Quarters, where they gave me excellent treatment. My foot and ankle were X-rayed and I found that I had a small broken bone, however it healed very quickly and within a fortnight I was able to go on sick leave.

For many years I believed the bodies of Baird and Roskrow lay in the wreck of the Blenheim at the bottom of the Channel. However, some two or three years ago I went to Runnymede Memorial, which is a memorial giving the names of all Allied airmen who have unknown graves. I failed at that time to find the names of either of them on the panels. I have recently spoken to the War Graves Commission and it told me that Baird's body was recovered and that he is buried in the communal cemetery at Malo-les-Baines, which is two miles east of Dunkirk. His remains lie at Plot 2, Row A, Grave No. 30. Roskrow's body was never recovered. However, his name was engraved on Panel 19 of the Runnymede Memorial. I had been unable to locate it as I had been looking under the rank of 'leading aircraftsman' but Roskrow's name was engraved under the rank of 'sergeant'. I imagine he had been promoted to this rank during the period when he was listed as missing in action.

Despatched to bomb Calais–Boulogne on 28 May, Swordfish K5982 of 825 Squadron crashed in the sea not long after take-off. Fortunately the crew were rescued; however, G5-P, their aircraft, was lost. Swordfish K8865, crewed by Lt R. G. Wood and Lt A. D. Neeley, were taken prisoner when they were brought down by AA fire. Naval Airman V. S. A. Moore, the third crew member, returned unhurt. Alexander Neeley later became one of the escapees from Stalagluft 3 during the well-known 'Great Escape', and although he was recaptured, he survived his internment.

The Goodwin Sands claimed another victim when K6009, flown by Sub-Lt P. H. Rylands and Capt. W. G. S. Aston, had to ditch in bad visibility, following a sortie to attack E-boats off the coast of Ostend. Both men were rescued, although the Swordfish probably remains trapped in the sands to this day.

An unfortunate incident occurred on 25 May when a Skua Mk II of 806 Squadron FAA Detling was attacked by overzealous Spitfires of 610 Squadron RAF during a shipping protection sortie. The Skua's crew were unhurt and were rescued. Sadly, the same Spitfires shot down another Skua of 806 Squadron piloted by LAM J. B. Burton, who was so badly injured he died later the same day.

Failing to return from a patrol over the Dutch coast, Anson N5227 MK-N's fate is not clear, although LAC F. H. Giles was killed. The other crew members, P/O I. S. Wainwright, Flt Sgt R. G. T. Sopier and Sgt H. W. Johnson, were missing. Ditching in the sea off Ramsgate at 6.05 p.m., Anson N5065 MK-L of 500 Squadron was lost. The crew, P/O A. Leeson, Sgt J. H. Hoskins, Cpl R. G. Rogers and LAC R. G. Honnor, were all injured. However, they were rescued by the *Royal Daffodil II*, which witnessed the aircraft being attacked by F. W. Meyer of 6-JG26.

On 29 May, Avro Anson K8773 of 48 Squadron RAF was severely hit, sustaining damage to wings and ailerons. It fell victim to Lt Hillecke of 6-JG26 off the coast of Zeebrugge. At 6.05 p.m., the battered Anson ditched in the sea near Deal with engine failure. The crew, LAC L. S. Dilnutt (wounded), F/O S. Wherry, P/O G. Allington and Cpl A. D. C. Harding, were all rescued soon after by a passing 'drifter' and taken to Ramsgate harbour.

An unfortunate accident occurred on 29 May at 7.15 a.m. when Blenheim IV P6909 of 225 Squadron hit trees returning from offensive patrols near Sittingbourne. Flt Lt R. P. Y. Cross and Sgt A. V. Slocombe were killed. Another crew member, LAC J. North, later died of injuries. One of the Blenheims later claimed as shot down by Hauptmann Galland crashed in the sea off Gravelines having been intercepted by Bf 109s of JG27. The crew of L9260 were on a coastal patrol off Calais at 12.00 a.m. and were later rescued from their dinghy. P/O J. R. Cronan, Sgt A. D. Lancaster and LAC Pebbles were uninjured; the Blenheim LA-E was lost.

Galland also shot down Blenheim L9397 of 225 Squadron. The crew, P/O A. F. Booth, Sgt D. J. Elliot and LAC E. R. Scott, were lost with their aircraft. The German ace also claimed Blenheim L9397, shot down off Calais. P/O A. F. Booth, Sgt D. J. Elliott and LAC E. R. Scott were declared missing. It was a sad day for 225 Squadron, as during the same patrol Blenheim L9401 was shot down in the sea by Lt Zirkenbach of 1-JG27. Its crew, Flt Lt G. A. P. Manwaring, Sgt I. MacPhail and AC1 D. B. Murphy, were all killed.

Not all losses to squadrons engaged on coastal patrols from Detling were attributed to enemy action. On Thursday 30 May, Anson N9919 of

48 Squadron was hit by AA fire from a friendly trawler and was forced to ditch in the sea off Ramsgate at 8.00 p.m. Fortunately, the Navy came to the scene and the crew of HMS *Vega* rescued P/O Tilson, Sgt Ardene, LAC O'Reilly and LAC Smith, taking them to Sheerness. Their aircraft, OY-J, was lost. The Skuas of 801 Squadron FAA, based at Detling, were tasked on 31 May with destroying pontoons that had been spotted over the Nieuport Canal, and suffered some losses. It was reported that Skua L2917, flown by Sub-Lt J. B. Marsh and Naval Airman G. R. Nicolson, crashed into the sea following an attack by Bf 109s of 3-JG20 and was claimed by Oberleutenant Lignitz. Skua L3005 was shot down by Lt Kolbow of 3-JG20 and crashed in the sea west of Nieuport. The crew, Lt R. L. Strange and Petty Officer N. R. Reid, were reported missing.

The pilot of Skua L2881 and his crew, Sub-Lt R. M. S. Martin and Naval Airman Hedger, managed to limp back to Detling. Not only was their aircraft riddled with bullets from ground fire as they dived the piers at Nieuport, they also received the attention of Unteroffizier Heilman of 3-JG20. Although Hedger was wounded, the crew of the Skua survived to fight another day. Far from being a fighter sweep that was cut to pieces, this was a highly accurate dive-bombing attack that possibly saved the Dunkirk perimeter from collapse at the cost of only three Skuas.

At the beginning of June, a detachment of Lockheed Hudsons from 206 Squadron arrived at Detling to provide additional air cover for the retreat of the British Expeditionary Forces at Dunkirk, the only escape route after the fall of Boulogne and the imminent fall of Calais. Coastal Command satisfied the need for air cover for British troops, to a degree. One of the most celebrated operations took place on 3 June 1940 and involved the three Hudsons of 206 Squadron on detachment. Flt Lt Biddell, F/O McPetrie and F/O Marvin were on patrol when they encountered Me 109s, which were attacking Skuas of 801 FAA Squadron, also from Detling.

The Skuas were returning from a raid and were low on ammunition; Coastal squadron records give an account:

Our machines intervened and numerous hits were scored on the enemy aircraft, two of which were destroyed and others damaged. The enemy broke off the engagement. All our machines returned safely to RAF Detling.

Biddell's gunner, LAC Caulfield, and McPetrie's gunner, LAC Freeman – both airmen – were awarded the DFM.

Sqn Ldr D. H. Clarke DFC AFC recalls events at Detling during the dark days of May and June 1940 with No. 2 Anti-Aircraft Co-operation Unit:

In those fateful few days at the end of May and beginning of June 1940, when the British Expeditionary Force lay crammed on the Dunkirk beaches entirely at the mercy of the German Army, Britain could have lost the war. That she did not was due to German lack of foresight – and the tremendous efforts made to save the men on the beaches. The soldiers, huddled together on the shell-strafed beaches, were well aware of the efforts being made when they saw the shoals of boats, naval and civilian, queuing to take them off. But, as they were strafed time and time again by enemy aircraft, the cry went up: 'Where's the RAF?'

The fact that the RAF was at Dunkirk and played a leading role in the success of the operation is now part of history, although perhaps their part was not obvious to the men on the beaches. But I was there too, flying through the misty vastness of the night skies. And if the men below could not see my own aircraft, at least I was in a position to know what happened to the pilots who flew in the daytime. Despite the fact that Dowding was anxious to husband his front-line fighters for what was to be the Battle of Britain, 11 Group alone maintained a daily average of fifteen Hurricane and Spitfire Squadrons over Dunkirk.

But there were also other types capable of carrying guns, and it makes not a jot of difference if most of them were antiquated, obsolete or totally unsuitable for the task. These aircraft flew over Dunkirk, apparently unrecognised by our troops – so that in retrospect it seems as if I flew with ghosts. I operated from Detling, a small aerodrome on the escarpment near Maidstone, and normally used by one squadron of Ansons only. I flew there in a yellow- and black-striped target-towing Blackburn Skua from my base at Gosport on the evening of 31 May 1940, and in company with me was a similarly painted Fairey Battle, also equipped with a D-type winch for target towing, and piloted by P/O Cliff Rendle. In the two aircraft we carried our winch operators, LACs Phelan and Verrier, Sgt Jefferies as general handyman, and Flt Lt Digger Aitken, who was in charge of our little unit.

Digger was a regular officer, but Cliff, like me, held a four-year short service commission. Although I was senior to him by a few months, we had roughly the same amount of hours in our logbooks – about 400, but neither of us had more than two hours night-flying experience. Our total operational experience was nil, so although we were rather surprised at the strange assortment of aircraft which were parked on the aerodrome, Ansons, Battles, a Gauntlet, Vildebeeste, Lysanders, an old Harrow, Swordfish and several other oddments – we certainly did not think of them, or of ourselves, as front-line fighters. We asked the way to the Navigation Room, and there we found a confusion of pilots and aircrew, struggling through the crowd we eventually located the station CO, to whom we had been ordered to report.

Gp Capt. Sainsbury was middle-aged, large and florid; his desk represented an oasis of calm in the surrounding tumult. Digger introduced us, and we saluted.

'I understand that one of you has been shown the flares this afternoon,' the group captain said. I was startled. It was true that I had been told to fly over to Lee-on-Solent just after lunch to have a look at a new idea for target towing at night, but I couldn't understand how he came to know about it. 'Yes, sir, it must have been me.'

'Well, don't you know?'

'I'm sorry sir, I was shown how we could tow lighted flares for night target practice – sir – but nothing was said about coming here to do it.'

'Hm, night target practice – someone has a sense of humour.' Gp Capt. Sainsbury accepted the joke, if a joke it was, without a flicker of emotion. Then he went on, addressing us all. 'You are no doubt aware that the British Expeditionary Force has retreated to the French port of Dunkirk just across the Channel – here'. He turned in his chair and stabbed a finger at a 4-miles-to-the-inch map pinned to the wall behind him. 'You are probably not aware that the Navy are doing their damnedest to rescue as many soldiers as they can from this untenable position. Now we at Detling are operating a selection of aircraft day and night to give air-cover, and your particular job, codenamed 'Flash', is to illuminate the sea north of the ferry lane so that our bombers can spot any enemy shipping which is likely to interfere with the evacuation.'

The sudden impact of the connection between what I had seen demonstrated only a few hours before and what we were expected to do with the flares made me feel sick – empty sick: a condition which I soon came to recognise as the twitch, and inevitable before any operational flight. The group captain continued. 'You will patrol between Dunkirk and the River Scheldt, about ten miles offshore, lighting your flares one at a time until they are all used. I understand that they burn for 3½ minutes, so take as many as you think you can manage in the rear cockpit – about twenty to thirty should do.' He paused and looked at me intently – then at Cliff.

'You realise, of course, that with 20,000 candlepower to light up the sea you will also light up yourselves. We don't know if the Germans have any night-fighters in the area, but if they have you will be sitting targets. Consequently I cannot allow you to take maps or documents of any sort with you – in fact, before you go I want you to clear out your pockets completely and check that your crew does the same. Your radio sets should have been removed at Gosport (Digger signified that they had), but I would like you to check through your aircraft and make sure that anything which might be of use to the enemy is removed. We can't be too careful.'

'How about armament, sir?' I asked. 'We're not fitted with guns.'

'I'm afraid that you'll have to do without them. We haven't any here, and in any case it would take too long to fit them.' *And what is more,* he seemed to imply, *it would be a waste of time and a waste of guns.*

Our first briefing (and brief was the operative word) was a waste of time – apart from the fact that it told us what we were there for. I scarcely had time to show Cliff and our crews how the flares worked before we were hustled into the air to follow six bomb-laden Swordfish apiece. I found the night take-off a terrifying business, my previous one being at FTS nearly two years before, and I didn't improve matters by doing it in coarse pitch. Unfortunately, nobody had thought of telling each Swordfish leader to keep his navigation lights on until Cliff and I had pulled into position, so neither of us found their faint blue formation lights and the first trip was a complete fiasco. But we were learning. In company with fifty other aircrews, we managed to sleep four hours on the floor of the ante-room in the officers' mess for the rest of that night. Three nights later I flew on my first operation of the war.

Three bombed-up Ansons led the way to Dunkirk, and I followed the leader's blue formation lights without difficulty. The weather was perfect, with the barest trace of a mist, but there was practically no horizon and my instrument flying ability was as poor as my experience of flying at night. I had a feeling of unreality – the darkness, no experience, no guns and navigating by guesswork – it was just like a dream. The Perseus droned monotonously and the instruments glowed their luminous messages with green confidence.

Dunkirk was an inferno of fires, surrounded by flashing pin-pricks of light which I assumed were guns hammering ceaselessly at our troops. We turned to port before we reached the land and the leading Anson blinked his formation lights. 'Stream all the wire,' I ordered Phelan over the intercom. When he reported that the 6,000 feet was out, I pulled clear of the Ansons. 'Right – let go the first flare.' Half a minute dragged in agony. I pictured the two-foot tube sliding through the darkness down the long wire. When it reached the toggle at the end, the jerk would snap the firing pin home.

Suddenly, the night sky vanished; the faint horizon disappeared. A billion misty droplets of water, almost invisible in the darkness, hurled back the glare of 20,000 candlepower so that I could see nothing outside the cockpit. We were locked in a bowl of brilliant whiteness, and it was as if we had flown inside an electric light bulb – even the instruments showed their black and white faces. Somehow I managed to keep straight and level. When the first flare died, the enveloping blackness which smothered my eyes was even worse than the glare. 'Don't wait for orders, keep 'em lit,' I told Phelan, hoping that he wouldn't notice the tremor in my voice.

For three-quarters of an hour I sweated a blind course up the Belgian and Dutch coast. I never saw a thing, on land or sea, nor Ansons. All I had for guidance were my instruments – how I wished that I had spent more hours under a hood – and some rough courses worked out by the navigation officer at Detling. Then I did see something. A vague blur of movement over the silver disc of the spinning airscrew – half seen through concentrated attention on the instruments. What was it, a night fighter?

There was a sudden jolt. For a moment the engine note changed – then it resumed its steady beat. 'Sir – an aircraft's fouled the wire. The flare's gone and the blackness once more the green instruments [*sic*].' I told Phelan to reel in, and he reported that only a few hundred feet of wire were left. Whatever it was I had seen must have flown into the wire and snapped it. With the toggle at the end gone, we could light no more flares that night. I turned on to the reciprocal course. As the pupils of my eyes slowly dilated I began to see again: a faint glow in the sky, Dunkirk, a dark mass over my port wing – land. Thankfully I straightened from my crouch over the instrument panel and flew visually – it was a strain even then, because there was no moon, but with the fires of Dunkirk as my guiding star found my way back to England.

My orders on approaching the English coast were to fly at 4,000 feet, switch the navigation lights on and off three times and then leave them on, and then to fire a two-star colour-of-the-day cartridge from my Very pistol, which was fixed alongside my seat and discharged through the bottom of the fuselage. When I saw the dim outline of home looming ahead I did all these things, confident that the worst was behind us and that soon I would be despatching a beer.

A white slash of incredible brightness battered into my already over-strained eyes. This time I could see nothing – not even the instruments. I was completely blinded by our own searchlights. I slammed the seat-positioning lever to the bottom notch, but the low sides of the cockpit, designed for maximum visibility when flying from aircraft carriers, gave me no protection. I flicked the strap release and strained forward over the stick, my face only inches away from the green messengers of flight. But even in that position the glare was dazzling; the instruments were blank-faced.

I had already fitted a red/yellow cartridge into the Very pistol and I fumbled around until I found the trigger. The discharge thumped. I felt for another cartridge in the rack. Then, quite suddenly, there was an uncanny silence, which even overwhelmed the droning Perseus. A stall. Mentally I felt for the position of the stick and rudder bar. Then we were diving. I closed the throttle as the engine over revved, easing back on the stick. She flicked into a spin. I corrected. She went the other way. I got her out. She dived, stalled, spun again – and all the time the white finger of blindness followed. And then, miraculously, the lights were switched off; in the few seconds that the carbons glowed, I caught the glimmer of water.

God knows how we escaped! Perhaps we were at 100 feet, maybe less. I corrected the spin instinctively, hauled back on the stick and gave her full throttle. There was a shattering bang. Water showered into the cockpit; the engine vibrated furiously. And then we were clear. Searchlights at nil feet picked us up again. Some shone down on us so that once again, blinded, I flew without knowing what I was doing or what was happening. I only wanted to land – a ploughed field would have done – anything to escape from the unreality, which had turned into a nightmare.

The lights shining down on us switched off; but those behind lit another whiteness ahead, whiteness which stretched up, up. I slammed the throttle open again, dragged back on the stick; we climbed steeply and below, stark in the bleak brilliance, I could see crumbling chalk, tussocks of grass, some sand-bagged pits, white staring faces and then nothingness. The lip of the cliff slashed the beams and we were heading inland into blackness.

We had no further trouble from searchlights; I switched my navigation lights off. At zero feet, in the blackout, without maps, after following several wrong creeks, roads and railway lines, I found my way home. I was furiously determined to get there so that I could express an opinion about our reception over the coast; perhaps I would never have achieved it if I hadn't lost my temper. But a temper lost in the panic of danger is soon dissipated by the comforts of safety; and the relief which came when the wheels of my Skua rumbled across the grass between the flaring goosenecks can only be known by those who themselves have returned. Late the next day, June 3rd, we returned to Gosport Cliff in formation as we flew westward into the setting sun.

On 31 May, ten Albacores and nine Skuas bombed German pontoon bridges over the Nieuport Canal, near the coast north-east of Dunkirk. Direct hits were claimed. Returning home, the Skuas were engaged by twelve Messerschmitt Bf 109s of 1-JG20, and two Skuas of 801 Squadron (L2917 and L3005) were shot down. Another Skua crash-landed back at Detling. The battle was not all one-sided: the Skuas claimed one Bf 109 shot down and another damaged. It seems the Messerschmitt may have broken off the chase to go after three Coastal Command Hudsons. The Skua that crash-landed back at Detling is probably the one described in Capt. Eric Brown's *Wings of the Navy* and Alexander McKee's *Strike from the Sky* as providing an example of the Skua's sturdiness, with nine bullet holes in one propeller blade alone, the top cylinder of the Perseus engine shot away, along with the pilot's windscreen and canopy.

On this very day, the British 12th Infantry Brigade (consisting of 2nd Battalion Royal Fusiliers, 1st Battalion South Lancashire Regiment and 6th Battalion the Black Watch) were holding the sector of the Dunkirk perimeter opposite Nieuport. They had just beaten off a strong German attack but at 5.00 p.m. massive German reinforcements were observed moving along the canal. Just then, bombing by British aircraft stopped the enemy movements and the Germans turned and fled. If this was the attack by the Skuas and the Albacores, then this one single incident alone justifies the British taxpayer's investment in the poor, maligned Skua.

One of the most celebrated operations undertaken at Detling involved three Lockheed Hudson aircraft of 206 Squadron, which were detached from Bircham Newton. The squadron, operating with 220 Squadron, was put into action as part of Operation Dynamo – the evacuation of Allied troops from Dunkirk. Flt Lt Biddell, F/O McPetrie and F/O Marvin took off from Detling and encountered nine Me 109s, which were attacking the Fleet Air Arm Skuas, based at Detling. They were returning from a raid and short of ammunition. The squadron recorded:

> Our machines intervened and numerous hits were scored on the enemy aircraft, two of which were destroyed and others damaged. The enemy then broke off their engagement. All machines returned safely.

A tragic incident occurred on 31 May 1940, when an Anson Mk 1 of 500 Squadron – serial number R3389, code MK-W – crashed at Detling while returning from a night patrol. The aircraft, piloted by P/O David E. Bond, had taken off at 11.38 p.m. Approaching the airfield, it hit trees, crashed into a field, and caught fire when a bomb exploded. The pilot was seriously injured and the navigator was killed; two other crew members were injured.

Cpl Joan Pearson, despite being told there were bombs on the stricken aircraft, fought her way into the wreckage without thought for her own safety. She managed to release the pilot's parachute harness and dragged him clear of the inferno. When they were only 30 yards from the crash, a bomb exploded. She threw herself over the injured pilot and remained with him until help arrived. Returning to the aircraft to look for other members of the crew, she found that the wireless operator, F/O Richard C. Chambers, was dead. Cpl Petts and LAC Fish, the other crewmen, were not seriously hurt.

It was a remarkable act of bravery for which Pearson was awarded the George Cross. Some weeks later, she received a commission in the Women's Auxiliary Air Force and was posted to Bomber Command, where she remained until the end of the war. At a reunion of the Victoria Cross and George Cross Association, her exploits were reported in the press, and as a result she was reunited with the pilot, P/O David E. Bond.

On Thursday 13 June, 500 Squadron was engaged on North Sea patrols when Anson N5225 crashed into the sea. The circumstances of its loss are not known but the crew – F/O R. K. Curzon, Sgt N. J. Sparks, LAC G. A. Mitchell and AC1 L. V. Pepper – and their aircraft MK-M were lost. Lt Savage of 801 FAA Squadron was startled when the windscreen of his Skua was smashed by ground fire during a photo-reconnaissance sortie between Boulogne and Calais on 18 June. Although injured in his face, with encouragement from his fellow crew member Lt Hayes, who was unhurt, he limped back to Detling and landed safely. The aircraft, code letter 'F', was quickly repaired and returned to service. The following morning, during a similar mission, a Skua of 801 Squadron, code letter 'P', was hit by AA fire. The aircraft's wing was damaged and its crew decided to head for RAF Manston. The aircraft was repaired. On Friday 21 June, Lt. A. V. M. Day and Naval Airman F. Berry, flying a Roc, were lost during dive-bombing attacks on gun positions at Cap Griz Nez. Oberfeldwebel Buhl of 1(J) LG2 intercepted them over Estables.

CHAPTER 6

1940–1941

*The Battle of Britain – Detling bombed heavily –
new units include a Polish squadron*

The summer months of 1940 – i.e. the evacuation of Dunkirk and the Battle of Britain – will always be associated with Kent and the disastrous events that took place at RAF Detling on 13 August, or 'Eagle Day'. Hitler knew he had to destroy RAF airfields in South East England if he was to consider an invasion. At 4.00 p.m., shortly before teatime, a force of eighty-six Ju 87 Stuka dive-bombers of Luftflotte 2 appeared in the skies over Detling. They had been fortunate, and were able to use the cloud cover for maximum surprise. The Stukas destroyed the airfield's runways, which were covered in craters, and twenty-two aircraft were destroyed. Hangars caught fire and a direct hit on the Operations Room killed the station CO, Gp Capt. Edward Davis.

One eyewitness, a local based with 500 Squadron at Detling, was Cpl Foster, whose home was at Bearsted near Maidstone:

I arrived at Detling in June 1940. I had been evacuated from Dunkirk because I was a medic with the RAF in France. We came up on the train from Dover to Paddock Wood, where the soup kitchens were set up for the men returning from Dunkirk. Someone mentioned that German aircraft had got through and were approaching the airfield. The sick bay was not directly hit, but rubble from the Operations Room fell onto the roof. Many Army men who manned the Bofors guns defending Detling were killed.

It was a busy day for my RAF chum and I, many of the injuries were bad, and many dead. There were many buildings on fire after the raid and it was decided to disperse much of the camp around the area at Detling. The sick bay was moved to house called Woodlands. Nizzen huts [*sic*] were erected in the gardens. The WAAFs were moved to Binbury Manor. Those moves most probably saved further serious injury and loss of five during a later raid. Members of 'B' Flight 500 Squadron had a lucky escape. They were being driven over to work on an Anson parked close to the Yelsted road when they realised the incoming aircraft were about to attack the airfield. They jumped off the lorry and ran to the nearest shelter as bombs fell close by.

The day before the raid of 13 August, an observant officer of 'B' Flight, Sqn Ldr Douglas Pain, had seen aircraft circling the dummy airfield at Lenham. They were in fact Stukas, possibly preparing themselves for the attack on Detling. The convoy patrol was uneventful and landed at Bircham Newton to refuel. It was a pleasant day and the crew decided to stay for lunch and a drink. The Anson took off to return to Detling, flying leisurely along the coast. As they approached the airfield, the sky clouded over. Pain and his crew realised that Detling was under attack and could see the damage to the runways and the demolished Operations Room. They were very lucky to have escaped the raid. Without hesitation, the Anson's crew joined the rescue work, but they were told to return to their own mess.

One amusing incident occurred when Peter Duff Mitchell of 'A' Flight 500 Squadron was having a bath. Hearing the tremendous roar, he leapt out of the bath and looked through a window. He didn't waste time grabbing a towel – he left the building and ran stark naked, in view of

The groundcrew of 53 Squadron during the summer of 1940. Cpl Jack Price (front centre) was one of those killed when Stuka dive-bombers attacked Detling on 13 August 1940.

some WAAFs, for the nearest air-raid shelter. A WAAF who was there at
the time said:

> I looked out of my bedroom window ... and saw a soldier running.
> We take very little notice of the noise of aircraft for they are about
> continuously, but to see a soldier run was unusual. Looking out further, I
> saw more soldiers running and realised there was a raid right on us – we
> had had no warning. I dashed down into our dug out only just in time.
> The noise was terrific, and I was deaf for two days afterwards. When I
> came out, I shall never forget the sights which met my eyes.

Not only were the hangars, workshops and quarters laid flat, but taxiways
and hard standings had been turned into a cratered mess. A total of
sixty-seven service and civilian personnel had been killed in the raid, and
work went on for hours to rescue the injured. The award of the Military
Cross, rare in RAF history, went to P/O D. Elliot, who had helped rescue
some of the injured in the ruined Operations Room even though he was
injured himself. Military medals were presented to Cpl B. Jackman, who
had operated his twin Lewis guns until the gun post was wrecked by a
direct hit which severely injured him, and to WAAF Cpl J. Robins, who
gave first-aid to the wounded when a shelter was hit, remaining with the
injured until all of them had been evacuated to hospital. Lt D. Curry RN,
one of the Naval Officers attached to RAF Detling, was awarded the DSC
for his outstanding coolness in the face of danger.

Twenty-eight aircraft had been destroyed at Detling and Eastchurch,
but Detling, not even a Fighter Command airfield at the time, was soon
repaired – a tribute to all who were there on 'Eagle Day'. Meanwhile,
Flt Sgt J. C. Thompson of 'A' Flight was enjoying tea at the back of a house
in the woods behind 'A' Flight's dispersal area. The lady of the house often
supplied airmen with cake and tea. As Thompson was tucking into his
cake, the owner's son, a small boy, kept tugging his sleeve, trying to get
him outside. Not wishing to give up his break, Thompson ignored the boy
until the latter said, 'Mister, they ain't our'n.'

They left the house and saw the raid taking place. Thompson told the
boy to get his mother and to shelter in the cellar. He ran over to a small
gun pit where there was a Lewis gun, amazed to see the gun was deserted.

Mrs Sylvia Yeatman's husband was based at Detling in 1940 and she
remembers:

> When my husband was at RAF Detling, I did coding there. I had done
> coding at the Foreign Office before the war started. The CO found it out.
> They were short of WAAFs at Detling then, so I did night and day duty.

In the hut were I worked there was a row of hockey sticks. I asked the CO what they were doing there. He said, 'That's in case the Germans come. They're for the WAAFs. We haven't got enough revolvers to go around.' I didn't want a hockey stick to hit a German with. I had a friend who worked in the small arms school at Hythe, so I got hold of a revolver. The chaps on the base used to look through the window at my revolver on my desk. I don't think they liked it at all. It made them nervous.

My husband was due for leave. He kept saying he couldn't possibly take it, in view of what was happening. I said, 'You must. It's probably the last chance you'll get for a long time'. So I bought tickets for sleepers on the night train to Scotland and we set off to Argyllshire to stay with cousin, taking along bikes and dog and all.

Just as we arrived, a message came through. My husband was recalled. No reason given. We went back to London by train from Glasgow. I went to stay with my sister-in-law while he went on to Detling to see why he was recalled. He told me he'd send a coded message to tell me what it was about. He said if he'd made a mess of things, he'd say the message, 'I lost my uniform.' If it was the aerodrome, he'd say, 'I've lost my vest.' If it was a general recall, he'd say something else – I can't remember what it was.

I went out to dinner. When I came back, my sister-in-law said, 'I've had the most extraordinary message from Harry. He said he's lost his vest but he's left his string jersey on the train. When I got to Detling, I realised he wouldn't have been there at all if I hadn't taken him off to Scotland. The Germans had bombed it. The CO had been killed. The Ops Room was gone. His office, his bedroom, everything had gone. Detling was a silly place for an airfield. We were up on a hill.

When Germans started bombing it, they had things all their own way. We used to call the German attacks our medicine – they came at eleven in the morning, three in the afternoon and seven in the evening. Of course, they didn't always come as regularly as that, but they did raid us often. My husband had a lot of fights with the Air Ministry, which he finally won, to take his men workshops in Maidstone, so they could get on with the job of repairing damaged aircraft. They couldn't get much done at Detling; they were always going in the bunkers during the raids.

LAC Frank Conn had been serving with 2713 Squadron RAF Regiment HQ Fighter Command in RAF Bentley Priory when he was ordered to report to Detling:

There I was given a 3 ton Crossley lorry, which had been converted to a mobile workshop, plus three armourers, and I was then told to take the lot back to RAF Eastchurch to be on call to service any defensive guns in the area. We had no tents, so it meant sleeping in the lorry, but we had a bit of luck because we found a Nissen hut at Eastchurch, so we set up our HQ there. We managed to get some mattress covers from Detling and some straw from a local farm to stuff them with, and some empty wooden boxes for bed lockers to make ourselves comfortable. It was a very busy time as the guns never seemed to stop firing except when they needed attention. My job, besides driving and getting the armourers onto the various sites, was servicing the generators that worked the predictors.

In addition I would drive down to Detling, pick up the mail and distribute it to the sites. It was not long before our team was ordered to France, but not me, I had to report back to my Squadron at Detling. I had become quite attached to the airfield. As I drove over Detling Hill and looked down on the village with its church and pub, I would say to myself – I would love to live there one day.

Frank did indeed fulfil his dream and forty-four years later, he and his wife bought a house in Detling village.

Plans for conscription were announced on the same day as Dave King's nineteenth birthday. He lived with his family in Maidstone. He had completed an apprenticeship with Frank East of Tonbridge in September 1938 and found work with Collets – a firm with fourteen branches – at Jermyn Street. He had to leave the firm because his brother had strained his heart. He returned home to help with his parents' business.

At the end on May 1939, I went to the Army recruitment depot, the drill hall in Boxley Road. The sergeant, who was very polite, explained that there were vacancies only in the searchlight branch, and if I came back on the following Tuesday they would produce the papers and I could sign on. A few days later a friend of my father said, 'Have you thought about joining 500 (County of Kent) Squadron AAF, which has recently moved from Manston to Detling?' The answer was no. I had never heard of the AAF, 500 Squadron, Manston or that Detling was being opened again, but I was mad keen on aeroplanes and the Army didn't stand a chance. 'SB' Fletcher, who knew the CO, Sqn Ldr Hohler, phoned him and was told I should present myself at Detling next Sunday morning, which I did. I was told there had been no vacancies but twelve new ones had just come through, and I could have one if I could pass the medical.

The vacancies were for Clerks (Special Duties) and we would be working in the Operations Room. What Operations Room? Nobody seemed to know, but I was told that once in the Squadron I could re-muster to any other trade of my choice. I rather fancied the photographic section. I was sworn in that afternoon and went home as Service No. 812354 (all airmen of 500 Squadron had service numbers beginning with 812) Aircraftsman 2nd Class u/t (under training) AAF, having undertaken to attend all day on Sundays, plus one evening a week in Maidstone, and fourteen days in camp in August.

On Sundays we were all drilled on the Parade Ground for an hour or so, and then told we could wander round and see what other sections were doing as we had no Operations Room, no officers, and no information. We also had no uniform, and we were not required to attend on weekday evenings. In August 1939 we went for a fourteen-day camp at RAF Warmwell, near Dorchester. We were introduced to our duties as Ops Room people, but although we now had an officer, there was virtually nothing he could tell us, so we resorted to our other duties as cleaners to the tented camp, picking up litter, a task that didn't take long. The hours of duty were from Reveille at 6.30 a.m. until 1.00 p.m., when we had a twelve-hour pass. We had a great time and wished for another one soon.

We were called up ten days later on 22 August 1939. For a week nothing happened and we wondered whether Hitler had lost his nerve. On 1 September Poland was invaded and Britain declared war on Germany on 3 September. On that day we were already in our Ops Room – a wooden hut, the purpose-built concrete block at Detling, lay in the future. We had nine officers and twelve ORs (other ranks) and operated in three watches on a 24-hour basis. We started with four hours on and eight off, but this changed quite soon. We ORs slept twelve to a bell tent, feet in the centre, which meant that during the night some were getting dressed and undressed clambering over sleeping bodies. But we soon had longer spells of duty and longer spells off; we had our own hut and beds. We soon learnt that we were the link between Group HQ and the squadrons, and our work was not difficult but there was no room for mistakes. People's lives depended on our doing things right.

We were part of RAF Coastal Command, which consisted of four groups covering the whole of Britain and Northern Ireland. No. 16 Group was based at Chatham, where there was an Area Combined HQ, in which an RAF officer (Controller) sat with a Royal Naval officer. The Naval officer told the RAF officer what needed to be done and the RAF officer gave orders to the stations, which in our case were Thorney Island (Chichester harbour), Detling, Bircham Newton (Norfolk) and

North Coates (Yorkshire). When Detling received its orders in the Ops Room, our senior officer (also called the Controller) gave the order to the squadron and the squadron CO or his deputy gave orders to the aircrew(s), which then came to the Operations Room for details.

Under orders of the Navy our work was the protection of shipping from U-boats. For this purpose 500 Squadron had recently been equipped with Mk I Avro Ansons, twin-engine monoplanes, slow but with all-round vision. We were a GR (General Reconnaissance) squadron. By flying around and ahead of a convoy a U-boat on the surface would be spotted easily, so it would dive and thereby its speed would be limited and it would be unable to get into a position to attack. Ansons would escort a convoy sailing around the coast from the nearest RAF station, so in the first six months of war Detling would take over from Thorney Island. Somewhere near Brighton for convoys going to London or up the east coast, and off Harwich for convoys going south.

On day two of the Phoney War, not so for us, one of our Ansons dropped its two anti-sub bombs on a U-boat, but unfortunately the bombs were dropped without first having the fuse switch turned on and consequently the bombs were harmless. On day six a number of our Ansons were out on a combined patrol in the dusk and they had difficulty finding their way home. The orders were strict that they could not use their WT (wireless telegraphy) because of German operators listening in, so they could not call up and ask for a course to steer to get back to Detling. Six either crashed or force-landed, with about half of the crew members being killed.

By now we had received half of 48 Squadron to bolster our numbers; a squadron was twelve aircraft and crews with perhaps another twelve in reserve and under training. It was soon realised that Operations Room personnel had no place in a squadron (which essentially was mobile) so we were transferred from 500 Squadron to RAF Station Detling. Our task was to load the navigator with his equipment. This consisted of the 'Syko' (Cypher/Code) portable machine for encoding and decoding messages, using a different card every day; 'Very' light cartridges for recognition, to be fired when being fired on by our own forces, changed every six hours; letter of the day to be flashed, especially at night, similarly for recognition. Also to advise if there were lights or balloons newly installed near their course overland.

There were of course periods of time when nothing was happening, and we were free to study the air navigation manual and aircraft recognition books. I reckon I would have needed very little training before I could navigate an aircraft completely, because I knew it all in theory. I wanted to fly and applied to become aircrew, but I suspected that with short sight and the need to wear glasses I would be turned down, and indeed I was, to my mother's great relief, but I felt I had to make the bid. During the ten-day period of the Dunkirk evacuation we went into top gear; we had no less than thirteen squadrons operating at one time or another. Our Ansons maintained air-search patrol over the area, three at a time from before dawn until after dusk.

Allowing one hour to get there, two hours on the job and one hour to return, crews would report for briefing one hour before take-off and again attend for de-briefing afterwards. During those six hours, further flights of three would have taken off, and this would go on until after dark, which at the end of May meant that we saw the last of them just before midnight. Added to this was a similar pattern for two squadrons of twin-engine Blenheim fighters. These had four machine guns firing forwards and were not very effective, but the RAF used everything they had got. These aircraft followed the same pattern as the Ansons, a flight of three continually over Dunkirk from before dawn to after dusk. In addition we had visitors from the Fleet Air Arm, two squadrons of Swordfish, which could carry four 250 lb bombs under each wing. They went on patrol twice a day, twelve to a squadron, day after day. They flew to Calais, where German tanks were stationed, and usually returned to base without casualties. With these and other squadrons now based at Detling, resources were stretched to the limit.

Following the miracle of Dunkirk, Detling went back to its usual routine of guarding ships from submarine attack. Except that everything had changed, as the Germans were just across the Channel. No ships crossed the Channel to supply the troops and as the summer of 1940 wore on, bombing attacks on British ships meant that convoys ceased to sail between Southampton and London, although they still sailed from London up the east coast. During these months of 1940 we were all given lessons in actual fighting. Firing rifles at targets on the firing range was fun. We were also taught how to bayonet and how to fire a Lewis machine gun and the 'Tommy' gun (Thompson sub-machine gun).

We were also given instruction on the use of hand grenades, throwing them from behind a wall onto a mattress placed some distance away. When I was promoted to sergeant I was issued with a Smith & Wesson 0.38. These weapons belonged to Detling and I had to hand my revolver in when I left Detling, because the airfield was in the danger zone, with invasion in mind. By July 1940 we moved into our new concrete Operations Room, which we shared with telephone exchange, WT Section, Met Office, Cypher Office and Teleprinter Office. It had air conditioning, six feet of reinforced concrete on the roof, and blast-proof, non-opening windows, and as one Sqn Ldr Controller remarked, 'If a bomb lands on top of us, we just raise two fingers in the air.'

In August we were visited by the AOC-in-C, AM Sir Frederick Bowhill, who came to inspect Detling airfield and the new Ops Block. The teleprinter office was where we received all communication to and from Group HQ by landline and therefore needed to be secret and secure, and consequently was placed adjacent to the Ops Room, with a hatch through which messages were passed. One day during the summer I opened the hatch and found a beautiful smiling face on the other side and was smitten. The face belonged to a WAAF named Valda Hardy and before long we were going out together.

The air raid warning system was 'yellow' (a preliminary warning that aircraft were active) and 'red' (imminent danger of attack), sent by telephone. In practice this meant that we would be given the 'red' warning when enemy aircraft were attacking shipping off Dover, because they were only a few minutes time away. The station commander arranged that the Observer Corps, whose HQ was in Maidstone, should phone us when there was a real threat because he could not allow work on the station to be disrupted constantly and unnecessarily by all and sundry going to their air raid shelters when no enemy aircraft had crossed the coast. But he did not arrange for a telephone line to be installed exclusively for the Observer Corps, with fatal consequences for RAF Detling. The question could be asked, was Detling a vital target to defend?

Dave King was told when he visited the HQ of the Observer Corps above Maidstone GPO that there was a squadron of Hurricanes flying towards the Detling, but they were apparently recalled and turned back. So the answer has to be no. So what defence was there for the airfield? Just a few machine gun posts.

King reflected further on the attack of 13 August 1940:

Working three watches over a three-day period meant that I came off watch at 2.00 p.m. on 12 August and was due back by 10.00 p.m. on 13 August, and I spent the day at home in Tonbridge Road, which was fortunate. My first glimpse of the airfield after the raid was from the top deck of a bus. When I left there was row of six Blenheim bombers of 53 and 59 Squadrons, all nicely lined up alongside the road. On arriving back at Detling, all I could see were just twelve engines – no aircraft. Every building was damaged or destroyed and sixty-seven people dead, including the station commander, two squadron leaders and a flying officer. All four were killed in the Operations Room; none of the staff were killed. All members of 'C' Watch had the distinction of being Mentioned in Dispatches because of the number of raids that we endured.

I have the certificate to prove it, mounted and framed by my mother, [who] was so proud – and that's why I have the oak leaf on my medals. Sometimes we would gather at Mrs Payne's house. [She] lived in the lane running west from the top of Detling Hill just off the perimeter. [We would] phone the Ops Room to find out if a raid was impending before travelling along the exposed mile of road alongside the airfield. Once 'A' Watch phoned from Mrs Payne's and were told there was no warning in force, but their arrival at the guard room coincided with that of a dozen Me 109s armed with bombs. They leapt from the car and sought shelter in the nearest ditch, later arriving at the Ops Room, scratched and bruised. August wore on; there were no more raids on Detling. However the Battle of Britain raged above our heads and throughout the South East. As for Detling, through the autumn of 1940 the Ansons continued to give protection to the convoys north of the Thames, and the Blenheims bombed the barges collecting in the invasion ports on the other side of the Channel at night. We went to bed wondering if an invasion would come.

But Detling's busy days were over and as the threat of invasion lessened, so our squadrons left the airfield. We were available for our bombers returning from raiding Europe, and we were also host to the naval aircraft. The main role of some of the Blackburn Sharks at Detling was for towing drogues for the Navy to shoot at … I went on one of these trips, the crew was pilot and wireless op, but they had three seats, one for the navigator, so they could take a passenger. It was a lovely day and we flew to Harwich where naval ships were waiting for us. We flew at 5,000 feet and let the drogue out a mile, and later 2,000 feet with the drogue brought in to 440 yards, this being for the benefit of quick-firing cannons and smaller weapons. Their aim was OK and the shells never came anywhere near us, nor of course could we hear the explosions because of the noise from the engine.

Blenheim Mk IVs of 53 Squadron (16 Group) operated from Detling between July 1940 and August 1941 as part of Coastal Command, later being joined by 59 Squadron (15 Group), from Thorney Island, flying the Blenheim Mk IV. Their task being anti-invasion Channel sweeps, they attacked shipping and targets north of France. During the summer, the squadrons became more involved in day and night raids on the Channel ports, where invasion barges were being massed.

The main ground and air party, consisting of twenty Blenheims, moved to Detling on 3 July 1940. The HQ was established at Owen's Garage on

Ready for a night sortie to Channel ports in September 1940 are, from left to right, Sgt D. Smart (observer), P/O R. V. Muspratt (pilot) and Sgt R. Cole (WOP/AG). The aircraft, a Blenheim Mk IV, had black under-surfaces for night-flying and flew with 53 Squadron.

the south side of the airfield and the personnel were accommodated in tents. Army officers seconded to 53 Squadron from the School of Army Co-operation at Andover had to brush up on ship recognition on arrival. Nine Search and Rescue (SAR) patrols and a reconnaissance flight off Boulogne harbour were flown on 5 July without incident. The patrol area ran north-east out over the North Sea from Manston to a point some 50 miles off Den Helder. Returning from an attack on a canal near Amsterdam, Flt Lt Bartlett in Blenheim L8789-J in the early hours of 7 July was unable to find Detling in bad weather. He had to land at the disused civilian airfield at Ramsgate and the aircraft was damaged when it hit several anti-invasion obstructions.

Fog at Detling made it difficult for pilots to find Detling airfield. P/O H. M. Newton returned from a raid on vessels at Ostend in R3678-Y at 1.30 a.m. and landed heavily in heavy rain, the aircraft tipping onto its nose. On 13 July, Wg Cdr Edwards was returning from a raid on Leidam Island in L9474-L and was unable to obtain any bearings. He ran out of fuel at 2.45 p.m. and the crew abandoned the aircraft near Bulpham, Essex. All landed safely. The WOP/AG had control of the radio. It was mounted on a shelf behind the turret and was completely out of sight when he was in the turret. It needed both hands to tune it and each hand was encased in many pairs of gloves. It is hardly surprising that obtaining bearings was difficult. Six Blenheims of 53 Squadron attacked an oil refinery at Vlaardingen near Rotterdam on the night of 20 July. Storage tanks were damaged and blew up. P/O D. B. Starky, Sgt H. W. Hunt and Sgt B. Moriarty went missing in R3836-X on 25 July; they were shot down and killed by a German convoy.

P/O J. C. Mallon found the flare path at Detling obscured by low cloud on his return from a raid in R3660-K on 31 July. He landed across the line of 'glim' lamps, ran off the airfield and collided with a sandbag emplacement. P/O Ritchie flying PZ-P could not find Detling and landed at Weston Zoyland, Somerset.

Sqn Ldr Oliver led seven Blenheims on an attack on Emden harbour on 3 August. The weather was deteriorating and two were unable to locate the target. P/O H. C. Corbett and crew of L9475-V made an attack on the airfields at Schiphol and Haamstede instead. They didn't come home; it was thought they were lost at sea.

On 4 August, Sqn Ldr Oliver in L8794-T, also unable to find Detling and without any bearings, ordered his crew to bail out when they ran out of fuel. He managed to put the aircraft down between Farnham and Petersfield.

A crew abandoned Blenheim T1937-E on 13 August. As with other aircraft, the pilot was unable to locate Detling. The crew landed safely and P/O Jameson was found hanging upside down from hop pole wires in the dark. The aircraft came down near Hawkhurst. During the raid on 13 August by Stuka dive-bombers, 53 Squadron lost two officers, Sqn Ldr D. C. Oliver (Operations) and F/O H. M. Aspen (signals officer). Of the twenty aircraft destroyed that day, five were of 53 Squadron. They caught fire after being hit by incendiary shells.

The same month, six members of the squadron were awarded the DFC, including Sqn Ldr W. B. Murray and Flt Lt A. C. Brown. DFMs were given to Sgt B. J. Brooks, Sgt G. H. Cooper, Sgt R. A. Latham and Sgt W. P. Whetton.

P/O Dottridge and Sgt Freddie King managed to return to Detling despite the damage to the starboard wing of their Blenheim T2132-L. King helped the pilot with the control column in a desperate bid to level the aircraft.

High above Detling airfield on 17 August 1941, Sgt C. Webb was on an authorised flight with his observer, Sgt J. Mathers. The pilot was practising slowing down the speed of his aircraft by lowering the undercarriage of his Bristol Beaufighter Mk I, serial no. X7564. On reaching an altitude of 10,000 feet, he inadvertently caused the flaps to be lowered at a speed

Sgt Lionel Louis Benjamin (observer) of 53 Squadron in July 1940. He was killed in Blenheim T1940 PZ-D on 31 August 1940 with Wg Cdr E. C. T. Edwards at Vlaardingen, Holland. Lionel was twenty-two years old and was buried at Rotterdam (Crooswijk) General Cemetery.

20 mph in excess of that permitted by the manufacturers, and failure of the flaps occurred. At this point, the aircraft flicked over on its back, stalled and spun. The crew were both based with 29 Squadron at RAF West Malling, a short distance from Detling, which was the satellite airfield for this famous airfield. Sgt Webb was an experienced pilot who had nearly 290 hours' flying experience and had flown many aircraft types.

In a report by the Accident Investigation Branch, it was concluded that the pilot had selected 'flaps down' instead of 'undercarriage down'. Sgt Webb stated that the immediate effect was for him to be thrown violently forward and for the aircraft to flick over onto its back in a roll to the left. In this position it stalled and went into a tight left-hand spin. Realising the mistake he had made and after selecting the 'flaps up' position, he eased the aircraft in the spin and went into a spiral from which he was able to regain control after dropping 8,000 feet. On close inspection of the flaps mechanism and design, it was noted that there was no relief system. It was recommended that Beaufighters should be fitted with a separate relief system to relieve loads imposed on the mechanism when the flaps were lowered at speeds in excess of that recommended by the Bristol Aircraft Company.

F/O S. C. Rochford, Sgt W. Briggs and Sgt D. Brooks of 53 Squadron were not so lucky when returning from a night patrol over the Hook of Holland to Ostend on 24 August. Their Blenheim T2035 hit houses at Dover and all were killed. It is thought the aircraft collided with a barrage balloon. Unfortunately, the Blenheim fell on 15 Chevalier Road, Dover, killing the residents – Police Constable William Maylock and his young wife Mary.

During the high-level attack of 30 August, AC2 B. Stone was killed; AC1 Jones and AC2 Johnson were injured. The airfield was again attacked the following morning by Bf 109s and Bf 110s. The fuel dump was ignited and the main electrical power cable to the airfield was cut. August ended in further tragedy when 53 Squadron lost five Blenheims flown by, among others, Wg Cdr E. C. T. Edwards (the CO), Sgt L. L. Benjamin and Sgt J. T. Beesley. They were all killed. Edwards was a very popular and respected leader.

One of the most famous and successful pilots of the Battle of Britain period was undoubtedly Flt Lt A. C. Deere of 54 Squadron. On 28 August 1940, he was flying from RAF Hornchurch in a Spitfire Mk I – serial no. R6832 – when in the vicinity of Detling airfield he was attacked and shot down by Spitfires. He managed to bale out without serious injury. This was one of several narrow escapes he had. The identity of the pilot and aircraft that shot him down are not known. He was attacking a Me 109 when his aircraft was hit by bullets in the fuselage and port wing, cutting his control wires. He had no option but to take to the silk. Landing safely, he was back at Hornchurch by 3.00 p.m., having been flown back from Detling airfield in an Anson aircraft.

The airfield was again put out of action for three hours on 2 September. The day before, the officers' mess had been set on fire during an attack. This time the airfield was hit by high-flying Dornier Do 17s. On 5 September 1940, at precisely 3.55 p.m., no less than twenty Me 109s dive-bombed Detling airfield. During this attack, 337 Gun Battery, based at Hartlip, got lucky and shot one of the intruders down. The same afternoon, Oberleutnant Karl-Heinz Metz, a pilot with 8-JG2, collided with another aircraft flown by Flt Lt Cotz during combat. P/O Johnson of 46 Squadron also attacked Metz, and the aircraft crashed-landed at Detling.

This machine was later removed from the airfield and transported to RAE at Farnborough for evaluation. Later that afternoon, at 4.00 p.m., two high-explosive bombs exploded close to the Harrow Inn, Stockbury, and another exploded further east. Two more fell near cottages at Thurnham, near Detling vicarage and less than a mile from the airfield.

Windows were shattered and ceilings damaged. Other bombs fell close to Beaux Aires Farm, Detling, destroying farm buildings and killing nine sheep. Thirty-six HE bombs exploded in the southern area of the airfield, but mercifully there were no casualties.

At Thames Haven, heavy and light bombs were dropped in a line almost east to west. The bombs were dropped about 200 yards too far north to obtain maximum effect on the oil tanks, but unfortunately two heavy bombs straddled the power house, which was temporarily put out of action. Bombs hit the tanks in two places. A 5,000-gallon tank full of lubricating oil caused the main fire, which was not extinguished until 4.00 p.m. on 6 September. A smaller fire about 150 yards further west was extinguished by foam before nightfall. One of the boiler houses was damaged and several other tanks were punctured by splinters. One oil incendiary bomb was found, but it had only caused a grass fire. At the conclusion of the main attack described above, between 3.55 p.m. and 4.05 p.m., when British fighters had returned to their bases to refuel, a 'sneak' bombing attack was made on Detling Aerodrome by Me 109s diving from 5,000 feet to 3,000 feet from different directions.

These were engaged by AA guns, which put up a barrage over Detling Aerodrome at 3,000 feet against a force of twenty Me 109s. This appears to have been successful in some measure, as only five aircraft carried out the actual attack on the airfield. Guns engaged six Me 109s at 3,000 feet. Three waves consisting of three Me 109s dived from west to east. One Me 109 dived from east to west and south-east to north-west and another dived from south to north. No hits were claimed, but although fifteen to twenty bombs were dropped on the landing ground, damage was negligible and no casualties were reported. Another gun battery during this raid brought down a Me 109 at 7,000 feet with barrage fire. The aircraft crashed near Detling. It had been a hectic day.

However, perhaps the most spectacular incident involving a German aircraft occurred on 30 September 1940. RAF fighters engaged a Bf 109E of 4-JG52 during a bomber escort sortie over London and damaged the aircraft's radiator. It was claimed that Gefreiter Erich Mummert had been hit by another Bf 109, but it is believed that Flt Lt E. Holden of 501 Squadron, based at RAF Kenley, caused the damage. Mummert overshot the airfield while attempting to land at Detling and force-landed near the airfield boundary at 2.00 p.m. The pilot was taken prisoner and his aircraft was a write-off. The first-aid kit and leading-edge wing panel 'liberated' from this aircraft were donated to the Kent Battle of Britain Museum at Hawkinge, Kent, in 1980.

Two Blenheims of 53 Squadron were shot down in the sea on 7 September, killing Flt Lt I. H. Bartlett, Sgt R. E. Aldridge and Sgt E. D.

This Bf 109e of 4-JG52 was damaged in combat and brought down at Detling airfield by Flt Lt E. Holden of 501 Squadron, based at RAF Kenley. The pilot, Gefreiter Erich Mummert, overshot the airfield while attempting to land at Detling.

Sheldrick of R3779-Z, and P/O R. G. Hall, Sgt J. D. Randall and Sgt M. B. Conacherin of T2042-H.

On 19 September, P/O C. F. Tibbits and his crew went missing. He was on his first operation with the squadron.

Six crews were briefed to attack Den Helder docks on 27 September. The raid was aborted when the second aircraft, flown by P/O P. J. E. Ritchie, hit a tree on take-off in poor visibility, Sgt. R. H. Trafford (WOP/AG) was seriously injured and Blenheim T2221-J was wrecked. The crew of T2044-G failed to return on 30 September. Sadly, Sgt H. A. Shaw's body was never found. Blenheim R2771-A, unable to make it home to Detling, crashed in flames at RAF Manston on 5 October. P/O K. A. Faulkner and Sgt G. B. Fielder were seriously injured; Sgt A. R. S. Hall was killed in the inferno.

On 21 October, P/O H. J. Meakin (pilot), Sgt G. Hutson (observer) and Sgt G. T. Hadman (WO/air gunner) of 53 Squadron took off from Detling in T2132-R on a routine coastal patrol over the Channel. Meakin had been trying out the new Mk XI bombsight. At 10.30 a.m. the returning Blenheim clipped the chimney of Osborne's grocer's shop on the corner of Dernier Road, Tonbridge, close to the cemetery, and crashed onto a terrace of houses. The crew had managed to bail out from their stricken aircraft.

According to the squadron records, the Blenheim had suffered control failure – the precise cause was not clear – but before the crew jumped to safety, the bombs were jettisoned. P/O Meakin reported that the damage

A scene of devastation is self-evident at Dernier Road, Tonbridge. At 10.30 a.m. on Monday 21 October 1940, Blenheim Mk IV R3699 of 53 Squadron crashed into houses.

was due to being hit by gunfire. Whether this was due to enemy action or fire from British guns is not verified, although 'friendly fire' was not uncommon during the war. The young pilot was injured and both his crew members escaped major injury. Unfortunately, the residents of Dernier Road were not so lucky. An eyewitness, Mr Skinner, remembers:

> The aircraft demolished the several houses and damaged many more. Two occupants were killed, Mrs Couchman and Mrs Alice Ford. Mrs Harris and Pat Atkins, a young girl, died later of their injuries.

A local baker's deliveryman, on his rounds for E. W. Edwards & Son, sustained a broken hip; other victims later died of their injuries. Royston Newman, a Wolf Cub, was awarded the Scout Silver Medal for an act of bravery when he shielded his baby brother in his pram from the Blenheim's falling debris and exploding bullets. Both boys were injured. Owing to censorship imposed on the press in those days, a detailed report was not printed in the papers. A few weeks later, a local paper printed a photograph of the devastation in Dernier Road, with the following caption: 'Havoc caused in south east town when plane crashed on the roof tops. Four homes were completely demolished.' After the war, the houses were rebuilt and became homes for local firemen – a fitting tribute.

On 27 October, P/O Plumtree, flying T2132-R, was sent on a routine mission over Den Helder. In fact, he was to try out the new Mk XI gun sight. He was attacked by three Bf 109s of ZG76, during which Sgt Wood and Sgt Kinsey were seriously injured. The pilot managed to land at Martlesham Heath. For his actions, he was awarded the DFC and Sgt Kinsey the DFM. The same day, seven aircraft of 53 Squadron attacked a convoy off Calais. P/O R. L. Buckley, Sgt C. Henderson and Sgt P. E. J. Neale were shot down and killed in Blenheim L8789-E.

Following an attack on Le Touquet airfield on 4 November, T1992-S was pounced on by a yellow-nosed Bf 109 piloted by Unteroffizier Rolf Klippgen of 9-JG53. The chase ended near Dover and the Blenheim's hydraulic system was damaged; however, the pilot made a safe wheels-up landing at Detling. The last raids by 53 Squadron took place on 7–8 November, when it attacked the Lorient U-boat base. All aircraft made it back to base. On 20 November, the squadron left Detling for Thorney Island, where once again they shared the airfield with 59 Squadron. They had suffered terrible losses in Kent, but had distinguished themselves in action.

It was unusual for Blenheims to carry bombs on anti-invasion patrols, but they soon found a use for them when they attacked an airfield near Boulogne. German coastal airfields around the Cherbourg and Le Touquet area, including Caen and Brest, became suitable targets when there was no shipping observed. During the first week of August, the squadron attacked Cherbourg. All aircraft bombed the target successfully, but WO Weldon Smith was shot down. Other duties involved escorting Channel convoys. Both E-boats and dive-bombers attacked the convoys and the squadron often searched for survivors of sunken ships.

In the same month, 53 Squadron was involved in special air strikes on Flashing's oil stores and the docks at Den Helder. Detling airfield was attacked late on the afternoon of 13 August and the squadron's Blenheims were severely damaged. Five of these aircraft were bombed-up. Me 109s also damaged two others during the attack. Four airmen were killed and Sqn Ldr D. C. Oliver died. Five other airmen were seriously wounded. Despite this setback, patrols and strikes continued, and on 21 August five Blenheims attacked Abbeville. The following day, St Omer airfield was bombed.

The Royal Artillery was based at Detling during the Battle of Britain. The following account was jointly written by Syd Ashby, George Wooton and Ron Allen, who were soldiers with one of the airfield's AA units, for the BBC WW2 People's War website. Their weapons were Bofor guns.

In August 1940, during the period which became known as the Battle of Britain, Detling received the attention of the Luftwaffe. We were extensively dive-bombed by Stuka aircraft. The first raid was the most disastrous. All three of our hangars were damaged, several aircraft were destroyed and there were many casualties. I believe that some thirty or so personnel were killed, mostly in air raid shelters, which received direct hits. Following this, most personnel never again entered a shelter during a raid. I and several workmates found a small hollow at the edge of some woods, just across the tarmac from our hangar, which we considered to be an excellent hidey hole. Every time the air raid 'red' sounded we ran like the wind to this hollow. All went well for several days, then, during an early morning raid, we were shaken out of our skins by a series of loud explosions and severe vibrations. We thought, 'This is it – goodnight nurse.' However, we found out that during the hours of darkness the ack-ack battery of the Royal Artillery had positioned two Bofors guns about two yards from the edge of our hollow. We had to find a new hidey hole.

I recall one memorable character at Detling, George Wooton, a reservist called up at the outbreak of war. George had left the RAF in 1924, working as a London bus driver, a real 'dyed in the wool' Cockney. If there was any fiddle going on you could guarantee George would have organised it or at least be deeply involved. The most lucrative was the section 'tea swindle', which George took over. He 'won' supplies of tea, sugar, milk and cake and expanded the swindle to serve the whole of Maintenance Flight, making huge profits for the members (the Instrument Section). If anything was in short supply, George could invariably obtain it (at a price). Near the end of August 1940, I was informed that I was to be posted overseas and was granted 4 days' embarkation leave. Having been issued with tropical kit I was sent to RAF Uxbridge, which was used as a personnel dispatch centre. I spent my nineteenth birthday at Uxbridge.

While at Uxbridge, London received several air raids, both by day and night. At night the sky was red from the many fires. I saw the aftermath of the raid on the East Surrey Docks, which set fire to Tate & Lyle's refinery. I was at a searchlight site on the perimeter of Detling airfield at a place (farm) known as Beaux Aires. This was shortly after turning into a lane on the left when passing the entrance to the airfield, travelling from the Maidstone direction. I was there both before the war and on final mobilisation in the Territorial Army, although I had been posted before the Battle of Britain started, actually on 12 November 1939. One of my companions on the site was called Ron Allen, but I expect that is a coincidence. My time there was during the Phoney War so I had lots of trips into Maidstone on short leaves. I think there was a searchlight site actually on the airfield. For us the rehearsals were now over and we were at war.

This news was received on 3 September 1939 by our searchlight detachment in the field at Beaux Aires (on the perimeter of airfield), where we had been since the small hours of Friday 25 August 1939. Nobody knew what to expect on that first day, but the day was spent in checking once again that all the equipment was functioning properly, was clean and ready for action. My own job, apart from guards and other jobs around the site, was to see that the generator was ready. At Beaux Aires this was a four-cylinder Lister diesel generator, rather than a searchlight lorry. Also, although there was no enemy activity, the usual drill was followed in running the engine (the same applied if it was a generator lorry) for ten minutes every hour during the night so that it would be warm and start immediately when required. There would thus be power whenever needed for the searchlight to engage hostile aircraft.

Things had improved considerably since the Munich Crisis in that the sites were complete in terms of equipment, but also we were accommodated in a wooden hut just large enough for a detachment of ten men, rather than the barn at Key Street during the Munich Crisis. The beds were three wooden planks with supports quite close to the floor with straw-filled palliases as bedding. In the centre of the hut was a cylindrical coke burning stove for heating. This had a removable round lid at the top for refilling with coke and a hinged flap at the bottom for removing the ashes and lighting it.

We naturally followed our training for night operations and had a sentry posted who also acted as an 'air sentry'. His job was to call the rest of the detachment out if he saw or heard any air activity. In the early morning of 5 September 1939, he proved to be superfluous when AA guns firing wakened everybody. Being unused to this sort of thing and seeing and hearing no aircraft activity, everybody dived for cover while we thought this through. (Slit trenches had already been dug). The only danger we were in, though, was from our own shrapnel.

Some time shortly after hostilities commenced, we received 'Rules of Engagement'. I remember one, which was to the effect that aircraft were not to be fired on unless they committed a hostile act. The displaying of the German cross on an aircraft would be a hostile act. For most people in the country … things were different from before 3 September. In the case of the forces the training and build up of material continued. We know now that we were in the period known as the Phoney War. However, had this description been known then, it would not have seemed a phoney war by any means to a number of people even on that first day. The sinking of the SS *Athenia* on 3 September by the U-boat U30 being a case in point. There were others, a couple of which, one personal, will be mentioned later.

Nevertheless, it is true that none of the intense air activity, which had been anticipated at this time, developed. Other than training periods there was no night activity as far as we were concerned. The maintenance of the site and equipment, with training, could mainly take place in the mornings. This allowed half the detachment to have approximately 3 hours leave on alternate days, except when there were alerts. There were a few occasions when we had 24-hour leaves enabling us to go to Gravesend – all of our detachment came from Gravesend. On the short leaves Maidstone was not far away so we were able to go there. Just prior to the war, I had bought a new Royal Enfield motorcycle and after a week or two ([on] 23 September 1939), on one of the 24 hour leaves I rode it back to the site.

This meant that two of us – I and somebody else on the pillion seat – could have longer in Maidstone on these short leaves. Checking my diary for the period, we very quickly found that our uniforms attracted the girls in the shops when we spent our time off in Maidstone. Some of the time there was spent in having hot baths in the public baths. On 6 September, after the bath, two of us went into a café where I thought one of the waitresses was very nice. Ernie (Cpl O'Connor), who was my companion, said that she seemed to like me – quite a morale booster. The following day I went again into Maidstone, this time with Ron Ashby. We did some shopping and got on fine with all the girls in the shops. Herbert's Café and Phyllis and Woolworths and Jean occur fairly frequently in my diary at that time. Altogether, with lack of action and fairly frequent short leaves, this period, as far as we were concerned, earned its subsequent title of the Phoney War.

However, Beaux Aires was on a perimeter of Detling airfield and it was not unusual to see the obsolete Avro Ansons returning to the airfield with signs of damage. Not a phoney war for the aircrew. Toward the end of the Beaux Aires posting the weather was showing signs of the winter to come. The nights were cold so one of the additional duties of the air sentry was to revive the coke stove if it had been a quiet night, as it usually was, before the rest of the detachment got up to face the day. The winter of 1939–40 had the coldest January since 1895 and eventually the second coldest of the century. The River Thames froze over for the first time since 1880.

At some stage during this posting, the Lister stationary diesel generator had been replaced with a generator lorry. Before this the fuel for the diesel had been supplied and kept in two-gallon petrol cans. Naturally, the petrol for the lorry was also kept in 2-gallon petrol cans. The method adopted by the air sentries each morning to revive the coke stove was to remove the lid and pour a little diesel oil onto the fire, which worked quite well. Came the inevitable day when the air sentry got the cans of fuel muddled up and poured petrol on instead. The resultant flash and bang as we woke hurriedly convinced the detachment that we had been bombed with a near miss. Fortunately no harm was done other than a severely shaken detachment and an air sentry who for the rest of the day had a very red face and burning ears not caused by burns. His knowledge of Anglo-Saxon English also probably increased considerably.

At the end of August, Detling was again the target. Me 109s shot up the airfield, and on 1 September it was dive-bombed. During this raid, which took place in the dark, incendiaries and high explosives damaged the MT Section.

Although these raids did not cripple the airfield, the Luftwaffe appreciated Detling's importance in the event of the Germans' planned invasion, observing that the RAF was keeping a watch on their preparations. With this knowledge, it was no surprise that the Luftwaffe bombed the airfield again, and inflicted damage to dispersal areas, but without casualties. The following afternoon the 109s were back attacking the remaining buildings. The massed barges for the imminent invasion of Britain became the target for both squadrons, but they continued their attacks on Channel shipping. Between 1 July and 30 September, 53 and 59 Squadrons had operated eighty-one Blenheims; nineteen of these were lost on operations. Some thirteen other aircraft were written off due to combat, with two more crashing during operational flights.

On 31 August 1940, a Blenheim Mk IV, T1940, squadron code PZ-D of 53 Squadron – with the CO, Wg Cdr Edwards, at the controls, and his crew comprising Sgt Beesley and Sgt Benjamin – crashed. The crew were buried close to airmen of 600 Squadron RAuxAF at Pernis. Locals regularly placed flowers on the graves, which became a symbol of remembrance and resistance. Later in the war, the Germans moved all five airmen to Crooswijk Cemetery, Rotterdam. They placed a shield on the graves with a simple inscription that read, 'Resting place of two English Pilot Officers, fallen 10 May 1940, and an English crew of a Bristol Blenheim that was shot down by AA fire on 31 August near Nieuwe Sluis.'

The AA defences of RAF stations like Detling were severely tested between July and August 1940, although the claims made by stations during this period amounted to only fifteen enemy aircraft destroyed and six damaged. The volume of ground fire undoubtedly had a considerable deterrent effect. The first gallantry award to a ground gunner occurred when Cpl Jackman received the Military Medal for operating his Lewis gun at Detling. Jackman served with the RAF regiment located on the airfield. He had remained at his post until it was destroyed and he was severely wounded. Ground-to-air engagements by AA machine guns were recorded at RAF Manston, Biggin Hill, West Malling, Hawkinge, Driffield, Dishforth and Leeming. During this period, the Army's Inspector of Fortifications and the RAF's Director of Ground Defence conducted a joint investigation into the requirements for airfield defence.

The Taylor Report, as it became known, advised that a single organisation should be provided either by the Army or the RAF. Both councils accepted the report and the Air Ministry set up a committee to examine how best to form an airfield defence force based upon the 35,000 ground gunners then serving in the RAF. At the same time, the War Office prepared to strengthen the forces available for airfield defence by raising 'young soldier' battalions for the task. Flt Lt Don Rogers, who had completed a short detachment at RAF Bircham Newton with 500 Squadron, remembers that the squadron used the airfield in Norfolk as a stop-over between patrols over the Thames Estuary.

On one such occasion on 3 January 1941, Rogers had been ordered to cover a southbound convoy north of the Thames Estuary. Having completed the patrol, he told his crew that they would head back to Detling as it was becoming dark. Approaching the airfield, he was unable to see the beacon that helped guide aircraft into land. He circled Detling, but there was still no sign of the beacon. After three and a half hours on patrol, fuel was getting low, so it was decided to bail out. Their altitude was 5,000 feet. Unfortunately, it was realised with horror that the Anson they were flying had just had a major overhaul and parachutes had not been installed. It was at this point that one of the crew finally spotted the beacon and landed without further incident. They had been airborne for three hours and forty minutes.

On the 19 June 1941, a flight of 59 Squadron Blenheims acting as convoy escort flew three sorties. During these missions, three aircraft were attacking shipping when TR-M hit the sea and took evasive action. It crash-landed at Shoreham. Fortunately, the crew – F/O Miles, Sgt Lewis and Sgt Mikklesen – were unhurt.

Night patrols were flown on various occasions. On 30 June, three Blenheims on one such patrol were involved in a tragic incident when P/O Whitmore and his crew – Sgt Dulley and Sgt Truman – did not return. Their aircraft was reported to have hit a barrage balloon at Dover. The body of P/O Whitmore was later recovered from the sea. One unlucky crew, flying a Blenheim Mk IV, serial no. Z7450, code TR-O, took off from Detling at 3.03 p.m. on 7 July 1941 on a routine reconnaissance flight and was shot down by a German destroyer off the coast of Gravelines. The crew, Flt Sgt (OBS) George Thomas Wood, Sgt John Henry Brown (WOP) and their pilot Sqn Ldr Lionel Aitkin, were all killed.

From May 1940 onwards into the succeeding months, Swordfish squadrons were loaned to RAF Coastal Command and conducted mine-laying operations and convoy patrols in the English Channel and North Sea against German, Dutch, Belgian and French ports. The Nazi Blitzkrieg against the Low Countries and France forced the RAF and FAA to call on every resource they had to stave off complete disaster. In all, four squadrons of Swordfish were attached to RAF Coastal Command, operating out of RAF Thorney Island, North Coates, Detling and Manston. They were put to every task for which they were capable: mine-laying, bombing of naval and ground targets, spotting, and reconnaissance, often flying individually with pilot and observer alone throughout the night.

With the threat of invasion from Europe, these four squadrons were called upon to bomb the build-up of invasion barges in enemy ports and to lay mines in the harbours. Their task went on into the Battle of Britain period, July–October 1940. This period was particularly difficult for the aircrews. On 26 May 1940, Swordfish '5H' of 825 Squadron, flown by Sub-Lt J. B. Kiddle from Detling, was spotting for HMS *Galatea* off Calais when it was attacked at 8,000 feet by two Bf 109s north-west of Songatte. During the violent evading action of diving and turning at sea level, the observer, Lt G. N. Beaumont, was thrown out of the aircraft and killed. The aircraft returned safely.

Sgt Aubrey Lancaster, who had recently moved to Detling with 235 Squadron, recalls the events of 29 May 1940:

We, three Blenheims, flown by Flt Lt 'Wigs' Manwaring, P/O Tony Booth and P/O John Cronan, took off with instructions to patrol from Calais to Dunkirk for the duration of our fuel. Of course, from Detling (we were detached there on 26 May) we were soon over Calais and heading up the coast until we could see the huge pillars of smoke from the burning oil tanks at Dunkirk. About 5 miles short of Dunkirk, we spotted lots of fighters heading our way and I alerted our gunner and he told us they were coming round onto our tails but until then was unable to definitely identity them. However, this was soon made clear as one of their number swooped across our path and it was obvious that we were dealing with Me 109s in too large a number for us to deal with. As I realised what we were up against, I happened to look to starboard and there was a fighter fastened on the tail of our number two.

It seemed that a solid sheet of flame erupted from the nose of the fighter and bits started flying off the Blenheim. At this point we were being molested and John Cronan put the aircraft in a dive and then we were really being plastered. The three Blenheims of 235 Squadron did not stand a chance as the attack was led by Hauptmann Adolf Galland, the famous ace, flying with JG27 and [he] claimed two Blenheims. [Leutnant] Igor Zirkenbach of 1-JG27 shot down the third. Both Manwaring and Booth and their crews were all killed whilst John Cronan ditched and he and his crew were rescued. So in one day we lost the most of those who have been the backbone of our squadron round whom we had hoped to build a useful fighting unit.

For the remainder of May and until the day 235 Squadron moved – 10 June 1940 – things were fairly calm, but the squadron's short time spent at Detling was indeed a sad one. There were many forced landings at Detling airfield. On one memorable occasion, Flt Lt H. S. Giddings of 111 Squadron, based at Debden, was forced to land following an attack on a He 111 over the Thames estuary. He managed to vacate Hurricane R4228, only to see it caught in an attack on the airfield. Not all aircraft that crashed or landed at the airfield during the hectic months of the Battle of Britain belonged to the RAF. Following an attack by P/O J. Johnson, Oberleutnant Metz of 8-JG2 collided with another Me 109E, flown by Feldwebel Gotz. He then did a circuit of the airfield and landed. Metz was immediately hauled from his aircraft by station personnel and remained a prisoner of war.

Following the Munich crisis and the German occupation of Czecho-Slovakia in the spring of 1939, Britain at last realised that preparation for war should be taken more seriously and conscription was introduced. All young men were to be conscripted at the age of twenty for four years, serving full-time for six months and then three and a half years on reserve. However, they could join one of the auxiliary forces before the age of twenty, and deduct the time from their later period as a reserve. It was reasonable to expect that the six months' full-time service would be spent with the auxiliary unit you belonged to. The auxiliary forces were the Royal Naval Volunteer Reserve, the Territorial Army, the Auxiliary Air Force and the RAF Volunteer Reserve. The difference between the latter two was that the AAF was formed in squadrons; those who joined the RAFVR were trained and then sent to any unit the RAF wished.

On 8 November 1940, Sgt Kosarz, a Polish pilot of 302 Squadron flying a Hurricane Mk I, serial no. P3538, force-landed at the airfield following combat with Me 109s. Shortly after, Kosarz was dismayed to see his comrade, F/O Wezelik, forced down at Detling while flying Hurricane Mk I V6860. Fortunately, both pilots – who were based at Northolt – were uninjured.

As it was gradually realised that Hitler's invasion was on hold, 4 Squadron settled down to what may be termed an intensive peacetime

Lysander V9587 of No. 4 Army Co-operation Squadron parked just inside a blister hangar in January 1942.

programme. But there occurred occasional excitements. Two days before Christmas, the flying programme was curtailed, owing to a red warning. Later, a Whitley returning from an operation – with a full load of bombs – struck a stationary Lysander. Both went up in flames, with bombs exploding every so often. A German bomber joined in the fun, but his aim was so bad that he missed the airfield completely.

The year 1940 began with another tragic loss, P/O Tennent. While ferrying a new Lysander to the squadron, he flew into a hillside at Ilkley Moor during a snowstorm and was killed.

A lot of work was done in attempting to keep the runways free from snow and one of the most successful methods was found to be spraying them, from the air, with brine.

Moving from Eastchurch on 14 August 1939, 4 Squadron arrived with seventeen aircraft. They were to remain until 20 August 1939; their task was to seek out enemy shipping. On return to Eastchurch, they were given notice to move. The main party of twenty aircraft moved to Thorney Island, but 'B' Flight, consisting of six Lysanders, moved again to Detling on 30 August 1939. They were to be based there for an indefinite period.

Then, on 1 September 1939, general mobilisation of the RAF was ordered, and by 22 September 1940 the squadron was in France. Following the evacuation of Dunkirk, two flights led by Flt Lt Campbell-Voullaire and Flt Lt Fuller left Clairmarais at 6.00 a.m. for Hawkinge; both officers were later flown to Detling. During May 1940, the squadron carried out many sorties over France and continued an intensive programme of night-flying training and Army Co-operation exercises.

In 1942 Army Co-operation Training was given to 4 Squadron for many months, but on the operational side the ASR Flight at Manston was still busy. A move was made to Clifton, York, and, by the spring of 1942, anticipating being re-equipped with single-seat aircraft, the pilots were busy with cockpit drill and passing out on a Miles Master and a Curtiss Tomahawk. The first four North American Mustangs arrived from Speke on 25 April 1942, and another five came three days later. Most of the beloved 'Lizzies' (Lysander aircraft) were flown away to Elstree and the air gunners posted to 296 and 297 squadrons.

By 2 July, Sqn Ldr Saunders was leading squadron formations of nine Mustangs. The squadron role was for the first time fighter-reconnaissance. Low-level attacks against enemy establishments started in October, and detachments of flights came south to Gatwick and Detling airfields for this work. It must have been a peculiar life for the pilots in this period; they were playing with the Army in training, and flying on operations at the same time – trying to remember which the enemy was. A number of operations were made against shipping off the Dutch coast.

The commanding officer at the end of 1942 was Wg Cdr G. E. Macdonald, a New Zealander. He was killed while on an operation over Holland. Sqn Ldr A. S. Baker wrote the following account of an undoubtedly great character:

> Wg Cdr Macdonald was the most vivid and invigorating person who came to 4 Squadron in my time. When Mac first joined us in October 1942, we were based at York but used to detach flights, for a month at a time, to Gatwick or Detling, to take pictures and, as a sideline, to beat up trains. Mac had little interest in cameras, except camera guns, and in his sudden visits to the detachment he set a splendid example of zeal and skill in finding Germans and killing them. One day he and C. T. P. Stephenson came upon a parade on Poix airfield, which they joyously attacked. The next day, Sunday, the picture papers bore the headline, '"We dismissed the parade," says Wing Commander.' In fairness to Mac, I should say that I believe this to have been an invention of the sub-editor.
>
> Mac was a splendid pilot and shot and an inspiring if impetuous leader. We were all the better for trying to live up to the standards he set us and achieved himself. His passion was guns. He loved using them, harmonising them, talking about them, and, I have no doubt, dreaming about them. When off this one subject his mind ricocheted from topic

to topic with a speed which left his audience speechless. His adjutant, 'Arty' Fischel, was the chief sufferer, and after a session of trying to get a decision on an administrative matter, ' Arty' would be quite distraught. One day a new pilot asked Mac how to go about shooting down a Hun. Mac's reply went like this: 'What, shoot down Jerries? Too easy. Go to the French coast fly up and down slowly at 5,000 feet for an hour or two. They will come up, shoot a couple down, come home. No trouble.' All this was delivered with such a serious air that for a little while it was taken to be serious advice.

His death was spectacular and typical. He was on 'Rhubarb' (low-level fighter reconnaissance) with Brian Slack (later killed in a Typhoon in Holland) as his number two. Mac found some barges on a canal between Zwolle and Deventer. He opened fire at 1,000 yards. Instead of dropping his opening burst half-way, as most of us would have done, his first rounds were on the target. The barges were full of ammunition and as Mac arrived they exploded. I was in the Operations Room that morning, and when we heard that only one of this pair was coming back, we assumed we had lost Brian Slack, for to our minds Mac was indestructible. We had cursed him often when he was with us, but missed him when he was gone. We yarned about him for years.

July 1943 found the squadron under canvas at Gravesend, and they were told that the Mustangs were to be changed for DH Mosquitoes. A month later, the unit was back at its peacetime station, Odiham, with one Mk II Mosquito from 140 Squadron for practice flying – though, of course, operations with the Mustangs continued. At the end of November, the squadron was at Sawbridgeworth.

The Coast Defence Co-operation Flight was formed at Eastchurch on 1 December 1924 for the purpose of co-operating with the Coast Artillery School at Shoeburyness, and was transferred from 22 Group to Coastal Command in 1933. In 1934, two more flights were added and the unit became the Coast Defence Development Unit. No. 1, the original flight, was still primarily employed in co-operation with Coast Artillery. During 1935, No. 1 Flight was ordered to Malta as a result of the Italian–Abyssinian War. It returned to Gosport in August 1936 and rejoined the Coast Artillery Co-operation Flight, where its role was training personnel and the formation of Coast Artillery units in an emergency.

When war came on 1 September 1939, No. 1 Flight was at Gosport, equipped with Avro Ansons, and a detachment was moved to Detling on 2 September to co-operate with the Thames and Medway defences. The main unit moved to RAF Thorney Island; its role was to carry out anti-submarine and convoy duties. By May 1940, the detachment became

No. 1 Coast Artillery Co-operation Flight, with permanent headquarters at Detling. In May 1940, working with the established defences at Medway and the Thames, the new unit co-operated with those at Dover and was on standby from dawn to dusk at short notice. In August, two Ansons were detached from Detling to RAF Hawkinge to co-operate with the Royal Marine Siege Regiment at Dover.

During the Battle of Britain, the role of the unit was spotting for the Royal Marines at Dover, whose 14-inch guns bombarded the French coast. In August and September, the unit carried out ten sorties, observing the fall of shot on the targets in the Cape Gris Nez and Calais Harbour area. German aircraft harassed them during these operations, and the final operation resulted in both Ansons landing near Dover. An air gunner was killed, the remaining crew injured. For this action, the pilot was awarded the DFC. Later in November 1940 at Detling, Blenheim aircraft replaced the slow Ansons, and later in April 1941 Defiant aircraft were added to the establishment at Detling. At the beginning of August 1940, two aircraft of No. 1 CACU were standing by daily for co-operation with the Thames & Medway Fixed Defences, in accordance with an order received on 2 July 1940. During the heavy raid of 13 August 1940, one of the Ansons, N5279, was damaged but later repaired. On 23 September, when Ansons were working with the Royal Marine Siege Regiment, another, N4914, force-landed in a field at East Langdon. Sgt J. H. Dowley (wireless operator/air gunner) was killed in action. Sgt J. McAllister and LAC John were admitted to the Royal Victoria Hospital at Dover, both wounded. They had been attacked by four Me 109s, diving for the sea and heading for the English coast. Shells burst into the fuselage, killing Sgt Dowley, injuring other crew and igniting the dinghy housing. However, one of the enemy aircraft crashed into the sea, possibly as a result of the Anson's return fire.

Returning from a raid on Düsseldorf with a damaged engine, Sterling W7643 of 3 Group had to make an emergency landing at Detling on 13 October 1941. Not long after this incident, the aircraft was repaired and safely returned to RAF Oakington, Cambridgeshire. Other aircraft operated by No. 1 CACU were Blenheims, and in November 1943 one of these, Z5749, was seriously damaged when it crash-landed at Detling in heavy fog. During this period the unit experimented with new equipment and on one occasion Sqn Ldr Morse, Admiralty Compass Observatory, arrived at Detling to fit an experimental mounting for the compass in the Blenheim. Early in April 1941, the unit carried out air-to-ground firing at Leysdown range. Defiant, Blenheim and Anson aircraft took part in these exercises. Following one such training session, Blenheim Z5756 crash-landed at Detling. The crew, Flt Lt Holt (pilot) and Sgt Yates (WOP/AG), were both uninjured.

The same month, Anson N5203 crashed at Detling after taking off for routine escort duties. Only one of its crew, Sgt Wood, survived, seriously injured. Sgt C. R. Blake, Sgt A. J. Pryer and Sgt H. L. Beach were killed. Aircraft of No. 1 CACU, while based at Detling, were often called upon to operate from other airfields, and on 7 May 1941 a Blenheim and a Defiant were flying from RAF Hawkinge when the Blenheim was attacked by enemy fighters. F/O Hicks, the pilot of Blenheim Z5758, was declared missing, believed killed, when his aircraft was shot down into the sea. Other crew members Sgt J. M. Macdonald, Sgt C. V. R. Scott and Sgt R. C. Livings, were also killed.

In February 1942, targets on the French coast were selected and a suitable location at Dover was found for a VHF Ground Station, which was vital for operations. But owing to heavy snow and bad weather, it was difficult to erect the VHF aerial, and when the work was completed there were technical problems. This delay had dire consequences when, on 12 February, a request was received by telephone from 12th Corps for air co-operation from Detling against the German battlecruisers *Scharnhorst*, *Gneisenau* and *Prince Eugen*, which were passing through the Strait of Dover. It became impossible to supply 'spotting' aircraft for the following reasons: the VHF Ground Station was unserviceable; there were no personnel to man the station even if it had been serviceable; the target was out of range; and the guns available were not manned.

The unit was really non-operational on this date but, had forty-eight hours' warning been given that the ships were likely to break through the Strait, the station could have been erected at Dover with personnel and equipment borrowed to man it. Aircraft and pilots were available at RAF Detling.

F/O R. Turner returned to the airfield on 2 January 1943, having been on attachment to AFDU at RAF Duxford. He later had reason to regret his return. The following morning, he was flying Spitfire 11b, serial no. P8262, when he collided with a Gladiator of No. 2 AACU. Fortunately, both pilots escaped serious injury and the aircraft were quickly moved from the dispersal area for repair.

During a routine operation from Detling, F/O J. L. Murray was rather shaken when his Spitfire 11b, serial no. P8476, was struck by seagulls but was able to return to base, where groundcrew quickly removed the gulls' remains and repaired the damage. The following day, P/O P. P. Sewell's Spitfire 11b (P8325) was hit by flak during a 'Rhubarb' operation but returned home and landed without further incident. At the end of January, F/O Turner in Spitfire 11b (P8372) and F/O R. J. Gee (in P8643) carried out another Rhubarb operation in the Dieppe–Le Tréport area. Turner was hit by enemy fire and had an unfortunate accident – he crash-landed at Brookland, Romney Marsh, after hitting a tree over the target. The pilot was slightly injured. F/O E. M. Cuff had a lucky escape when he crash-landed at Detling in a Spitfire 11b (P8476) on returning from firing practice at Leysdown ranges on the Isle of Sheppey. The pilot was uninjured. A special parade was arranged on 1 May 1943 to celebrate the twenty-fifth anniversary of the formation of the RAF.

Two weeks later, F/O L. D. Turner was involved in a mid-air collision in a Spitfire 11b (P8548). Seriously injured, he later died, a sad loss for No. 1 CACU. This unit was disbanded on 11 October 1943, having been in service with the RAF since 1 December 1924. It was left to F/O Gee to complete the unit's work at Detling, and when he returned from operations, he flew low over Bell Farm. The unit's history was compiled and forwarded to the Air Ministry and today, as with most RAF records, it is held at the National Archives in Kew.

On 15 June 1941, the unit transferred from No. 17 Group Coastal Command to No. 70 Group Army Co-operation Command. On 16 August 1941, a detachment of twenty-two personnel were sent to RAF Budergan, equipped with two Blenheim aircraft, one Anson, and one Defiant, to establish a training flight for work in conjunction with the Coast Artillery Training School at Llandudno. This unit was divided into an operation flight at Detling and a training unit at Budergan, transferring again in January 1942 to No. 70 Group in No. 35 Wing Army Co-operation Unit.

In 1942, the unit took part in various exercises with the Army and Navy. A number of practice shoots were carried out with 540 and 520 Coast Regiments at Dover. The unit was also involved in Rhubarb sorties in the autumn of 1942, and in November that year the flight returned to Detling with all aircraft. Back at Detling, it flew Spitfires on night-flying practice to find out if spotting in Spitfires was feasible at night, but this was found to be impracticable. From January 1943 until the unit's disbandment, flying duties were mainly practice shoots with Coast Artillery, the Army and Royal Navy, as well as the occasional Rhubarb and 'Jim Crow' sortie. On 1 June 1943, Army Co-operation Command was finally disbanded and No. 1 Coast Artillery Co-operation Unit was transferred to Fighter Command.

A sad loss to the unit occurred on 23 June 1942, when Spitfire Mk IIb, serial no. P8531, flown by P/O David Malloch RNZAF, crashed at Camer Farm near Maidstone. This aircraft was test-flown by Alex Henshaw on 15 May 1941 prior to being accepted by the RAF. Money for this aircraft was raised by the people of Blandford, Dorset, and a presentation Spitfire was christened *Who's A Feard*. In 2007, a memorial plaque was unveiled close to the site of the crash.

P/O D. Malloch RNZAF from Dunedin South Island, New Zealand, was killed on 23 June 1942 when he crashed at Camer Farm near Maidstone, Kent. He was twenty-one years old.

The only known photograph of Spitfire Mk IIb P8531, which was based at Detling with No. 1 (CACU) Coast Artillery Co-operation Unit and flown by P/O David Malloch RNZAF.

An exercise was carried out on 22 September 1942 with the Army Battle School involving a low-flying attack on troops. Spitfire 11b P8372 collided with a bird and the pilot was lucky to escape with only damage to his aircraft. On 9 November 1942, Flt Lt D. J. H. Miltch was killed when his Spitfire 11d, P8333, crashed near Dover while engaged on operational co-operation at night with the Coast Artillery. He was later buried on 13 November at Brookwood Cemetery; his funeral was attended by several of his fellow pilots.

In August 1939, 48 Squadron, with its Avro Ansons, was based at Eastchurch, but was moved to Detling on 14 August to take part in large-scale exercises, which lasted until 20 August. The squadron arrived at the airfield with seventeen aircraft; its role during this period was to seek out enemy shipping. 48 Squadron returned to Eastchurch on 21 August and was placed on War Station. When hostilities commenced, the squadron was again detached to Detling. On 29 May 1940, three aircraft were on Dutch patrol and engaged with nine enemy motor torpedo boats. The Ansons dropped eight 100 lb bombs, but the result of this action is unknown. The wireless operator and air gunner of one aircraft were wounded by concentrated AA fire from the boats and one aircraft was badly damaged. A second aircraft in the formation was seen to be hit and did not return. The crew reported missing were Flt Lt S. T. Dodds, P/O B. Booth, LAC A. M. Gumbleton, LAC Jacobs and LAC Brass.

During a patrol on 30 May, an Anson was engaged by three Me 109s and suffered severe damage to the wings and aileron controls. LAC Dilmot shot down one enemy aircraft and although he was wounded in the leg, he managed to get his gun into the cabin to free a stoppage and returned to the gun turret to continue the fight. Eventually, a British destroyer was seen and the Anson made for it. On seeing the ship, the Me 109s ceased their attack. The Anson force-landed in the sea. The crew were rescued, transferred to a Drifter and taken safely to Ramsgate.

During the short period 48 Squadron was based at the airfield, it flew mostly Channel 'sweeps' and convoy patrols, escorting shipping to and from France. However, the squadron had an interesting sideline in flying at night over Thanet to check up on the efficiency of the blackout restrictions. The busiest day was 16 June, when it flew no less than thirteen convoy patrols, sixteen French coast search patrols and three night searches for downed crew. In July 1940, the squadron moved from Detling to Carew Cheriton, where it converted to Beaufort Mk I aircraft.

In late 1941, the RAF set up a flight of German aircraft to assist military personnel in recognition and to study the aircraft under operational conditions. During the three years and two months the flight was in existence, it met with many maintenance difficulties, due to the lack of spares and maintenance details. Tools and equipment had to be specially made and all engine and airframe spares had to be obtained from crashed and unserviceable aircraft. It was necessary to assemble aircraft that had never previously been in Great Britain and about which little was known from a maintenance point of view. No. 1426 (EAC) Flight, as the unit was designated, became known as the 'Rafwaffe'.

The unit was formed at RAF Station Duxford on 21 November 1941 when F/O Forbes, F/O Kinder, P/O Lewendon and Flt Sgt Gough were posted from AFDU, to which they had been attached for eleven days for flying experience on German aircraft. All the pilots had been in 41 Group as maintenance unit test pilots. The aircraft were allotted to the flight early in December, first the Heinkel 111 on 7 December, then the Messerschmitt 109 and the Junkers 88 on 11 December. The Heinkel, which had been flying for about two years, came from RAE Farnborough, the Messerschmitt 109 (captured in France) from AFDU, and the Junkers 88 from RAF Station Chivenor, where it had recently landed, almost intact, the crew having lost themselves in the night.

A Monospar was delivered to the flight on 17 December 1941 for communication purposes and collecting spares. The posting of maintenance personnel commenced on 22 December 1941. It was decided that a programme be set up for 1426 Squadron to visit RAF airfields with the captured aircraft to enable RAF personnel to familiarise themselves with enemy aircraft. There were in fact eight tours arranged and the unit arrived at Detling on 15 June 1941. It also visited West Malling and many other bases, returning to Duxford on 3 July. One of these aircraft, Bf 109E-4, serial no. 3417, was the machine that made a wheels-down landing at Detling on 30 September 1940, and was flown by Gefreiter Erich Mummert.

Another aircraft demonstrated by the unit was Bf 109E-3/B, serial no. 4101, flown by Leutnant Wolfgang Teuner on the afternoon of 27 November 1940. Flying over the Thames, he was attacked by Spitfires and forced down at Manston. The Canadian pilot credited with this successful engagement landed to check that Teuner had been taken prisoner. After the war, this aircraft was put on display at a number of locations and at one time was crated up in storage at the Imperial War Museum in London. Eventually, it was put on display at Biggin Hill, where it remained for ten years. It was eventually restored at St Athan in 1976.

Two bombs were dropped close to the Operations Block on 12 January 1941, which interrupted the communications and caused the lights to fail. Emergency lighting was switched on and there was no serious damage caused to the building. On 20 January, Detling got a new CO, Gp Capt. E. A. Hodgson, who took over command from Vice Wg Cdr C. H. Turner,

The operations board, which recorded events at Detling from 6 June to 21 August 1940. Details of squadron operations and their results on missions can be read.

who relinquished command of 500 Squadron to Sqn Ldr G. I. Pawson. The *London Gazette* recorded the award of the DFM to Cpl L. A. C. John of No. 1 CAAF. F/O C. S. S. Rendle, also of No. 1 CAAF, was Mentioned in Dispatches.

AC O. H. Hewitt, Station Headquarters, was awarded the Military Medal for the following action, which is recorded in the Detling Operations Record, preserved at the National Archives:

> Immediately after a heavy bombing raid on an RAF Station (Detling), this airman volunteered to control a fire which threatened an ammunition store. Without hesitation, he drove the station crane from its partially demolished garage, though the petrol was pouring towards the fire. His calmness and courage in spite of continued enemy air activity undoubtedly saved the ammunition store.

In the early evening of 3 March, a Spitfire of 92 Squadron stationed at RAF Biggin Hill caught fire in the air and force-landed at Detling. The pilot, Sgt Le Cheminant, although shaken by the experience, was uninjured and the fire was successfully extinguished on the airfield with little damage to the aircraft. P/O J. T. Davison RNZAF was awarded the George Medal. He and Sgt Brazier (wireless operator/observer) took part in a bombing attack on two heavily armed merchant vessels. P/O Davison was wounded in the foot and thigh but succeeded in flying his aircraft back to Detling. Owing to severe damage sustained to the hydraulic gear, he was compelled to make a crash-landing, not knowing that a bomb remained 'hung up', i.e. had not been released. It exploded on landing, severely wounding the rear gunner and setting the aircraft on fire. With Sgt Brazier, the crew jumped clear, but then discovered that the gunner was still in the aircraft.

Regardless of the fire and the likelihood that the petrol tank might explode, they succeeded in extricating the wounded rear gunner from the rear turret and dragging him to safety. By their courage and gallantry, they saved the life of their fellow crewman.

At 10.55 p.m. on 25 July 1941, following take-off for 'Operation Habo', a call was received from the pilot of Blenheim TR-K of 59 Squadron, reporting that his aircraft had crashed at Boughton Monchelsea, having previously dropped his bombs 'safe'. The cause of the crash appeared to be engine failure – one engine cut out when crossing the coast and the other some minutes later, during the return flight to base. All the crew were safe and uninjured except for minor bruises. Secret documents and equipment were removed from the wreckage and brought back to base; the aircraft was a write-off.

During early October 1941, a Stirling bomber of 7 Squadron, serial no. W7445, squadron code MG-V, stationed at Oakhampton, landed at Detling late in the evening with engine trouble. The primary target was Düsseldorf. Both the aircraft jettisoned bombs south of Liège and returned. At the beginning of the New Year, a Spitfire of No. 1 PRU (Photographic Unit), while on a delivery flight to Detling, overshot the runway on landing. It hit the wire defences and suffered damage, but the pilot was unhurt.

The same month, Exercise Winkle was put into operation. Germany was supposed to have established beachheads in Kent after enormous losses. Both sides were temporarily exhausted, and the enemy held Harrietsham, Wormshill, Bredgar and Sittingbourne. The 5th Wiltshires (i.e. the enemy) were patrolling and testing station defences. Contact was first made soon after 6.00 a.m. The enemy advanced from all directions, and were wiped out in every locality without doing damage except to 'B' Flight, to the east of the airfield. Several casualties and considerable damage were caused before the enemy were put out of action. At 8.15 p.m., the operation was over.

A photograph of RAF Detling taken on 10 September 1942, looking towards Detling Hill with the A249 on the left. Aircraft dispersal areas can be seen. Bottom right is a hangar, and upper left is the site of the First World War airfield used by both the RNAS and RFC.

In September 1941, No. 609 (West Riding) Squadron moved to Biggin Hill to take over the offensive with 'circus' operations. One of the squadron's pilots, P/O Roger Malengreau, a Belgian, recalls one incident that took place on 4 September 1941:

> Circus 93, Biggin, acting as Escort Cover Wing to twelve Blenheims raiding Mazingarbe. More 109s are seen than for some time, and these come down and attack in threes and fours. Wg Cdr C. Robinson is leading the squadron, Sqn Ldr Gilroy Yellow section, which bears the brunt of the attack, and gets split up. Sqn Ldr Gilroy expends all his cannon ammunition in defensive warfare and considers he was lucky to get back. Sgt Palmer causes one EA to go down seemingly out of control with its airscrew stopped, and P/O Dieu is unfortunate in having another Spitfire flying right between him and a 'sitter' just as he has got it nicely lined up. Blue section is also attacked, P/O Sanders suffering damage to the tail unit of his a/c and landing with some difficulty at Detling. One Blenheim is seen to suffer a direct hit from flak, and a Spitfire (probably 92 Squadron) going down in flames. Mist causes one or two pilots to get a bit lost returning to base.

CHAPTER 7

1942–1943

Aircraft dispersal – squadrons and units detached to Detling for AA co-operation training

Information arrived by signal to 280 Squadron (Air–Sea Rescue) that it would move to Detling on 14 February 1942. This unit was equipped with Avro Anson Mk I aircraft during its stay at the airfield. Like many of these special squadrons, it was previously based at Thorney Island, where it had been formed in December 1941. By 22 February, six Ansons had arrived. Many of the squadron's pilots would need flying instruction, which was led by two officers, one of which was Wg Cdr R. E. Rogenhagen, the CO. Some of these pilots serving with the unit had in fact not flown for nearly nine months. Despite this, they were keen and eager to commence operations.

On 24 February, eight heavily laden trucks arrived at Detling with equipment for the squadron. The following day, the medical officer arrived. As luck would have it, flying was delayed for three days due to poor weather, shortly after which seven pilots were off on their solo flights. By the end of the month, 280 Squadron consisted of sixteen pilots, four air gunners, two gunnery officers, six Ansons (used for training), and other ranks amounting to eighty-seven airmen. During this period some operations were flown in co-operation with Army units. Capt. P. Livry, previously of the Free French Air Force, joined the unit on observer duties, for which he had already been trained. He was an excellent observer/ navigator. Livry had been an artillery officer in the First World War and was awarded with the Légion d'honneur, Croix de Guerre.

Advanced training of crews was delayed due to equipment shortages. However, this was to be resolved when the three fully equipped Ansons arrived on 28 April. Prior to that, no less than eighty Air Training Corps cadets arrived at Detling for flight experience with the squadron. They joined the crews on cross-country and Army Co-operation flights. During April, two experimental flights took place, which involved dropping a

Mustang Mk I AM171, which hit a tree taking off from Detling on 4 February 1943 and overturned. The pilot standing nonchalantly on the wreckage is Peter Bagshawe, who survived the crash and went on to command a South African fighter squadron.

dummy set of Lindholm dinghies and a container over water. It was the first time this had been attempted by Anson aircraft.

On 6 June 1942, a consignment of thirty-two Vickers 'K' guns arrived with pans as beam guns, to be fitted the squadron's Ansons. On completion, the modified aircraft commenced gunnery training. Sadly, on 26 June, the squadron suffered its first casualty during 'canopy' exercises with local searchlight batteries. Sgt Christison RAAF, while taking evasive action, crashed and was killed with his crew, Sgt Norwich RCAF, Flt Sgt Bell (observer) and Sgt Rookes Clarke (WOP/AG). This unfortunate exercise came shortly after months of intense training and just as the squadron became operational. The crew had completed a successful communication flight carrying AM Maynard as passenger. This was indeed a tragic loss of both a keen pilot and a well-trained and reliable young crew. Returning from detachment on 28 June, from Squires Gate, 'B' Flight had no less than 290 flying hours.

Seventeen Lindholm dinghies arrived, which completed the equipment of the squadron and thus enabled it to become fully operational again by 1 July. At this time, six aircraft of 'A' Flight were detached to Bircham Newton to replace those away on detachment. Meanwhile, ATC cadets had arrived again at Detling for flight experience and set up their Air Camp. Operations during this period consisted of camouflage flights,

No. 1 PRU (Photo Reconnaissance Unit) Training Flight during its stay at the airfield in 1942. Front row, from left to right: Sgt Chambers, P/O MacLaing, Flt Sgt Martin. Standing, from left to right: P/O Weber, P/O Walker, Sgt Cusack, P/O Greenwood, Sgt Sabourin, P/O Clifton, P/O Fortt.

canopy exercise flights, co-operation flights with the local Home Guard and photographing naval vessels.

The squadron was at last considered fully trained and equipped and put on operational basis, and on 22 July they were responsible for sighting two dinghies in the Channel. The survivors, nine airmen and pilots, were rescued successfully. By the end of July, 280 Squadron (Air–Sea Rescue) were moved from Detling to Langham and Bircham Newton. From there they moved to Thorney Island, where they converted to the Vickers Warwick. For the first time, 280 Squadron was involved in an experiment to drop a dummy set of Lindholm dinghy gear onto water from an Anson.

During its brief interlude at Detling, the squadron also took ATC cadets on flights that had been arranged by the Army. Shortly after, it was moved again to Langham.

Most airfields were visited on occasion by VIPs and Detling had a rather unusual guest, the Maharajah of Kashmir, who was touring airfields. He was met by the station commander, Wg Cdr M. N. Crossley DSO DFC, accompanied by Lt-Col. N. S. Rawat, Wg Cdr W. E. N. Crowdon and Maj. Upson of the India Office. Following an inspection of the airfield and aircraft, the Maharajah was introduced to pilots in the Operations Block following a pilots' briefing.

One of the lesser-known squadrons operating from Detling, 239 Squadron, arrived from Gatwick in May 1942. This was Exercise Tiger; the task was to move the whole squadron to Detling by 4.00 p.m. on 19 May 1942. The move involved transporting all the squadron's equipment and laying out the encampment on arrival at the airfield. The operation was carried out with the assistance of 12 Corps and the 11th Armoured Division of the Army. At that time, the squadron was flying Mustang Mk Is and still had on strength a few Hurricanes. Until September 1943, this unit was equipped with the Mustang Mk I – an aircraft suited to tactical reconnaissance tasks, which was the main role of the squadron. Despite the short notice given to the squadron, the temporary move had gone according to plan.

Their success was marred when P/O McKeown made a heavy landing in Mustang AG417 but was not injured. Following inspection, his aircraft was soon airborne again. But F/O Carpenter, flying AG439, was not so lucky. When his aircraft dived out of low cloud into a hillside about four miles from Maidstone, killing the pilot, the aircraft burnt out. Led by Wg Cdr Donkin, the squadron, saddened by the loss of a popular pilot, flew back to Gatwick. A convoy of vehicles and men returned on the evening of 31 May 1942. 'K' Flight, No. 1 PRU, had moved into Detling

Mustang Mk Is of 26 Squadron at rest close to the blister hangars at Detling in 1943. The pilot on the aircraft's nose is Gus Sheret.

on 23 January 1942 and they remained until 1 August 1942, when they moved to Mount Farm.

On 4 June 1942, Flt Lt F. G. Fray was posted to 'K' Flight, No. 1 PRU Detling, at the beginning of June 1942. He was immediately put on PR operations and practice-flying. Initially he was taking high-altitude photographs of the Gatwick area and the Great Western Railway at Swindon. He flew an assortment of Spitfires, mostly Mk I and Mk V, and usually at an altitude of 30,000 feet. These flights were fairly uneventful until 26 June. Flying Spitfire Mk I, serial no. R6968, he flew back to Detling following a PR mission over the Grantham district. On touchdown, an undercarriage leg collapsed, but he managed to land safely and the aircraft was soon repaired.

Heading east over the English Channel at a height of 24,000 feet, aircraft of the 407th Bomb Squadron, 92nd Bomb Group, had enough to worry about as the crew scanned the skies for fighters AA fire. They had just flown over the French coast when they witnessed a mid-air collision between two of their own flight. At the time, visibility was marred by the sun and frost on the aircraft windows. Lt Eugene M. Wiley reacted quickly and peeled off, diving straight down. The aircraft was seriously damaged, having been holed in the fuselage. The vertical stabiliser or fin was almost cut off and the rear gunner's hatch was wrecked. Despite this, the pilot managed to return and made a successful landing at Detling.

With two engines vibrating, wing dripping gasoline, propellers bent and nose hatch torn off, the pilot of the other aircraft tried to jettison the bomb load. Frantically working the emergency release, he eventually dropped the bombs over the Channel, just in time. As can be imagined, those who witnessed the aircraft's rapid descent were expecting an inferno. Mercifully, none of the crew members were killed.

On 1 January 1943, Detling was taken over by Army Co-operation Command from Coastal Command. The CO was Wg Cdr H. R. A. Edwards AFC. The unit comprised HQ 2751 Squadron RAFR, 2822 Squadron RAFR, and AA Flight. Attached were also No. 1 CACU, No. 2 CACU and a section of MORU 8008 crew signals.

A strange incident occurred following an air raid at the start of March 1943. A German body was found in the vicinity of the sergeants' mess. A second body was found near the WAAF officers' mess. Both were examined by the CO and station adjutant and it appeared that their aircraft had a received a direct hit, damaging the parachutes of the crew, who then sustained fractured spines on impact with the ground. The two unfortunate airmen were removed to the camp mortuary and subsequently inspected by Mr Rogers, Deputy ARP Controller, Maidstone, and Inspector Wood of West Malling Police. Later the same day, two Butterfly Bombs were found

'A' Flight of 26 Squadron in 1943. The aircraft in the background is a Mustang Mk 1; the squadron had previously operated the Curtis Tomahawk Mk I. Flt Lt Terry Spencer is seated in the centre of the front row.

Flt Lt Terry Spencer escaped serious injury when he crash-landed his Tomahawk Mk IIb AK125 at Detling while returning from photo-reconnaissance over Calais on 27 January 1943. He was rather upset that the recovery crew seemed more concerned with extricating the camera than the pilot.

close to some parked aircraft. They were made safe by Sgt Dockery, station armourer, and subsequently used for demonstrations at the station.

On 14 April 1943, the bodies of two Canadian NCOs from a crashed Wellington bomber were brought to the station chapel, St Nicholas and All Angels. The funeral was conducted by the station padre and an escort and firing party was provided by 2773 RAFB Regiment.

An operational Wellington bomber – HE159 of 'B' Flight, 424 Squadron, based at Topcliffe – crashed at Lambsland Farm, Rolvenden, Kent, on 11 May 1943. P/O A. W. Thompson and three Canadian NCOs were killed. A. G. Lee was injured. Another funeral was arranged at Detling. Nearly sixty years later, a memorial was erected in honour of the dead, close to the crash site of the aircraft. Flt Lt H. L. D. Tanner CAAU, flying a Spitfire, collided in mid-air with a Spitfire piloted by P/O R. J. Fowles, based at RAF Eastchurch. Both aircraft crashed at Frinsted, Doddington, and were totally destroyed by fire. Both pilots were killed.

In September 1941, the Americans shipped the first RAF Mustangs to the UK, and on 5 January 1942, 26 Squadron became the first unit to be equipped with the new aircraft. Since 26 February, the squadron had been flying Curtis Tomahawks, which were based at Gatwick and were later

Pilots of 453 (RAAF) Squadron at Detling in March 1944. On the cowling, left to right: WO J. W. Scott, WO R. Lyall, WO J. P. Iver, WO G. J. Stansfield. Standing and seated on the wing, left to right: F/O L. J. Hansell, Flt Sgt B. Gorman (who was killed a few days later), F/O K. K. Lawrence, Flt Sgt J. A. Boulton.

Sqn Ldr Jack Rose DFC – CO of 184 Squadron from December 1942 until July 1944 – with his Hurricane Mk IV. Unlike the squadrons it served with at 125 Airfield Detling, the unit converted to rocket-firing aircraft.

detached to West Malling, Lympne and Manston. They had been involved in supporting British forces at Calais until its capture.

It was some relief when the squadron was ordered to regroup at Detling in January 1943, although this move was short-lived. In March 1943, it again moved to Stoney Cross and shortly after back to Gatwick. However, 26 Squadron returned to Detling in June 1943 and remained until July 1943. Its new task, operating the Mustang Mk Is, was the resumption of dawn and dusk coastal patrols, this time to intercept both Bf 109s and Fw 190s fighter-bombers raiding coastal towns. During this period, the squadron flew Rhubarb, Ranger, Intruder, Jim Crow and convoy patrols.

One pilot who remembers Detling with just cause is Terry Spencer, who was with the squadron from 12 January to 27 February and from 21 June to 30 June 1943. He recalls:

On January 15 1943 we moved to Detling. Soon after arriving I made my first official Rhubarb, over the Dieppe area, but I got lost and spent 50 minutes shooting up trains, until being jumped by two Fw 190s. It got a bit hectic as they chased me halfway across the Channel at wave-top height, and by the time I lost them I had taken my first half-dozen hits. As well as the Mustang Mk I we still had a Curtis Tomahawk fitted with vertical cameras. On 27 January 1943, I was unlucky enough to be sent out on a tactical reconnaissance mission over the Dunkirk area, flying the Tomahawk. After taking the pictures I arrived safely back into the circuit at Detling, only to have the engine catch fire as it throttled back on the approach. I had to drop it on the threshold pronto, wiping out the undercarriage. I vacated the thing pretty sharpish, to the indifference of the rescue crews, who were much more worried about saving the camera than me.

On 21 June with Colin McGee I took off on yet another sortie, shot up four trains, a truck and a charabanc full of German soldiers. Later in June I was promoted to 'B' Flight Commander 26 Squadron, returning to Gatwick on 30 June 1943. During our time at Detling we drank at the George & Dragon at Ightham. The pub was then run by 'Door Knob Dora' and her mother 'Pissy' May. It was on another such mission on 5 July to Le Treport when we shot up four trains and, returning across the Channel, David Bell hit the sea in his Mustang – an idea of how we lived and flew in those days.

In January 1943, the squadron was engaged in many sorties over France, attacking trains, barges and even dredgers. They usually took off from Detling in groups of three Mustangs, and were airborne for less than two hours. These raids were officially known as Rhubarb operations, and proved very successful. The Mustang Mk Is of 26 Squadron frequently came under attack from German Fw 190s, which were formidable fighters, but as often as not the Mustangs returned safely to land at Detling. Aerial photography played an important role in the squadron's work, usually with success. Although, on one occasion in February 1943, two Mustangs flown by F/O T. Spencer and P/O P. Arkell were assigned to take oblique photographs over the Dieppe area. Spencer took his photographs with no trouble, but the unfortunate Arkell's camera load fell out of his aircraft. But both returned to Detling with no further problems.

In late February, personnel from 26 Squadron were assigned to 129, 124 and 123 Airfield Headquarters to take part in Exercise Spartan. The purpose of this was to refine the organisation for the possible invasion of Europe in 1944. There were two sides in a mock conflict, Eastland and Southland, the former being the Germans. Eastland forces occupied an area bounded by Cambridge, Coventry and Gloucester, while Southland forces occupied the 'front line' from Swindon through Hungerford, Newbury, Reading and Maidenhead. The CO of 26 Squadron, A. H. Baird, remarked in the squadron's ORBs:

During the month of July 1943 occurred what might be the decline of the squadron. At the commencement we had our complete period of training and settling in of regular 'Op' in our mess at Detling. 'Spartan', 123 Airfield, tent life and all our troubles were forgotten. We seemed to be on the threshold of a new life, which would add renown to the name of 26 Squadron. At the end of the month, two flights were in Yorkshire, flying exercises for the Army, and 'B' Flight was in Ireland. Some twenty-two sorties were flown getting in trim for coming operations. P/O W. A. C. Phillips had been killed and we only had twelve serviceable aircraft.

Not all problems at Detling were related to operations. On the night of 27 July, a robbery took place. Over £50 was stolen from an airman's billet, including £27 from LAC A. G. Russell. Special Police had to be called in, but with little success. In May 1944, Terry was posted to 41 Squadron at Bolt Head, Devon. He also flew from RAF Lympne and West Malling on anti-diver patrols. Sadly, one of Terry's fellow pilots at Detling, Tim Phillips, crashed into the middle of Gatwick airfield at 500 mph after an aerobatic display in which he did a roll off the top. He had failed to pull out of the dive.

On the BBC WW2 People's War website, Neil Gladman relates the story of Ronald Eric Pope, who was posted to Detling in 1943:

At the age of twenty Ron started his pilot training with a Mr French at the RAF Civil Training College in Desford, Leicester [in September 1939]. Before this he was a draughtsman working in Hatfield, living with his mother and Auntie Silvia, who used to rent rooms to airmen and staff the of de Havilland. At one time the now-legendary pilot Johnny Johnson was staying and Ron caught sight of his uniform hanging in the wardrobe. He always said it was this that inspired him to join the Royal Air Force Volunteer Reserves and learn to fly ...

[Ron was] posted to 26 Squadron Detling near Maidstone, Kent [on 1 July 1943]. Flying mainly solo operations predominately in a Mustang but occasionally in Proctors, Domines and Oxfords. At this time he saw a fair bit of combat ... Still taking aerial photography, including vertical photos of shipping in Relle, Tessell and Ijmuiden around the coast of Holland. His flight logs show this was a busy time, with 26 Squadron listing many ops and increased surveillance photography of German occupied areas and shipping.

He remained with 26 Squadron until demobilisation in November 1945.

Although not based at Detling, 85 Squadron, which was operating from West Malling, had considerable success with regard to the destruction of enemy aircraft in 1943. As with many combats over the county of Kent, victory in the air was very often followed by the loss of pilots and crew. One such incident occurred on 9 July 1943, when P/O J. P. M. Lintott and Sgt G. Gilling-Lax shot down a Dornier 217K of 6-KG2. The German crew were killed. But on this occasion, Lintott and Gilling-Lax also died. The GCI (Ground Control) had put Lintott onto the intruder and he saw two blips on his screen. Both stayed together for seven minutes, then faded. The crew were found dead among the wreckage, following the destruction of the Do 217K. It appears that they tangled with an Fw 190 close to Detling, which probably brought down the Mosquito.

In early summer, the squadron was enjoying considerable success against the German intruders, but in early July the weather broke. On the afternoon of 9 July, in driving rain and low, scudding clouds, two experienced crews from 85 Squadron stood at readiness as an 'all-weather' section. The 'B' Flight commander was Flt Lt Geoff Howitt, and his radar operator was F/O G. N. Irving. They were joined by Flt Lt Lintott and P/O Gilling-Lax. They scrambled in the bad weather to intercept a wave of sneak raiders coming up the Medway under cover of the weather. Twenty minutes after take-off, the sounds of air combat could be heard from the airfield, above the cloud and rain, together with AA fire, cannon fire from a Mosquito, and the rising scream of a descending aircraft cut short by an ominous 'thump'.

Neither aircraft returned to West Malling. The frustration and concern on the airfield was considerable. After a short while, the RAF base at Detling, just across the Medway Valley, reported that a Dornier 217 had crashed close to the airfield. Local AA batteries were claiming the kill, but it emerged that the local GCI at Wartling (F/O Norman) had guided Lintott onto this aircraft and he had been tracking and closing on it for seven minutes before it crashed. The controller had followed both blips on his screen, but both had disappeared at 5.27 p.m. A telephone call from RAF Bradwell Bay on the other side of the Thames Estuary brought confirmation that Howitt and Irving had landed safely – flying in under the low cloud, having pursued the raiders out to sea.

Then, finally, came the news that everyone had been dreading. Lintott's Mosquito was found less than two miles from the wreckage of the Dornier at Boxley near Maidstone, with both crew dead in the cockpit. Later examination of the Dornier revealed that it was riddled with 20 mm cannon rounds, and the AA gunners sensibly withdrew their claim. The armament officer from Fighter Command HQ later inspected the wreckage of the Mosquito and determined that Lintott had indeed fired his guns. Lintott and Gilling-Lax were credited with their fourth and final victory (one short of being an ace) before their crash.

The inspection of the Mosquito revealed that it had partially broken up before it hit the ground. There is the possibility that in his determination to shoot down the Dornier, Lintott may have collided with it. Alternatively, it is also possible that the Mosquito could have been damaged by debris from the disintegrating bomber. It does seem, however, that an error of judgement in appalling weather conditions and at very low level, combined with the distraction of an eagerness to shoot down the intruder, cost Lintott and Gilling-Lax their lives. They were a bitter loss to the squadron; Gilling-Lax had only recently been commissioned, just in time for both himself and Lintott to be recommended for the Distinguished Flying Cross the week before.

Lintott and Gilling-Lax's victim was Dornier 217K-1 (4519) (U5+FP) of 6th Staffel KG2, which crashed at Bicknor Court Farm, Detling. The aircraft disintegrated upon impact and the crew were all killed; they were Oberleutnant H. Zink, Unteroffizier W. Bernhardt, Unteroffizier E. Freiermuth and Obergefreiter E. Stiermann. The Dornier 217 was one of ten aircraft dispatched by KG2 on 9 July in appallingly bad weather, and one of these raiders was eventually responsible the bombing of the Whitehall Cinema in East Grinstead. This was a tragic incident caused by a bomber circling the town before dropping a stick of eight bombs across the town centre. It is still unclear what the target was. A convoy of trucks in the High Street? Or perhaps a train that had pulled into the station? The cost was terrible for so small a town. No fewer than 108 people were killed and 235 injured, requiring a communal burial of some of the victims on the following Wednesday.

It is perhaps comforting to think that the perpetrators of such an infamous attack failed to escape and many Banstead villagers believe that this raider was the one shot down by Lintott. But while there is a very slim chance that this is so, it seems unlikely. The aircraft had been pursued by Lintott for seven minutes as it looked for targets of opportunity over the Medway area; it was brought down at Detling. East Grinstead, Sussex, is about 30 miles south-west of Detling, which means that had it dropped its bombs on East Grinstead, it would have been flying north-eastwards (away from its French base) when Lintott shot it down. Regardless, Lintott and Gilling-Lax's achievements were considerable.

No. 1624 (Anti-Aircraft Co-operation) Flight was formed at Detling on 14 February 1943 by rededicating 'D' Flight of No. 2 Anti-Aircraft Co-operation Unit. The aircraft flown by this unit were a Gladiator, Hurricane, Oxford, Defiant and Martinet. During its short existence, 1624 was to be involved with many operations, working with both the Royal Navy and the Army. On 1 December 1943, a new squadron was formed at Detling from 1624 Flight. 567 Squadron formed part of 70 Group. Its role was to carry out AA co-operation duties in South East England. During the war period, it used Martinets for target towing, Hurricanes for simulated attacks and Oxfords for gun-laying and searchlight practice.

The latter were retained after the war, but the Martinets were replaced by Vengeances and the Hurricanes by Spitfires until the squadron was disbanded on 15 June 1946. The squadron's first day at Detling got off to a slow start, as all flying was cancelled due to bad weather. To improve morale, an officers' party was held in the mess. By 5 December, all serviceable aircraft were moved from Detling to Short Bros Ltd at Rochester, as the airfield was again impossible to use, due to mud. It was not until 22 December that aircraft returned to Detling and normal flights took place.

At the beginning of January, Sqn Ldr Hill and Flt Lt Short were tasked with testing the camp's security. This entailed walking around the airfield dressed in authentic German uniforms. Personnel did not react to the masquerades very quickly, but merely stared, whispering among themselves that the strangers were most probably Norwegian or Dutch. At last, an airfield intelligence officer spotted the uniforms and several fights ensued, but much sabotage could have been done. A full report was filed. Later, news came in that Sqn Ldr Hill had visited the air officer commanding 70 Group and was complimented on the German uniform security exercise.

Heavy snow fell on 17 January, which stopped all flying at Detling. As a result, the squadron was given aircraft recognition lectures. Later that day, personnel were sent to Maidstone swimming pool to practise dinghy drill. During the bad weather, snowball fights kept the aircrew busy and there were many lectures on engines and airframes. There were several minor accidents. One occurred when Flt Sgt Hunt was taken ill while on a course, but AC1 Brakes helped to get the aircraft safely in by giving precise information to the pilot as he flew. The station medical officer grounded Flt Sgt Hunt; fortunately the aircraft was not badly damaged. By the end of March 1943, the squadron had totalled 636 hours of flying despite the appalling weather conditions; 485 hours were taken up by Army Co-operation flights. The month ended on a high when Sqn Ldr Cave flew in a new Hurricane.

March passed slowly. Again, weather created problems for flying operations and time was filled with lectures and courses on the camp's Link Trainer. Flt Lt Rankin arrived at Detling to investigate the crash of Martinet MS785.

In March 1943, 567 Squadron undertook bombing runs on the RNAA range off the Isle of Sheppey. During one such exercise, on 19 March, WO Collins had an unfortunate but lucky escape. When flying Oxford V4264, he experienced engine trouble and put down in a field near

Minster. He was not injured and his aircraft was only slightly damaged. It was later repaired.

The new station commander arrived on 12 May. Wg Cdr Crossley became very popular with pilots and groundcrew alike. Two days after his arrival, a tragic loss occurred when F/O Nichel and LAC Knight crashed in the sea off Sheerness. Both were killed. They were flying one of the squadron's Martinets – an aircraft type considered by most to be unreliable. Yet another replacement aircraft of the same type arrived from 695 Squadron, who no doubt were pleased to see it go. F/O Garrick, while on co-operation duty over the Channel, spotted an airman in a dinghy four miles off the coast at Deal. He was instrumental in the pilots' rescue, having radioed for help; an air–sea rescue launch was on the scene within fifteen minutes of his call.

On D-Day – 6 June – all co-operation flights were suspended at Detling until further notice. There was a feeling of great excitement. All personnel were issued with firearms. The following morning, an order was issued to paint all aircraft with black and white invasion stripes – a tedious task, but one essential for identification purposes during the weeks and months that followed. The Hurricanes flown by 567 Squadron were re-fitted with 20 mm Hispano cannons, giving an already successful aircraft more firepower. Despite D-Day operations, there were a few co-operations with the gunnery school at Barton's Point, Sheppey. P/O Garrick almost 'came a cropper' when during this exercise he selected undercarriage down rather than flaps.

On 9 June, WO Harvey and Flt Sgt Holding were posted to 695 Squadron at Bircham Newton and dinghy drill was held at Maidstone swimming pool. As a precaution, when the squadron was on target towing duties over the south and south-east coasts, they were escorted by Hurricanes. However, during this period the weather was so poor that some of these operations were not flown. Several flights were also cancelled as a result of V-1 activity, which had commenced on 13 June 1944.

Some aircraft are deemed to be unlucky. In the case of Oxford V4264 – previously mentioned – this was so. While taxiing out at Detling on 24 June, Flt Lt Mears, collided the Oxford with another aircraft. There were fortunately no serious injuries, but the aircraft had to be taken out of service.

On the evening of 5 July, no less than ten aircraft carried out a mass attack on the targets at Barton's Point, and the following day committee members of the Air Defence of Great Britain (ADGB) visited RAF Detling. The weather had improved, and all co-operation flights were carried out according to the squadron's programme. In addition, the squadron was able to practise formation flying. Following a visit by the CO and Flt Lt

Castle to 38 Brigade, further Army co-operation flights were organised and the Navy included two of its Barracuda aircraft in mass attacks at Barton's Point.

Following the poor weather in August – RAF Detling was at times unserviceable – September started fine. The squadron was visited by the captain of the 21 Destroyer Flotilla and it was arranged that the CO of 567 Squadron, Sqn Ldr Hill, would look into the possibility of a Martinet being detached to RAF Eastchurch, where it would be at the disposal of the 21 DF. As a result, and after talks with Gp Capt. Butler at Eastchurch, F/O Rippington was detached to Sheppey with Martinet TT-O – with groundcrew – to co-operate with the 21 DF. A Defiant Mk II of No. 1622 Flight, serial no. DR989, involved in target-towing operations, crashed at Detling on 7 September. Its pilot was not badly injured and the aircraft flew again on 21 September 1943.

Orders came on 22 September for both 'A' and 'B' flights of 567 Squadron to move to RAF Eastchurch on detachment. The following day, an advance party consisting of groundcrews joined them. By 27 September, the detached party had settled down at a temporary location and was already engaged in co-operation flights. Sub-Lt Ashton and F/O Sneyd, assigned to the 21 DF, were sent on a night patrol in a Martinet over the North Sea in search of E-boats, but found nothing in the reported area. Back at Detling, gale-force winds were so strong that on 7 October Flt Lt Castle and Flt Lt Mears organised a party of six men and proceeded to secure the aircraft, to prevent them from being blown over and severely damaged.

A few days later, WO Dandridge, while taxiing Hurricane KW816, managed to tip the aircraft on its nose in a soft patch near the watch office. Later that day, Lt-Col. Round and Sqn Ldr Hill watched WO Dandridge take off in a glider target without incident. On 3 November, it was clear that 567 Squadron would be on the move again and the CO went to RAF Gravesend to a meeting to discuss the suitability of the airfield becoming the next base. As it turned out, all aircraft from Detling and those of the squadron on detachment to Eastchurch were moved to RAF Hornchurch in Essex on 16 November 1944. Following its stay at RAF Detling, 567 Squadron could reflect on its successful record of co-operation flights, despite being constantly hampered by the curse of Detling airfield – i.e. the gale-force winds and rain.

Moving from Gatwick, 655 (Air Observation Post) Squadron arrived at Detling on 7 April 1943, en route to North Africa. Its role, as with other AOP units, was to be the eyes of the Army gun crews, a task the Auster Mk III aircraft were ideally suited for. The Auster had replaced the Westland Lysanders, which had proved too large and intractable for the task. Wg Cdr R. Noel Smith visited 655 Squadron at Gatwick on

4 April 1943 and informed the squadron that it was to move to RAF Detling by 6 April. Maj. B. Ballard (CO) visited Wg Cdr C. R. J. Hawkins AFC, who was at the time station commander at Detling, to discuss the squadron's move and accommodation. He was soon to learn that there was insufficient accommodation for the squadron and that approximately fifty ORs (Other Ranks) would have to live under canvas. It was also doubtful whether any storage space could be made available for the equipment section. As a result, it was decided to decentralise 'A' and 'C' flights to the 53rd Army Division and No. 3 AGRA.

The remainder of 655 Squadron and 'B' Flight moved to Detling, as planned, on 6 April. 'A' Flight moved to Lenham and 'C' Flight moved to Penshurst in preparation for Exercise Pilgrim. This was a Royal Artillery exercise of movement, which commenced at Alfriston ranges in Sussex and moved by way of Salisbury Plain to Senybridge in Wales. The squadron suffered its first major accident when, on 10 April, Capt. R. A. Lloyd of 'A' Flight crashed. He was uninjured and his Auster was repaired. The following day, the squadron was visited by Brig. S. P. Rawlins MC of 12 Corps, who inspected the stores and the airmen's billets and later discussed the unit's training at Detling.

Two officers were killed on 18 May. Maj. E. B. Ballard (CO) and Capt. J. P. C. Benson were carrying out evasive tactics in an Auster Mk III fitted with an Astrodome and rear-facing observer's seat. The accident happened at 11.25 a.m. at Chigwell Row church. Flight commanders met at Detling to discuss the situation arising from the death of the CO. Shortly afterwards, AOC Command ordered the termination at Detling to discuss the situation arising from the CO's death. Capt. Gordon and Maj. T. I. Tetley-Jones visited the CO's widow. Capt. R. C. Illingworth was promoted to acting CO during Exercise Stagger. The funerals of these two popular officers took place on 22 May at All Saints' church, Newmarket. Capt. W. G. Gordon and Brig. J. C. Frieburger took off from Detling to reconnoitre gun areas in South East England, while Capt. H. E. C. Walker and T. C. Bradley flew to Old Sarum to collect Auster ME169 for a 60-hour inspection.

In an Air Ministry minute dated 23 February 1943, authorisation was given to form 318 (Polish) Squadron, based at Detling. It arrived at the airfield on 15 March and was equipped with Hurricane Mk Is in April for tactical reconnaissance. The squadron formed part of No. 35 Wing and was to train at Detling before being sent overseas to Egypt. In fact, they were only at the airfield until August, during which time they were also detached to Weston Zoyland in April 1943. This unit was formed from NCOs and airmen of 301 and 305 squadrons and twenty-six airmen from 309 Squadron. At the time of its formation, it consisted of eight officers and 113 airmen. There were thirty-seven Polish pilots trained for tactical reconnaissance – no mean task in the time available.

Flight-testing the new Hurricane – which was fitted with two cameras – took place at Detling on 10 April 1943. Sadly, the first loss happened a few days later when F/O J. Jakubowski was killed flying Hurricane V6544. The aircraft struck and killed LAC James and LAC Hogarth of No. 2768 Flight RAF Regiment. Sqn Ldr G. P. Wildish, who commanded the CACU at Detling, held an investigation into the accident at the airfield on 22 April. Three days after the accident, a funeral Mass was held at 8.00 a.m. and twenty-six officers escorted the coffins to Maidstone railway station. F/O J. Jakubowski was interred at the Polish cemetery at RAF Northolt, the funeral being attended by F/O M. Urban and F/O Blaszczyk.

On return to Detling from Weston Zoyland, fifteen airmen were dispatched to RAF West Malling to attend a wing parade. By coincidence, all aircraft had to land at West Malling while returning from Weston Zoyland owing to poor weather conditions; they returned to Detling the following day. The unit, however, was poorly equipped, and it was reported that the squadron was short of five parachutes, had only two complete cameras, no tools for harmonisation and cleaning, and only two complete sets of tools for the Hurricanes.

Not all was doom and gloom for the newly formed squadron, as on 2 May a special Mass was led by Wg Cdr Plater to celebrate the anniversary of the Polish constitution. The CO of Detling, Wg Cdr Hawkins, took the colour-raising ceremony and the Polish flag was to be raised daily at 8.30 a.m.

Hurricane V6637, flown by F/O Czarnecki, was involved in a taxiing accident a few days later. The pilot was not seriously injured. The aircraft was badly damaged, as was its engine. At the beginning of May 1943, the squadron was visited by ACM Sir Edgar Ludlow-Hewitt KCB CMG DSO MC for an inspection. He also reviewed the work and progress of the newly formed unit. Fortunately, he did not witness the events of the following day, when Hurricane L1572 caught fire in mid-air and crash-landed on the Polish guardroom. The pilot, Flt Lt Nareski, was badly burnt, but was rescued from the wreck by Cpl Bress, Cpl Dutkiewicz and LAC Gustkowski.

Bress was recommended for the George Medal, the other two NCOs for the British Empire Medal. Their swift and fearless action saved the life of the unfortunate young pilot, who would certainly have perished in his aircraft. An investigation followed at Detling under the leadership of Wg Cdr Schofield from 11 Group HQ Fighter Command. On the same day, 318 Squadron was ordered to stand down and assemble at West Kirby on 6 July 1943 in preparation for movement overseas.

P/O Witke belly-landed on the airfield when he failed to lower his undercarriage correctly. His Hurricane L1742 was damaged, but although he was admitted to hospital, it was only the pilot's pride that was hurt.

RAF Detling was also home to 602 (Glasgow) Squadron RAuxAF, which, along with 132 and 453 RAAF squadrons, formed 125 Wing/125 Airfield. It had recently moved from Kingsnorth and Newchurch ALG, where they were billeted mostly in tented accommodation. They were pleased to be back on a permanent RAF airfield. Due to poor weather, the squadron's first operation since 24 October took place on 4 November. They were assigned to escort 72 Marauders to St-André-de-l'Eure airfield. On the return flight, three pilots – F/O Kistruck, Flt Sgt Spence and Sgt Remlinger – landed at Bradwell Bay to refuel. They arrived back at Detling some thirty minutes after the rest of the squadron. A quick turnaround was ordered at 5.30 p.m. and the squadron took off for Lympne, where it was to remain overnight. However, the recall was given, and all aircraft returned in the rapidly gathering dusk.

Members of 602 (Glasgow) Squadron RAuxAF, which moved from Newchurch Advanced Landing Ground to Detling in October 1943. Following a move to Skeabrae, Scotland, it returned to Kent in March 1944. The aircraft is Spitfire IX LO-R, serial no MH709. On the fuselage, left to right: F/O J. Kistruck, Flt Sgt J. Kelly, Flt Lt K. Charney DFC, Flt Lt F. Wooley DFC, F/O Jones, Sgt J. Ost, P/O P. Closterman C of G FFA. Seated on wing, left to right: F/O 'Moose' Manston RNZAF, F/O Frank Sorque RCAF, F/O Robbie Robson RCAF, F/O McConache, F/O 'Twopint' Thomerson.

Flt Lt F. C. Wooley of 132 Squadron took over as the flight commander of 'B' Flight, 602 Squadron, from 1 November. Sqn Ldr R. A. Sutherland became CO. Operations throughout November consisted mostly of 125 Wing escorting bombers into Europe. There were few encounters with enemy aircraft, although some were seen. An unfortunate accident occurred on 25 November when, while taxiing, P/O Gourlay collided with P/O Sorge due to skidding on Detling airfield's muddy runway. Both aircraft were damaged; neither pilot suffered any injury.

F/O P. H. Closterman, a Frenchman who had flown with 341 (Alsace) Squadron at RAF Biggin Hill, joined 602 Squadron on 28 September 1943. Pierre arrived at Ashford to join 125 Wing, which was based at Kingsnorth. In his book *The Big Show*, he recalls the event:

There was a mist and damp clouds scraped the treetops. At least we will get some rest today. Sitting in front of the bacon and eggs and several slices of toast done to a turn and dripping with butter, I was having breakfast in the mess, at the same time arranging the programme for the day. There would certainly be a general release, I would have a hot bath, and then, after lunch, Jacques and I would go – if the car had not fallen to pieces – to Maidstone. After a flick we would dine at the 'Star' and, after a round of drinks, come back to bed. 'Hallo! Hallo!' – Dam

Spitfire Mk IXb LO-D MH526 flown by Sqn Ldr I. Blair DFM, who served with 602 (Glasgow) Squadron at Detling in 1943 and 1944. Note the aircraft is connected to a starter, i.e. ready for action.

that blasted loudspeaker again. 'Operations calling – will the following pilots of 602 Squadron report to Intelligence immediately.' Seething, I heard my name among the eight called. I gulped down my coffee, spread a double layer on my last piece of toast and scrammed. Surely the GCC can't expect us to fly on a day like this.

They did fly that day. A No-ball target escorting eight 184 Squadron Hurricanes armed with rocket projectiles attacked the V-1 site at Hesdin. The mission was successful without any loss of pilots. Drenched in sweat, the men of 602 headed home. The aircraft landed at Detling in pouring rain and dense fog – home sweet home. During the return to Detling, Closterman bounced his Spitfire three times.

A few minutes before, Ken Carney had tried to land but wrote off his aircraft. The undercarriage had been jammed by a bullet, and would not lower. He belly-landed. A later inspection by groundcrew revealed that an unexploded shell had smashed one of the magnetos and gone through an exhaust pipe. Pierre's Spitfire IXb LO-D, serial no. MK611, would be out of service for a week; its controls had been hit by a bullet that had ricocheted off an oxygen bottle.

15 Fighter Wing Headquarters moved to winter quarters at Detling, the wing moving independently to the airfield. The winter of 1943 created problems at Detling. The runway was covered in ice in December, which caused several taxiing accidents and damaged undercarriages. By 21 December, 602 Squadron had only eleven serviceable aircraft available; to make matters worse, before any flying could be done the hot-air de-icing trailer had to free all aircraft of ice that had formed during the night.

On several occasions, pilots of 125 Wing escorted damaged bombers back to England; some landed at Detling. Without a doubt, the escorting Spitfires gave the crews courage as they struggled to make home and land safely. On 21 December, following a successful fighter sweep in the Cambrai area involving all three squadrons, they were attacked by no less than forty Fw 190s. Pilots took evasive action, some breaking to port, others to starboard. Unfortunately, some left it too late and were hit.

One Spitfire was seen emitting smoke, spinning earthwards; the pilot was Flt Sgt A. H. Morgan. During the initial encounter, it was believed another three received hits behind their cockpits and starboard wings. Capt. P. J. Aubertin found he was alone and promptly gave chase to an Fw 190, firing at it in short bursts as it dived to 500 feet. Eventually, the pilot was rewarded when it flicked over on its back and was lost to sight. Aubertin made for home, chased by two aircraft; climbing into cloud, he lost them near Le Touquet. A Spitfire was seen at 6,000 feet trailing black smoke. It crashed into the sea. F/O Robson circled the area, but no

The driver of a mobile canteen operated by the Church Army offers tea to a pilot of 165 Squadron, who is seated in Spitfire SK-H at Detling in 1944. Note that this aircraft is being fitted with a 90-gallon auxiliary fuel tank. (*IWM A3820*)

wreckage or dinghy was seen. In fact, the pilot was F/O G. S. Jones, flying Spitfire MH721. Both he and Morgan were killed. The rest of the section, on returning to Detling, were stunned by the loss of their friends.

It was Christmas 1943. The day's celebrations at Detling began when pilots and groundcrew took wine with the CO. Officers and senior NCOs served airmen Christmas dinner in their mess, which was followed by toasts to the King and absent friends. Some effort had been made to decorate the mess in festive fashion, which was appreciated by all in the squadron. Later, several airmen were joined by girls they had met in Maidstone and continued the party until late – it was perhaps the best way to say goodbye to friends and comrades. That's how the war went on.

By the end of December, the Spitfire IXbs of 125 Wing had been fitted with 45-gallon long-range fuel tanks, enabling the aircraft to remain with the bombers in their care as they penetrated even deeper into enemy territory. One such mission, on 7 January, involved 120 B-17s and Liberators. 602 Squadron escorted the second and third sections to the French coast near the Somme Estuary and returned to assist 132 Squadron, which picked up the remaining force. Wg Cdr Yule attacked an Fw 190, which he claimed, and a pilot of 132 Squadron destroyed another. P/O Closterman

Groundcrew watch as SK-H Spitfire Mk IXc MH849 of 165 Squadron taxies out for take-off in 1944, The ever-present Church Army's mobile canteen stands by. To the left stands a blister hangar, a structue adopted by many airfields during the war. In poor weather a curtain could be pulled over the entrance.

bounced three enemy aircraft and claimed one damaged. Flt Sgt Jenkins left the escorting Spitfires to return to Detling. Low on fuel, his engine cut out five miles off Dover. He tried to bale out instead, but with his aircraft in a spin, he decided to ditch. He was pulled out of the water twenty minutes later by an RAF air–sea rescue launch. Apart from shock and being cold and soaked, he was none the worse for the experience, and few of his fellow pilots had to land at advanced landing grounds on Romney Marsh to be refuelled.

Again, the poor weather at Detling hindered the wing's operations, but on 15 November they were ordered to pack up and fly to the Orkneys for intensive training. They were to remain at Skeabrae until 9 March 1944. However, pilots were not too pleased when they were told they would be flying Spitfire Vbs – 'clipped, clapped and cropped', as they had been dubbed by many pilots who flew this type (see Appendix 2). Skeleton staffs were to remain at Skeabrae on 10 March following the wing's departure for Kent, while the main body proceeded to Thurse. From there, the men caught a train to Jellicoe. They arrived in London too late to travel to Maidstone, and so stayed at the Endleigh Hotel overnight. After a hearty breakfast, they continued on their journey, arriving back at Detling in the early afternoon, only to be told they were off to Llanbedr for dive-bombing practice, returning home on 20 March 1944.

Back at base, they were soon attacking No-ball targets – flying bomb sights – for the first time. On one such occasion, attacking Abbeville Woods, two Spitfires led by Sqn Ldr R. A. Sutherland failed to release their bombs. Later, one pilot managed to lose his over the Channel. The other pilot, F/O A. P. Robson, landed at Detling with the bomb firmly in place, without any explosion. At 2.10 p.m., Sqn Ldr A. G. Page led six 132 Squadron Spitfires off from Detling on another 'Ranger' patrol, briefed to sweep from Eindhoven to Munster. Geoffrey Page had been shot down and severely burned on 12 August 1940 when his 56 Squadron Hurricane had been set on fire by crossfire from Do 17s.

Rushed to hospital, he became one of Sir Archibald McIndoes 'guinea pigs' at the new plastic surgery department of East Grinstead hospital. The next two years of Page's life were spent in hospital, where he underwent a dozen painful operations, but he returned to duty, first going to the Air Fighting Development Unit, thence to 122 Squadron. In January 1944, he took command of 132 Squadron. During his time in hospital, he resolved to destroy one German aircraft for every operation that he had undergone.

Airmen enjoying tea and rolls supplied by the Church Army's caterers. On the left is a Spitfire. The unit is not known, but under the nose the letter 'P' indicates the last letter of a squadron code. A Royal Navy air mechanic is seated on the aircraft's wing; the blister hangar dominates the whole scene.

A caricature of Capt. F. Read, who served with the Church Army and, with his wife, managed the airfield catering for the RAF. The sketch was drawn by Joe Thomas and is dated 1945.

His score was, at this time, four destroyed and 'shares' in three more, so he had some way to go to reach his twelve. Now, as the flight approached Deelen airfield, he saw his chance to improve.

A Bf 110 night-fighter was approaching the airfield, its nose bristling with radar aerials, and Page called 'Tally ho!' and led the flight down on it, picking up speed. The Messerschmitt was from Stab. NJG 1 and was flown by Hauptmann Hans-Joachim Jabs, who had taken command of the Geschwader on 1 March. He already had forty-five victories to his credit and had won the Ritterkreuz with Eichenlaub (Oak Leaves) on 24 March. He hadn't fought Spitfires since the heady days of 1940, but, warned by his gunner, he was ready for them. The Spitfires were going far too fast for accurate shooting and as Jabs broke, they overshot. One Spitfire swung into his gunsight and he took a snap shot. The heavy armament hit Spitfire MJ170, flown by P/O R. B. Pullin, and it went down in flames, too low for the pilot to bale out. Reefing his Spitfire around, F/O J. J. Caulton came back at Jabs head-on. He felt cannon shells smacking into his aircraft and the engine stopped dead.

He glided around and bellied MJ639 on the grass of Deelen airfield. Page, less headstrong, had curved around behind the Me 110 and now opened fire. Jabs knew that he had no chance of escape, nosed down, and also belly-landed on Deelen airfield, where he met John Caulton. Geoffrey Page had one less German aircraft to hunt down.

Many years later, the author was privileged to be invited to the Jagdfliegertreffen in Fürstenfeldbruck, where the ex-Luftwaffe fighter pilots held their annual reunion. They had invited people from the RAF, USAAF and RCAF, and the author found himself at a table beside Bob Tuck and directly opposite Geoffrey Page, who was drinking with a tall German. 'See this chap – I shot him down in 1944,' said Page.

Hans Joachim Jabs raised his glass and said, solemnly, 'On that day, he was the hotter man.' Page relates what happened:

> I had told Johnny Caulton that it would be a very bad idea ever to try things head-on with an Me 110. The nose armament was formidable. Better to go in from behind against a single machine gun. Johnny simply forgot about it.

John Caulton, first introduced to Jabs on Deelen airfield after belly-landing his Spitfire, also renewed his acquaintance many years later, with the same result. The two following accounts are typical combat reports by pilots of 132 Squadron during the period the squadron served at RAF Detling. Flt Sgt C. A. Joseph recorded in his account for 18 October 1943:

I was flying Blue 4 and, noticing the rest of Blue section jettison their tanks, I checked up and found my R/T u/s. Blue section then broke down to starboard and I followed noticing several e/a diving away. I then saw a Me 109 make an attack on me from the port beam. I broke upwards calling up Blue 3 in the hope he might hear. Enemy aircraft turned to port climbing rapidly and I followed closing the range. The e/a then started to dive and I began to give short bursts from about 300 yards, allowing one ring deflection until I got into line astern position. I continued to fire until I had expended all my ammunition. EA then began to emit greyish smoke from starboard side until it crashed into high-tension lines south of Bethune.

Sgt J. H. Williams's report for 18 October 1943 is as follows:

I was flying Yellow 3 when about twenty Me 109s approached head on. Yellow section broke right on to them and split them up, one Me 109 came up in front of me doing a steep turn. I followed him around giving him about six short bursts at about 300 yards' range and 20 degrees astern. Glycol started pouring out and it went down in a steep diving turn and I broke off and rejoined another Spitfire formation. This enemy aircraft was seen by Flt Lt Maggs and F/O Hanson of 602 Squadron. It was on fire, with glycol and flames pouring from the aircraft. It rolled over into a dive from 2,000 ft and was destroyed.

Sgt Williams was credited with the kill.

On 4 May 1944, 125 Wing moved on from Detling to a new home at Ford, not far from Brighton on the Sussex coast, and 4018 AA Flight, based at RAF Northweald, received orders to relocate at Heston. Accordingly, an advance party prepared for the move and stores and equipment were sent to Epping railway station for transportation. At the last minute, much to the annoyance of all concerned, a telephone message was received, redirecting the unit to RAF Detling. Under command of Flt Lt W. C. Coate, the main party set off for Kent, and arrived at the airfield by 2.00 p.m.

The flight's headquarters was established at Marrun Wood Dispersal Site; stores and equipment arrived later that day. Shortly after, Boors gun training commenced under the direction of Royal Artillery instructors. Brig. C. R. Britton MC and Col. Rocher DSO visited and inspected the No. 4018 Flight while they were undergoing training, and a detachment of personnel from the unit commenced rifle-firing practice at the War Course Range, which had been established at the Lower Halston Range.

On 16 June, a picquet was sent to Maidstone to mount guard over the Spitfire on display in connection with Wings for Victory Week.

Flt Lt W. C. Coate and Flt Sgt Simmons were in charge. They remained on guard duties until 26 June, when the Spitfire was dismantled for transportation. A few days later, the unit's HQ was moved to Newnham Court Farm. This unit was supposed to merge with that of 2877 AA, but the order was cancelled and 4018 AA moved to Kingscliffe. They had only been stationed at Detling for a month.

CHAPTER 8

1943–1944

USAAF bombers crash-land at Detling – activities during the
V-1 Campaign – other operations

In 1943, many RAF squadrons were moved frequently, none more so than 184 Squadron. From May to September, it was based at various locations in Kent, such as RAF Manston. However, it also spent time on Kent's Advanced Landing Grounds at Kingsnorth, near Ashford and Newchurch. The squadron was moved to RAF Detling in October 1943. Prior to moving to Detling, it had been equipped with the Hurricane Mk IV. In October, it was re-equipped with the Spitfire Mk Vb. The unit had carried out attacks on shipping, and by December 1943 it was attacking No-ball targets as part of the 2nd TAF (Tactical Air Force).

When pilots and groundcrew were informed they were moving to Detling, they were very pleased – at Newchurch and Kingsnorth they were billeted in tents, and it was now autumn. On 12 October, the squadron moved to Detling with 125 Wing Headquarters. Sqn Ldr Kemp arrived to take over from Sqn Ldr Rice, who became the officer commanding 124 Airfield. An exercise with No. 34 Tank Brigade was cancelled due to poor weather, so personnel settling into the new dispersal and organising their kit took up the remainder of the day.

On 14 October, many of the pilots and groundcrew set off to explore Maidstone for the evening. An exercise took place on 19 October when four Spitfires of 184 led a mock attack on the 53 Division Battle School at Leysdown, during which the ALO and CO entered the area in a jeep fitted with VHF. Later the same day, the CO borrowed Flt Lt F. Holland's aircraft and the tail wheel fell off, which meant the aircraft was unserviceable for a while. During another demonstration on 20 October, the Spitfires armed with 40 mm shells impressed the Army by destroying a Churchill tank that had been provided for the occasion.

13 November started well with the squadron watching several films, including one Russian film, *Defeat in the West*, which was seen in the Operations Room. The day was spoilt when an unfortunate accident happened at 10.40 a.m. Pamela Espent Barton was a well-known golfer who had joined the Royal Mid-Surrey Golf Club, London, with her older sister Mervyn at the tender age of twelve. They were both considered too young to have handicaps, so joined Richmond Park Golf Club. Pamela went on to win, with her sister, the Bystanders Foursome in the Girls' Golf Championship. By the 1930s, she had established herself as a fine golfer and in 1936 she won the US Amateur tournament, bringing the trophy back to Britain for the first time in twenty-three years. In the years up to 1939, she had taken part in many golf tournaments around the world and won both American and British Championships. When war was declared, her life changed dramatically.

In 1941, true to her spirit of adventure, Pamela joined the Women's Auxiliary Air Force, and became an ambulance driver in London during

A fine oil painting of Pamela Barton is on display at the Royal Mid-Surrey Golf Club, Richmond. Pamela, a successful golfer, died in a Tiger Moth crash at Detling on 13 November 1943 while serving with the WAAF. She is buried at St John's Cemetery, Margate.

the worst phase of the Blitz. After only serving for seven months, she was commissioned, and F/O P. E. Barton took command of more than 600 staff at RAF Manston. It was during her service at Manston that she lost her life. By then it was 1943 and F/O Barton was at RAF Detling. Records show that on 13 November she was a passenger in DH 82a Tiger Moth EM902. In fact, she was not authorised to fly that day. Shortly after 10.40 a.m., Pamela had taken off in this aircraft – which was piloted by Flt Lt A. W. Ruffhead RAFVR – from a prohibited area of the airfield. Although the pilot had not allowed sufficient room for take-off, the Tiger Moth took off from a dispersal area. The wet and heavy ground was a contributory cause of the disaster to come.

As this was not part of the landing and take-off area at Detling, it provided inadequate run for the aircraft to become airborne. The result was tragic. At 10.50 a.m., the Tiger Moth struck a petrol bowser. The aircraft caught fire and F/O Barton was killed. Acting swiftly and without concern for his own safety, F/O Goodger towed away a fuel bowser parked near to the burning wreckage. The tyres were already alight. Goodger saved lives as well as a vehicle full of aviation fuel. The pilot, who was injured, survived the crash, and was taken to the Royal Naval Hospital at Chatham. He was transferred to Princess Mary's Hospital, Halton, on 16 November. It was recommended that Flt Lt Ruffhead be court-martialled for the accident. He was serving with 184 Squadron at the time of the crash; the Tiger Moth was issued for service with his squadron as a trainer and communications aircraft. Pamela Barton was buried on Tuesday 16 November 1943 in St John's Cemetery, Margate, close to the war memorial.

The death of F/O Barton left a big gap when golf began again after the war. She was only twenty-six when she died, and without doubt she would have returned to her career as a golfer. Her memory lives on, and today, if you visit the Royal and Surrey Golf Club, a beautiful oil painting by T. M. Ronaldson hangs with pride. In her honour, the Pam Barton Memorial Salver is awarded to the winner of the British Ladies' Amateur Golf Championship.

Returning from a mission to bomb Bremen on 26 November, a B17 of 401st Bomb Group, 612th Bomb Squadron, had a narrow escape when struck from below by a B17 from another group, cutting off the ball turret and killing Sgt L. Baranik. The aircraft, 'Fancy Nancy', serial no. 42-37838 SC-F, had collided with B17 42-30317, but, despite the damage, managed to crash-land at Detling. The aircraft was beyond repair and scrapped. Fortunately, the remainder of the crew were not seriously injured. The 401st Bomb Group was based at Deenethorpe, Cambridgeshire. It was a bad day for the group, as two aircraft had collided during take-off, and one of the aircraft lost its tail section.

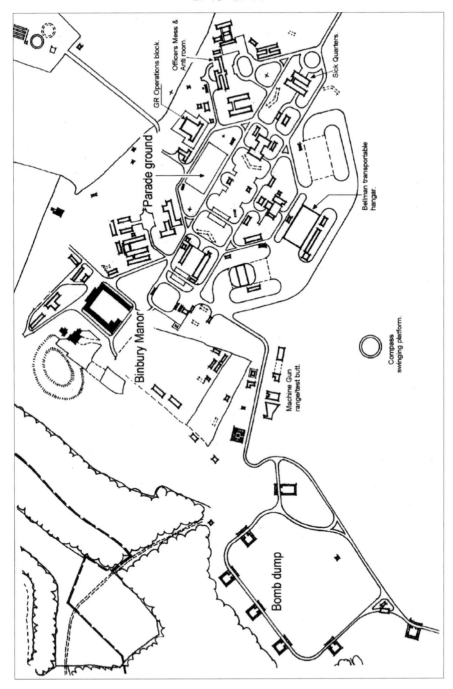

The general layout of Detling airfield in June 1945. Very few original buildings exist today, but the Bellman hangar remains intact. The bomb dump, or store, is on the left of the diagram.

Spitfire Mk IX SK-N, serial no. MK471, flown by Sergeant 'Wally' Marr, an Australian, who flew with 165 Squadron in late 1944. Note the wing stay – a necessary precaution at Detling when windy. Spitfire SK-V is standing in the background.

HRH The Duke of Gloucester inspects 453 Squadron pilots and aircraft.

On 6 January 1944, four Hurricane Mk IVs of 184 Squadron led by Flt Lt Ruffhead took off at 1.50 p.m. to attack a No-ball target. Ruffhead received a direct hit from heavy flak over Le Touquet. His aircraft, Hurricane KZ378, was seen to be hit by small arms and Bofors fire. He crashed on the sand dunes north of Le Tourquet and was killed instantly. P/O Carr and WO Sellers watched as he dived to his death. Flt Sgt J. F. Andrew, flying Hurricane KZ401, was also hit, and he crashed to his death near Le Touquet. WO Sellers, finding himself alone, turned back towards the flak to find his way home, but was hit. He had a large hole in his tail but was uninjured and made a forced landing at Lympne. The Hurricanes of 184 Squadron were armed with eight 61 lb rocket projectiles, which had a devastating effect when they found their target. The No-ball operations were carried out with 181, 175, 182, 56 and 247 squadrons, each flying sections of four aircraft during the attacks.

During yet another No-ball mission, F/O Downs received a devastating hit from flak and his Hurricane had both wings damaged. Unable to gain control of his aircraft, he was last seen spiralling down from 2,000 feet when a wing broke off. Fortunately, although the other aircraft got separated, they all made it back to Detling. An attack on No-ball V-1 sites was successfully completed on 21 January 1943 by 184 Squadron with Flt Lt Holland and F/O Cross leading the sections. They had taken off from Detling at 1.35 p.m. with eight aircraft and two in reserve. They were to rendezvous with 181 Squadron, a typhoon squadron based at Snailwell, and later New Romney ALG. Both had problems locating the target. Eventually, however, when they eventually did, they certainly made up for lost time.

The salvoes of one section landed between the launch platform and the control tower; other salvoes blew up buildings and structures close by. WO Sellers reported three circular stone towers about 100 feet high, some 15 feet in diameter across the top, their bases touching in triangular formation. These stood on the edge of the target area and were thought to be water towers. All aircraft returned safely to base, having been airborne for nearly two hours. A similar attack was planned for later that day, but the escort didn't turn up, so the squadron practised dive-bombing at Leysdown.

F/O J. Downes also lost a wing due to flak. Flying Hurricane KZ607 on 8 February, he crashed to his death near Zudausques during attacks on V-1 launching sites. On 9 February 1944, F/O Stockbury had a narrow escape when his Hurricane's engine cut out. At the time, he was on a night-flying exercise from Detling, but managed to crash-land at Manston. Two days later, during routine flight tests, WO Finch spun to his death while approaching Detling to land.

The squadron took part in an exercise with 59th Army Division, which involved low-level simulated attacks on its headquarters at Canterbury. The weather at Detling was a constant problem and many flights were cancelled. On one memorable occasion, when 184 Squadron was grounded, a party was thrown at the New Inn by the officers for the 'erks'. A much-needed break. A few days later, they were moving to Odiham to convert to Typhoons on 6 March 1944. Lt Samuel McRoberts, a pilot of the 381st Fighter Squadron (363rd Fighter Group, 9th USAAF), was killed while attempting to crash-land his Mustang P-51b, 43-6752, near Detling on 15 April 1944. This American fighter group had moved to Staplehurst Advanced Landing Ground from Rivenhall in Essex the day before.

Among the essential units formed as a result of the war were Repair and Salvage Units (RSUs), the personnel of which had one of the most unpleasant duties. Their task was to recover crashed aircraft that either could be removed and were considered repairable, were causing an obstruction, or were on the secret list. The RSUs were also responsible for recovering crew unable to escape from their aircraft. These units were particularly active in South East England and several were based on airfields in Kent, within easy reach of many crashed bombers and fighters. They would arrive at a crash site with trucks and heavy-lifting vehicles in order to dismantle the airframe and return to the required destination with it loaded on a Queen Mary aircraft transporter. Local police were usually on hand to assist; the crews were given a map reference to help locate the aircraft.

Some aircraft were buried, which made it difficult to identify the type. On occasions, if overwhelmed with work, the unit would just take down the details and fill in the crater. Any crew found would be removed from the site and given a Christian burial.

During 1943–44, three such RSUs were based at Detling airfield: 403, 405 and 410.

In June 1943, 403 RSU salvaged eleven aircraft; these included five Typhoons, three Spitfires, a Mustang and a Tiger Moth, all of which were speedily recovered and disposed of as required. This work included the salvage of one aircraft that ditched in the sea. Several requests were received for engine changes or removals of aircraft left behind on airfields when squadrons moved to other bases. It was heavy work. The Typhoons were considered beyond repair and were stripped down to their main components, which were later passed to an Inspection and Repair Unit, to be restored for further use.

An NCO and two airmen were continuously employed in changing Allison (US Aero Engine Type) engines held at RAF Gatwick – which had to be collected when required. Some aircraft repairs were delayed due to the lack of spares, which were delivered between two and twenty days after request. RAF vehicles were also repaired or modified by RSUs based at Detling. On one occasion, an office was constructed on the back of a truck. On top of all this work, airmen and NCOs still had to undertake defence training. At the beginning of July 1943, there was a break from routine when Cpl Marries was sent on an eight-week firefighting course and three airmen were sent on an anti-aircraft gun course at RAF Shoreham. Gunnery practice consisted mainly of shooting at drogues – targets towed by aircraft.

Sqn Ldr Saunders DFC, the CO of No. 3 Delivery Flight, also based at Detling, was seconded to assist No. 403 RSU by ferrying new and repaired aircraft to the allocated units. Shortly afterwards, an aircraft reception flight was formed as a section of 403 RSU; the main function was to receive aircraft from 41 Group ASUs and to test guns and wireless equipment. The new unit would also maintain a pool of aircraft for immediate issue to squadrons; F/O Dust was given command of the new flight.

The following day, four Typhoons that had not passed through 41 Group arrived from Gloster Aircraft Company. They required a lot of work, including gun adjustments. Unfortunately, vital tools and equipment had not arrived at Detling, and as a result they had to be loaned from

WO Len Tedder, who served with No. 2 Anti-Aircraft Co-operation Flight at Detling during the unit's stay at the airfield in 1943. He looks very proud of his new flying gear; the warm overtrousers would have been much appreciated.

other RAF units in Kent. Arrangements were also made at this time for serviceable aircraft to carry out air-firing to the east of Leysdown range on the Isle of Sheppey. On a lighter note, the 'mobile bath unit' paid a visit to the airfield on 30 July – an important occasion for all who did not have this facility at Detling readily available. This visit was soon followed by the arrival of the 108 Mobile Dental Units. This was the first time 403 RSU had its own dental facility.

At the beginning of August 1943, difficulties were experienced by the reception flight over the initial adjustment of 20 mm cannons not previously butt-tested in aircraft. This was overcome by flying the aircraft to West Malling and using the butts there.

This was a slow process, as these visits were subject to the flying conditions, and the aircraft were grounded at Detling until the weather improved. The first batch of aircraft was finally cleared and they were delivered to their squadrons; 403 awaited further aircraft delivery. The CO addressed the unit for the benefit of several newcomers, outlining the structure of the group. Transport to and from Maidstone swimming pool was arranged for twenty-four airmen under the control of an NCO and was paid for by the PSI funds, which was much appreciated by the airmen, who leapt at the opportunity.

Thirteen replacement Hurricanes arrived at Detling on 25 August; however, the unit, being undermanned, had difficulties coping with the additional work.

By 27 August, some sixty aircraft had arrived, considerably over the maximum holding number (thirty-six) and too many to allow safe dispersal on the airfield. HQ Command insisted that no more aircraft should be delivered until completed aircraft had been delivered to their destinations. The problem of servicing, refuelling and taxiing aircraft was only overcome by recruiting men from other RSUs and outside units. It was a welcome relief, at the start of September, when 83 Group HQ had notification that leave would recommence.

Sqn Ldr Revd R. M. Taylor, the station padre, and Lt Selva both escaped with their lives when the Auster of 655 AOP they were flying crashed on take-off. The aircraft came down at Hurst Wood, West Peckham. It was believed that the pilot stalled the engine and the aircraft landed on two trees. Both pilot and passenger were admitted to Orpington Emergency Hospital, suffering from moderate injuries. Later they were collected and returned to base. The station engineer and an ambulance set off for Yew Tree Farm, Wormshill, and the scene of a crashed Spitfire V of 313 Squadron, serial no. AA843, which flew into high ground in heavy mist. The aircraft completely disintegrated and the pilot, Flt Sgt E. Green, was killed instantly.

Two brothers who both died in the war – Sgt R. E. Yarra, killed on 14 April 1944, and Flt Lt Jack Yarra, killed on 10 December 1942. Both flew with 453 (RAAF) Squadron.

F/O S. R. Chambers, who served with 165 Squadron and No. 1 Photo Reconnaissance Unit at Detling in 1944. He was successful in destroying V-1s during the same period.

In September 1943, the station commander visited Ashford to inspect 305 Squadron ATC and present prizes to cadets at parade; it was a proud day for the boys. ATC cadets often spent time at Detling airfield for summer camp and, if they were lucky, this often included some flying. The following day, nine Spitfires of 124 Squadron arrived for air-firing practice with 1493 target-towing flight now based at Detling. This was followed by the usual gas practice, with tear gas and smoke being laid down.

Entertainment was an essential part of airfield life, and at the beginning of October 1943, an ENSA concert took place in the NAAFI, featuring Bobby Hind and his London Sonora Band – a break from the stresses and traumas of wartime.

It was a busy day, as it turned out. Earlier, twelve Mustangs of 414 RCAF arrived to take part in air-firing exercises with 1493 Flight. Unfortunately, F/O Gee of No. 2 CACU taxied his Spitfire into a hole on the side of the runway, and the aircraft tipped on its nose, damaging the propeller. RAF personnel witnessed many incidents and crash-landings, but, occasionally and increasingly, aircraft of the United States Army Air Forces (USAAF) would have to crash or force-land on the nearest airfield. So it was no surprise when a Marauder of 559 FS, returning from operations, put down at Detling due to bad weather and lack of fuel. The crew stayed overnight and were entertained by the RAF.

By November, the runway at Detling was in a poor state of repair and it was deemed essential to lay Sommerfeld Tracking, a wire mesh rolled out and secured with pegs driven into the ground. It was used extensively on Advanced Landing Grounds. Lt S. J. Thatcher of 214 Pioneer Corps reported to Detling with two sergeants and fifty-eight ORs to do the job. This coincided with a heavy frost and 768 Flight ATC visiting the station.

Sport was a popular pastime at the airfield; the following day, football, rugby and hockey matches took place against RAF Hawkinge as part of the 11 Group Challenge Cup. That evening, another ENSA concert party was held in the NAAFI, and a party of gunners and ATS from a local AA battery were shown round the station.

A USAAF aircraft force-landed at Cliff, near Rochester, on 20 November, and Flt Lt Hudson had to talk to the pilot by telephone with instructions to ensure his safe arrival at Detling. A short service was held at the airfield to commemorate the Battle of Britain on 15 September, followed by a football match and a dance at Bearsted village hall. October came and 403 RSU received orders to move to a new home at Biggin Hill. On 14 October 1943, the main party – consisting of forty-nine vehicles and 230 men – departed from Detling at 9.30 a.m. They arrived at Biggin Hill at 12.30 p.m.

Sqn Ldr C. L. O'Hanlon MBE and F/O D. N. Rushnorth of 405 RSU, stationed at Dunsfold, visited Detling on 27 June 1943 to inspect the new campsite. Arrangements were made for them to occupy part of the Coast Artillery Co-operation Unit dispersal as a working area; part of a field behind the dispersal, south-west of the airfield, became the domestic area. The site of the domestic area was owned by the landlord of the Three Squirrels Inn, Stockbury. Mr. P. Brown and the CO made arrangements to use the former's field. At the same time, arrangements for pay, rations and NAAFI facilities were made for the incoming RSU at Detling. A reception flight and MT light-repair unit would be on hand at the airfield.

On 2 July, 405 RSU moved into Detling. During the next few weeks, the unit's strength built up with the arrival of more personnel and equipment. It was not long before a few Typhoon aircraft arrived, but only one of these passed the air tests. Several aircraft had difficulties when air-firing the 20 mm cannon. During a routine air test, P/O Hallett was alarmed when the Spitfire VC BL897 started to swing violently in the air. On landing at Detling, the Spitfire was checked by riggers and it was found that the tail plane was warped and a new tail plane had to be fitted. This machine was later delivered to 127 Airfield at RAF Kenley. Spitfire IX, BN129 – based with 127 Airfield – was also fitted with a new tail section. At the same time, Mustang Mk I AG660 of 400 Squadron RCAF was flown and passed as airworthy by P/O Selvey.

A much-needed new aircraft transporter arrived, and was on loan from 404 ASP Unit until early September. Just in time, as Mustang Mk I AP420 of 231 Squadron – based at 128 Airfield Redhill and Woodchurch, Kent – was salvaged by the unit, repaired and, following the fitting of a new engine, returned to its squadron. By the end of August 1943, there were 312 airmen on strength with ten officers, Detling was becoming very crowded. An accident occurred on 19 September when two Mustangs flown by No. 1 Delivery Flight, part of 405 RSU, crash-landed at Croydon. Spitfires MN665 and MA232 were both fitted with new propellers and, following thorough checks, returned to service.

On 11 November, 405 RSU moved back to Biggin Hill, only to return to Detling on 26 January 1944. Although it was a brief stay at Biggin, they were extremely busy. Indeed, the day after arriving, Spitfire IX MA812 of 68 Squadron crash-landed at Gravesend with both wings broken off at the root ends and the fuselage in two sections. The pilot, F/O Cann, was injured. This crash was followed by Mustang Mk I AG539 colliding with cables over enemy territory; another, AG416, hit trees. All three aircraft were salvaged by 405 RSU before returning to Detling.

The accommodation for the unit was rather limited and, despite wet weather, tents were erected to enable work to continue and trucks and vehicles to be unloaded. The weather made the airfield virtually unserviceable and, the following day, Flt Lt Grehan arrived at Detling in a Piper Cub; he reported a very rough journey from Biggin Hill. However, six aircraft arrived safely from Biggin Hill, and work resumed again. On 28 January, five more aircraft were ferried from Biggin Hill. By the end of the month, over eighteen aircraft had been ferried back to Biggin due to the exceptional effort of the unit, working until late evening and taking very few breaks. In the first week in February 1944, the airfield was visited by AVM Elmhurst and Air Cdre Montgomery; both were satisfied by the work of the Salvage Units.

F/O Hallet went to RAF Gravesend to report on the damage sustained by Proctor Mk III LZ185 of 83 Communication Unit, which swung on take-off. The rear fuselage was badly damaged, and both undercarriage legs were torn off; the aircraft was Category 'E', a write-off. Shortly after this incident at Gravesend, F/O Price inspected a Mustang Mk III – FX115, operated by 19 Squadron – which crashed when its undercarriage collapsed, sliding along the runway, damaging the fuselage and wings and ending its tour of duty.

Some repairs were carried out by 405 RSU on aircraft that crashed at Detling, one being Spitfire IX MH456 of 453 Squadron. The pilot was uninjured. Then, on 14 February, a Hurricane Mk IV – KE559 of 184 Squadron, based at Detling – stalled on approach and was completely wrecked. F/O Hallet was very busy. The same day, Spitfire IXe KH452 of 118 Squadron and Spitfire MJ173 collided while taxiing on the airfield. Both were repaired.

A court-martial was held at Detling on 13 February. LAC Markham was accused of stealing and found guilty of five out of eight charges. He was sent to prison for seven months. Such incidents occurred even in wartime, and were unpleasant for all concerned.

A Spitfire IX of 118 Squadron, MJ257, was taxiing when its drop tank fell off, damaging its undercarriage – more work for the overworked RSUs. Collisions were common at Detling, probably due to overcrowding. Two Spitfires of 453 Squadron, MJ171 and MH504 paid the price on 21 February. Both aircraft had wings torn off – it was quite a sight. At RAF Sawbridgeworth on the evening of 4 November 1943, instructions were received by 410 RSU that it was to move to Detling.

There the unit would join forces with 403 and 405 RSUs, whose function it was to recover and repair aircraft damaged or in need of major work. Nothing new there – the war had been going on for two years already and most of the airmen were used to moving at fairly short notice. But things were 'hotting up'.

On Guy Fawkes Night 1943, an advance party consisting of F/O C. E. Hall and twelve airmen in three vehicles arrived at Detling at 4.15 p.m. The following day, a convoy of thirty-four vehicles accompanied by six motorcycles, led by convoy commander Sqn Ldr T. T. Kyle, left Sawbridgeworth at 8.00 p.m. The weather that day was foul and only five miles from base the fire tender broke down with ignition trouble due to heavy rain. This was soon fixed and the slow-moving convoy was met by a police escort. On reaching Lewisham Way, London, a tyre burst – another delay.

However, the day improved when the convoy stopped for tea and sandwiches. Eventually, it arrived at Detling at 2.00 p.m. The remainder of that day was spent sorting out equipment and accommodation. Later that evening, the remainder of the unit, Sgt Oglivie and thirty ORs, arrived. It was not long before the all-important cook house was established. No. 410 RSU became operational on 9 November. The following day, it was visited and inspected by the CO of RAF Detling, Wg Cdr Lapsley. Following a few days of settling in and lectures, the unit had an association football match against 409 RSU – an away game, played in the 83 Group Cup Competition. The result was a 4–4 draw.

Later that month, twenty-two new vehicles were collected from RAF Banforth and arrived at Detling during the early evening of 18 November. The unit carried out much work in November, including providing assistance to units at Detling. One incident of note was when a Tiger Moth crashed at the airfield. The tragic accident involved a pilot from 184 Squadron and a WAAF officer. Not long before Christmas 1943, the unit received a delivery of donated books, which had been given to the group welfare officer. Other gifts included weapons issued for personal charge; three of the senior NCOs received Sten Carbines – submachine guns.

On Christmas Day, the unit held a party at Astley House, Maidstone, and provided their own music. Despite the weather and the festivities, 410 RSU had repaired and salvaged eighteen aircraft in December, comprising sixteen Spitfires Mk IXs and two Hurricane Mk IVs. At the same time, engineers had designed a new lock for the Spitfire's drop tank, which was fitted and tested by the unit. The ARF (Aircraft Reception Flight) attached to the unit had accepted and delivered twenty-one aircraft during this period.

The New Year dawned with new faces. Sgt Vanuge, a Free French pilot, arrived, as did a sergeant of 2187 RAF Regiment to undertake weapons training. All personal were vaccinated against typhus. On 27 January, some 210 Canadian personnel arrived at the unit on posting. Unfortunately, the majority arrived in the late afternoon, when daylight was fading. This necessitated the sorting out of 400 items of kit with the aid of vehicle headlights. The unit was divided into two groups, which were posted away from Detling at the end of January 1944, to Biggin Hill and Kenley.

CHAPTER 9

1944–1945

Further operations – personal accounts of service –
incidents at the airfield – day-to-day events

On 28 January 1944, the crew of *Hula Wahine* – a B-24H Liberator of the 446th Bomb Group, 704th Bomber Squadron, 8th USAAF, based at Bungay, Suffolk – took part in a raid on Frankfurt. It was a tree-top flight over Belgium during which 1st Lt Ernest W. Bruce (the pilot) and his crew fought off several attacks by enemy fighters. The engineer, S/Sgt Eugene D. McGuire, had been injured and was suffering from concussion; four other men were wounded at their guns. Despite this, Bruce dropped his bomb load. Two of the aircraft's superchargers were out of action and the hydraulic system of the tail gun turret had failed twenty minutes before they reached the target. They joined other stragglers on the way back, and were attacked by an Me 110, which was chased off by P38s.

The same aircraft came in for another attack; this time the left waist gunner, Sgt L. M. Jones, fired at it and it spun away, trailing black smoke. The bomber remained in cloud cover until reaching Belgium, where the cloud cleared. It dropped to an altitude of 75 feet, dodging windmills and high-tension cable towers. Below, workers in the fields waved at the aircraft as it roared overhead. Suddenly, an Fw 190 appeared, but the gunners were ready and poured a hundred rounds into it. It was seen to break away in flames and got into a spin. Half an hour later, a second Fw 190 joined them. The pilot opened fire and hit the top turret and waist gunner positions.

Sgt Jones remained at his gun despite having a hole in his leg. Sgt F. R. McLaughlin, the right waist gunner, was knocked over and wounded by shell fragments; he received first aid from Sgt Edward W. Schuller, who relieved the injured gunner at his gun and was also hit. Sgt H. B. Renfroe, the ball turret gunner, took over from McLaughlin. By then, No. 3 engine had been hit, but remained running, yet S/Sgt McGuire was hit and out of his head. The co-pilot's controls were damaged, but both the navigator and radio operator got radio bearings and the B24 staggered home over the Channel. Seeing Detling, they swooped in to land at 200 mph. After the crash-landing, the crew couldn't believe their luck and thanked *Hula Wahine* for bringing them all back alive. Sgt Leslie M. Jones was awarded the first Silver Star in the 446th BG and 2Lt Ernest W. Bruce received the DFC. The bombardier, 2Lt Thomas J. Pretty, got the Air Medal for destroying one of the Fw 190s.

By February 1944, many raids were undertaken by the 8th USAAF on No-ball targets or V-1 launch sites. One such mission involved the 385th Bomb Group based at Great Ashfield, Suffolk. On 13 February, it launched two groups of eighteen aircraft as part of an attack on V-1 sites near Calais. Leading the high squadron of 'B' Group was Lt Leonard C. Swedlund and crew in their B-17 Fortress, *Star Dust*. Swede, as nicknamed by his crew, had been a flying instructor, and was made responsible for bombing accuracy.

No-ball targets were bombed from low altitude because the targets were small, which obviously made the aircraft vulnerable to ground fire. The bombers took off and left their home base at 1.25 p.m., climbing over the Channel in very fine weather, which meant they could be seen and it was not long before they were flying into light flak. As they flew on they could

The crew of *Star Dust*, the B17 that crash-landed at Detling. Standing, left to right: 'Gren' Hawes, Charles Day, Ernie Meyer, ? (groundcrew), Charles Thompson, ? (groundcrew), Jack Brutenback, Jack Osborne. Kneeling, left to right: ? (groundcrew), Fred Berlinger, 'Swede' Swedlund. George Guscatt, Andrew Minkus, ? (groundcrew).

Star Dust, the B17 that crash-landed at Detling on 13 February 1944. The crew survived to tell the story. The pillbox still exists today, despite the impact and the intervening half-century.

Star Dust's number one engine was named *Betty*, after the wife of Grendell ('Gren') Hawes, the tail gunner. The pillbox into which it crashed can still be seen from the A249, which passes the site of Detling airfield.

hear the shrapnel hitting *Star Dust*, but they were unhindered. Suddenly, the B-17 was hit by three bursts of flak close to starboard. Grendall 'Gren' Hawes, the tail gunner, felt the aircraft surge upwards before wallowing back. Fortunately, there were no serious injuries apart from the waist gunner S/Sgt Charles R. Thompson, who was hit in the right leg.

The transmitter was smashed and Swede was unable to hand over lead position in time to release the bombs on target. The aircraft drifted out of formation and as they crossed the Channel descending, they jettisoned the bombs and threw out equipment to lighten the aircraft. Swede ordered the crew to ditching stations. However, realising how cold the sea would be, they decided to fly on. The first airfield to come into view was Detling. Losing height and unable to make radio contact with the airfield, the crew indicated their intention to land by circling before descending for the final approach.

As *Star Dust* touched down, the crew made for their crash stations, at which moment the aircraft bounced skywards. The B-17 hit the turf and skidded out of control. With brakes applied, Swede saw that they were heading for a concrete gun emplacement. Both pilots and crew braced themselves as the aircraft ploughed into a concrete pillbox. Crew in the radio room were thrown into a jumble of bodies and equipment, and as the aircraft came to a sudden halt they managed to make a hasty exit. *Star Dust* had hit the pillbox with such force that the aircraft had broken her back, and from the smashed cockpit someone was yelling for help.

Smoke was coming from the port inner engine. Gren went back inside the smashed aircraft. Both pilots were uninjured, but the engineer, Jackson T. Osborne, had been catapulted forward and was trapped between the pilots' seats. The navigator, Lt Rex M. Cantrell, was also trapped in the cockpit, and Fred Berlinger, who had been ejected through the aircraft's nose, lay badly injured on the roof of the pillbox.

Gren managed to help Jack Osborne, although a tangle of wreckage prevented escape through the rear of the cockpit. Finally, the crew escaped through the left-hand window, with Swede helping them out. RAF personnel by this time doused the smoking engines.

The unfortunate Fred Berlinger had to have a leg amputated, but the other crew members were not seriously injured and spent the night as guests of RAF Detling. In the morning, Col. Vandevanter flew in to collect the lucky crew. Before flying back to Great Ashfield, he delighted all by buzzing the airfield. All but two of the crew completed their tour; sadly, *Star Dust* was never to fly again.

At the beginning of April, six Spitfires of 19 Squadron were flown to Detling to be replaced with Mustangs. Practice flying in the Mustangs was carried out one morning, and in the evening a squadron party was held in Gravesend. The groundcrew were guests of the pilots.

A damaged B17 made an unscheduled landing at the airfield on 13 April 1944. This aircraft – *Satan's Mate*, serial no. 42-110074, call sign P-Bar – was based at Hethel, Norfolk. The pilot was 1st Lt Elwood N. Whitbeck of the 567th Bomber Squadron, 389th Bomber Group. The post-mission form was never completed, so there was no explanation for the landing at Detling. A brief report from the 3rd Strategic Air Depot states that they worked on the no. 2 engine, a fuel cell change, and minor battle damage, so perhaps the aircraft was experiencing serious fuel leaks, and the reason for landing was fuel starvation.

On 10 April 1944, 274 Squadron embarked from its temporary base at Portici near Naples for the UK and reassembled on 24 April at Hornchurch, moving in May to RAF Detling. Equipped with Spitfire IXs, it was now part of 2nd Tactical Air Force and carried out the usual round of offensive operations in connection with the forthcoming invasion and it provided cover to the invasion forces themselves. In early August, a complete reorganisation occurred.

Tempest Vs replaced the Spitfires, and eighteen of the twenty-nine pilots left were replaced by others from 501 Squadron. A move to RAF Manston followed, and the squadron commenced operations against the V-1 flying bombs being unleashed against Britain at that time. By the start of September, the squadron could claim fifteen V-1s. When the V-1 threat abated, the squadron made sweeps over the Dutch coastal area and moved to Coltishall on 20 September. Nine days later, the squadron moved to the Continent and was posted to Belgium. It rejoined 2 TAF in September, and went to 125 Wing on 1 October. Based in the Low Countries, the squadron commenced operations over the Arnhem and Nijmegen area. A week later, a move was made to join the Tempest units in 122 Wing in the Netherlands, and here, from December onwards, Luftwaffe aircraft were frequently to be met. The unit saw much aerial fighting during the final months of the war. A total of 171 victories had been claimed by 3 May 1945, by which time the unit was operating from German soil at Quakenbrück.

When they moved to Detling on 20 January 1944, the pilots of 453 (RAAF) Squadron were anxious to fly the new Spitfire IXb, which was replacing the ageing Spitfire Vb. The previous day, 'A' Flight, based at Sumburgh, flew to Doncaster. 'B' Flight left Skeabrae and landed at Syerston. From there, both flights travelled to Maidstone by train, arriving at Detling at midnight. Having just arrived at the airfield, eighteen pilots flew to Hutton Grunswick. The remaining fourteen pilots joined them after travelling by road, and they were to spend two weeks on firing practice. They returned to Detling on 4 February 1944. The remainder of the squadron were pleased by their comrades' return. The first formation flying took place and, despite the squadron's lack of practice, it was a

Flt Lt Paddy Horbison is seated in the cockpit of a 118 Squadron Spitfire Mk IX, one of several new aircraft transferred from 132 Squadron. Stan Kirtley is on the right in a flying jacket. The squadron was moved to Scotland and reverted to Mk Vs and VIIs, leaving the newly squired Mk IXs behind.

respectable performance. Watched by AM Conningham, a practice move took place on 3 February with a convoy of some 160 vehicles stretched for five miles along the country lanes.

It was only a few days after arriving at Detling that 453 Squadron was assigned to escort Marauders over Amiens. Sqn Ldr Andrews DFC led them, and he and F/O H. E. Yarra had to return due to engine trouble. On the night of 13 February, enemy aircraft dropped incendiaries close to 'B' Flight Dispersal; fortunately, no one was injured. However, Flt Sgt A. H. J. Harris was rushed off to hospital with appendicitis. With heavy snow falling, the squadron was grounded until 20 February, when it returned to escorting Liberators and B-17s. An operation took place from RAF Manston providing escort to Marauders. The flight lasted two hours fifteen minutes and WO Scott, flying his first sortie, suffered severely from the cold. On taking off, Flt Sgt Kinross had to land again, owing to oil on his cockpit's hood, and he collided with F/O Baker, who was taxiing up the runway. Both pilots escaped uninjured.

At the beginning of March 1944, the squadron was flying 'Ramrod' missions, deep penetration flying using 45-gallon fuel tanks, of nearly two hours. These sorties, escorting B-17s going to Germany, were usually uneventful; many pilots complained of boredom. They also suffered from the extreme cold. Electrically heated jackets, boots and gloves were supplied, which were agreed by all to be very efficient. But F/O P. V. McDade – who had a badly blistered toe owing to a short circuit – missed the warmth after switching off and suffered from frostbite on his left thumb. Had there been a petrol leak into the cockpit, the short-circuiting may have proved dangerous.

On a lighter note, Operation Kingo took place on 5 March. All pilots were taken into the Kent countryside to pose as parachutists. They then had to make their way back onto the airfield undetected. About seven reached the Operations Room, but others were caught in various locations around the airfield. The majority walked about ten miles during the exercise; the police and the Home Guard stopped none of them. Later that week, Sqn Ldr Hilton arrived with two new wireless sets – one for each flight for use in the crew room – which cheered everyone up.

HRH The Duke of Gloucester visited 453 (RAAF) Squadron on 9 March 1944. Gp Capt. Willoughby de Broke, AVM Wrigley, AVM Dickson and AVM Elmhurst accompanied him. Spitfires were lined up on each side of the runway leading to 'A' Flight Dispersal. Pilots stood in front of their aircraft with groundcrews and came to attention as the Duke's car drew up. He was met by Sqn Ldr J. R. Lapsley DFC (the squadron's CO), Sqn Ldr D. C. Andrews DFC (flight commander), Flt Lt R. H. S. Ewins and the squadron's adjutant. Following the inspection, he walked to the dispersal, where a cup of tea was provided. After lunch, while photographs were taken, one pilot was heard to say, 'Don't you get fed up with this, Duke?'

'Yes – as far as having my photograph taken is concerned,' the Duke replied. He left RAF Detling at 2.00 p.m.

Orders were received on 11 March for 453 Squadron to fly to Peterhead for a few days' air-firing and bombing practice. It was during this break that Flt Sgt B. W. Gorman was killed during flying practice. He was a popular pilot and had just been promoted to warrant officer. The same day, Flt Sgt H. D. Aldred returned from Burn flying an Auster, which was placed on squadron charge for communication flights. At the end of the month, pilots and groundcrew were introduced to the 500 lb bomb that 453 Squadron's Spitfires would be carrying on missions. Not such good news was that Spitfire IXas were to be flown. The feeling was that flying as 'top cover' was a 'stooge job'.

Early April was a busy period for 453; it took part in Exercise Jim Cook, the object being to test out the GCC and wing organisation. The first sortie from Detling was flown on the afternoon of 1 April, with the wing commander leading. The target was successfully attacked on several occasions and much was learned, despite the poor weather.

Flt Lt R. H. B. Ewins was posted to No. 1 Delivery Flight, Croydon. Being one of the founder members of the squadron, he was given an appropriate send-off at the Star Hotel, Maidstone. The following day, despite the previous evening's party, a football match took place between members of 453 and 602 squadrons. Although it lost, 453 later restored its pride by beating 602 at rugby. Although 453 Squadron was the only Australian Spitfire squadron in England in 1944, there was little publicity about them. In an effort to improve this, P/O Toohey arrived on 9 April from Public Relations HQ to interview pilots and airmen, and generally boost their ego.

A dive-bombing mission against a No-ball target at Abbeville took place on 14 April; bombs were dropped from 4,000 to 8,000 feet and mostly undershot the target. To make matters worse, the flak was intense and accurate. One aircraft, Spitfire MK324 piloted by P/O R. E. Yarra, received a direct hit and blew up. Yarra had flown with the squadron for a year and was popular with pilots and groundcrew alike. His was a particularly sad loss, as his brother, Flt Lt J. W. Yarra DFM, also serving with 453 Squadron, had been killed in action on 10 December 1942. Flt Sgt F. F. Cowpe, hit by flak, was, although uninjured, unable to lower his undercarriage. He was forced to belly-land at New Romney.

16 April was indeed a busy day, as 453 Squadron was scheduled to move to Ford in Sussex. At 3.00 p.m., the adjutant moved off with a small convoy of vehicles carrying equipment of 453, 132 and 602 squadrons. The remainder of the squadrons joined them later the same day, although a skeleton staff remained at Detling until the move was completed.

Gp Capt. Wells, nicknamed 'Hawkeye', led the famous Tangmere, Detling and West Malling Wing in March 1944, equipped with the Spitfire IX, an aircraft very popular with pilots. On 28 March 1944, he was credited with destroying a Messerschmitt Me 410 on the ground, and he led the wing on many operations over France prior to D-Day. Following a well-earned rest in November 1944, he was posted to the Central Fighter Establishment to command the Day Fighter Leaders' School.

June 1944 marked the beginning of the V-1 campaign. 229 Squadron had arrived at Detling from Hornchurch on 19 May 1944 and was to remain at the airfield until 22 June, when it moved to Tangmere. On 17 June 1944, this squadron was the first to fly a sortie against V-1s from Detling, but this action led to the loss of a Canadian pilot, Flt Lt W. D. 'Wally' Idema, who had returned to Detling after providing cover for the Mitchells and Bostons bombing Mezidon. On landing, Wally overshot the runway, pulled up, and crashed unhurt at 10.20 p.m. Thirty-five minutes later, he took off alone to seek out V-1s. He informed control that he was heading south-east but was not heard from again.

Reports indicate that he had been killed when he attacked a V-1 and was caught in the explosion. Pte R. C. McKenzie, a soldier with the Canadian Infantry, witnessed the incident:

> My regiment, Calgary Highlanders, was billeted in the empty seafront hotels at Folkestone. Some of us were standing at the entrance to our hotel. One of the first V-1s we saw was flying straight at us across the Channel. Suddenly a Spitfire dived out of the clouds and fired at the 'Buzz-Bomb', which exploded, and the last thing I saw before being blown backwards into the hotel was the Spitfire being flipped into a backward loop by the blast.

Spitfire Mk IX, serial no. MH852-9R, was destroyed and the young Canadian pilot lost his life. Not long after this tragedy, two more Spitfires of 229 Squadron took off to patrol the Hythe area. They were vectored to a target, which turned out to be a friendly aircraft. Later that day, a V-1 crossed Detling airfield. Guns opened fire, but airmen in the vicinity were not amused as they were surrounded by flying tracer while watching outside the mess dispersal. On 21 June, a V-1 flew across the airfield and crashed on the north-eastern perimeter of the airfield. Fortunately, there were no casualties.

Sqn Ldr W. A. (Bill) Olmstead DFC DSO, a Canadian, joined the Royal Canadian Air Force in 1940. Following various postings, both abroad and in England, Bill was sent on a course at Central Gunnery School, Catfoss, near Hull. His CO was the famous fighter pilot Wg Cdr Alan Deere. By the end of the course, Bill felt he was capable of firing at an enemy aircraft and hitting it. His reward on graduation was to be sent to Detling in May 1944 as gunnery officer. Duties included sharing the briefing sessions with the wing 'spy' (RAF slang for the intelligence officer), setting up aircraft identification kits to help pilots recognise all the various types of Allied or German aircraft, and assessing the gun camera films taken by pilots during combat. When guns were fired, a camera located in the wing was automatically activated, photographing the target for as long as the gun button remained depressed.

After a film was developed, you could identify the target, range, angle of deflection and number the of bullet strikes. From that, you could make an educated guess as to the final result of the engagement. According to Bill Olmstead:

> Once I got my equipment and information organised and established, there was little for me to do. The Spitfire squadrons forming Detling Wing met little opposition to their sweeps over France, Belgium and

Holland, which meant that I had no film to assess, therefore took the opportunity to roam around Kent's lovely countryside. As May turned into June, we all knew that D-Day was approaching. In my case, although I appreciated being closely associated with operational fighter squadrons, I found it particularly frustrating to realise that I was only a supernumerary at best, unable to fly missions on a regular basis.

During this time, Bill pestered the Canadian (RCAF) Headquarters with telephone calls and visits to persuade them to let him return to operational flying. He was turned down as his superiors considered the period spent at Detling a well-earned rest. In desperation, he offered to join the RAF, but this appeal was also refused. Sqn Ldr 'Stocky' Edwards, CO of 274 Squadron Detling, intervened, but the request was rejected again. It wasn't until Wg Cdr E. C. 'Hawkeye' Wells got involved that Bill was granted permission to fly in one or another of the squadrons on 'sweeps'.

Bill Olmstead recalls the day before the D-Day invasion was to begin. It was a day he would never forget and the one he had been waiting for:

5 June and news of the impending invasion was released to the forces. We were confined to camp while groundcrews painted black and white bands on the wings and tails of the aircraft to identify aircraft for the invasion forces. The atmosphere at Detling was tense as we paced up and down, awaiting our briefing. Shortly after 1100 hrs we pilots made our way to the Intelligence Room. In the brightly lit room three walls were covered with coloured maps. Soon the wing commander, intelligence officers and Army liaison officers walked into the room carrying more rolls of maps and piles of books. Wells had a large map pinned to the wall displaying the Normandy coast. There was an audible gasp from the pilots, the CO talked for the next two hours.

On D-Day, 6 June 1944, the CO stood down one of his pilots, allowing Bill to fly. No. 2. Squadron records reveal that Bill was listed, on these operations, as 'Pilot X', which would have caused trouble had he failed to return.

The following week, on 13 June, the Germans were launching the V-1, which was to cause great loss of life and devastation in London and the South East. They were launched at ten-minute intervals from many sites in Europe, and Detling was often directly beneath their flight path. As the flying bombs shot over the area, aircraft from Detling scrambled to intercept this deadly menace. The noise was terrific, and Bill remembers that it was as though the 'bloody things' were flying right through the mess and barracks:

During the early days of the invasion I flew a number of patrols and sweeps with the Detling Wing, while still trying on a daily basis to persuade RCAF Headquarters to post me to a fully operational squadron. Then, in mid-June, I visited our headquarters in person. A squadron leader stopped me in the hall.

'Are you Olmstead?' he asked.

'Yes sir,' I replied.

'Where in hell have you been? We've been looking all over for you; you are to go back to Ops immediately.'

There had been some foul-up, but my prayers were answered and I was soon leaving Detling for 83 Group Supply Unit (GSU) in Redhill. From there I went to Bognor, Sussex, an Advanced Landing Ground.

In July, Bill Olmstead was posted to 442 (RCAF) Squadron, based at B3 at St Croix-sur-Mer, an Advanced Landing Ground located on the Normandy beachhead. His days at Detling were at an end.

On 22 June 1944, 165 (Ceylon) Squadron arrived at RAF Detling, having been moved from Harrowbeer to take part in anti-diver patrols. They soon found themselves very busy indeed.

23 June was a tragic day for the newly arrived squadron. WO A. E. Lamour-Zevacoo RAAF crashed three miles south-east of Canterbury and was killed. He was on diver patrol when his Spitfire Mk IX – serial no. MK738, code SK-L – was seen to spin into the ground. The following day, there were two non-operational flights and twenty-eight operational, of which twenty-six were anti-diver patrols. During one of these, Flt Lt Watson destroyed a V-1 near Tonbridge at about 6.20 a.m. It crashed north of Biggin Hill. The squadron settled into their new home at Detling, hoping it would be a long stay, as they were having considerable success with the V-1s. It was not long before both Flt Sgt Hughes and F/O S. R. Chambers destroyed two more 'divers' (another name for V-1s). They crashed at Tonbridge and Tunbridge Wells.

That evening, the squadron intelligence officer gave pilots all the available information regarding the V-1 and Operation Diver. The CO, Sqn Ldr M. E. Blackstone, who had considerable technical knowledge, was able to expand on the matter and explain in simple terms, how the propulsion unit of the Doodlebug worked. Several patrols undertaken by 165 Squadron were either Ramrod or Convoy patrols, which were, as often as not, uneventful.

It was a busy day on 23 June, when squadrons from Kent and Sussex airfields were engaged in anti-V-1 patrols. 165 Squadron entered the arena in the evening when five Spitfires took off on patrol from Detling. It was not long before Flt Lt Tony Holland, a Malta veteran, shot down a V-1

Not all V-1s exploded. After examination by technical experts, some were reconstructed and displayed to raise funds. This example was put on display at Maidstone during the summer of 1944. It gave the public the opportunity to get close to a 'Buzz Bomb'.

near the railway line at Rye. He recalled that the target was travelling at 300 mph and flying north-west. Another was destroyed by F/O 'Tommy' Vance, and came down south of Redhill. To his surprise, he noticed another, which had been damaged by a Tempest. He finished the task and the V-1 exploded. Vance remembers that a 5-foot piece of cable, similar to an aerial cable, caught the mirror of his Spitfire.

Sqn Ldr Maurice Blackstone intercepted another V-1 north-west of Beachy Head and gave chase, as did many other aircraft. It was flying at 375 mph at a height of 2,500–3,000 feet. He closed in and fired with no effect. He pulled away, but lost sight of the target. It was confirmed later by ROC that the V-1 had crashed near Wimbledon Common. Lt Selwyn Hamblett RNVR, who had been seconded to 165 Squadron at Detling, gave chase to another V-1 over Beachy Head. He waited until it was over open country. It came down in flames at Hailsham, some 150 yards from houses. The last target fell to Flt Sgt Hughes, who intercepted a Doodlebug over Dungeness; it crashed into woods.

On return to Detling, the pilots of 165 Squadron were upset to learn that their friend, French one-legged pilot WO Albert Zevaco-Lamour, was killed when his Spitfire IX, serial no. MK378 SK-L, crashed two or three miles south-east of Canterbury, it was thought that he was shot down by AA fire. The following day, Flt Lt C. Watson of 165 Squadron brought down a V-1, which dived into a balloon barrage north of Biggin Hill. Flt Sgt R. J. Hughes was back in action on 27 June when he sighted a flying bomb coming in east of Hastings at 1,000 feet. It was being chased by two Tempests and another Spitfire joined the pursuit. He attacked and the V-1 exploded in flames not far from Maidstone. F/O S. R. Chambers shared the destruction of another with a Tempest of 3 Squadron, Newchurch. The target came down near railway lines between Tunbridge Wells and Tonbridge. 29 June was to be a rewarding day for 165 Squadron. From early afternoon until late that evening, seven pilots of the squadron destroyed six Doodlebugs, with the loss of no pilots.

Following the squadron's success in June, the aerial assault intensified in July and the month began with eight more V-1s destroyed during an evening patrol. One of the pilots, F/O Armstrong, returned to Detling with his Spitfire covered in soot and with the elevators and rudder partly burned after his target exploded north of Hastings. He was just 50 yards behind the V-1 and couldn't avoid flying through the wreckage. It was a narrow escape. Later that month, P/O J. V. Tyran was forced to abandon a V-1 attack when the local AA fire was directed at him – a fairly regular occurrence during those hectic days. Flt Lt Tony Holland destroyed two 'Buzz Bombs' during the same patrol; one crashed at Beachy Head, the other near Eastbourne. The last V-1 patrols flown by 165 Squadron took place on Tuesday 11 July, when five pilots destroyed three V-1s.

To provide close support for the Allied forces fighting in Normandy following the successful invasion on 6 June 1944, 1 Squadron was moved to Harrowbeer near Plymouth in June 1944. Wg Cdr H. A. C. Bird-Wilson led them during June 1944. However, it was during early June that the first V-1s appeared in the sky over the South East. As a result, several squadrons flying high-speed fighters such as the Spitfire IX LFs and Tempests were assigned to combat the new threat. As a result, 1 Squadron was moved to Detling on 22 June, having only been at Harrowbeer for thirty-six hours. The squadron's first sortie against the V-1s took place on 24 June. During the first few days, pilots had problems turning into the targets, since the V-1s moved so fast. Tempests of 150 Wing at Newchurch ALG also hindered the Doodlebugs.

Luck changed for 1 Squadron on 27 June when both F/O Bob Bridgeman and F/O Batchelor shot down two V-1s. One crashed near Wadhurst, the other near Rye – both exploding on impact. Eight days after D-Day, two officers from the squadron (F/O Stuart and F/O Marsh) scored yet another first by becoming the first pilots to land on the emergency airstrip laid just behind the newly won beachhead. By this time, the Typhoons had been replaced by Spitfire IXs, and by using 150-octane fuel and running the Merlins with a 25 lb boost, the pilots were able to intercept the flying bombs. F/O Bridgman was the first pilot of 1 Squadron to be successful. He shot down a V-1 12 miles south of Tonbridge. The flying bomb was judged to be doing 360–375 mph.

By 30 June 1944, the pilots were more adept. Flt Sgt Hastings finished one attack on 5 July on the fringe of the London balloon barrage. He fouled one of the cables, which took off his starboard wing-tip and two airscrew blades. Despite this, he managed to land his aircraft intact at Gatwick. Altogether, 1 Squadron destroyed thirty-nine flying bombs. By late July 1944, Gp Capt. C. F. Gray had taken command of the Spitfire Wing at Detling to organise operations against the V-1s and to support the Army in operations over Europe. Gray had a distinguished flying career, and since May 1940 he had accounted for the destruction of no less than twenty-seven aircraft.

Many of these were Bf 109s, which crashed following combat with Gray over Kent during the Battle of Britain. By the middle of August 1944, the AA guns largely had the measure of the flying bombs, and 1 Squadron, now with Griffon-engined Spitfire XXIs, took on more bomber-escort work on daylight raids. One of the shortest sorties must be that of F/O McIntosh, who had not long taken off and had just raised his Spitfire's undercarriage when he noticed a V-1 approaching, so gathered speed and turned; the V-1 crossed his aircraft's nose. He gave it a short burst, and the V-1 exploded. He landed back at Detling, having been airborne a few minutes.

Many airmen who joined the RAF had previously been in the Air Training Corps, hopeful that they would later become RAF pilots. One such young man was P. J. C. Williamson, who joined the ATC at the beginning of the war. He later joined the RAF as a volunteer in December 1942. He failed to become a pilot, but qualified as an armourer. He was posted to Lympne with 1 Squadron, which was at that time flying the Typhoon Mk I. On 14 February, the squadron moved to Martlesham Heath, where it flew escort to many USAAF bomber formations. However, this was not for long, and they moved to North Weald on 2 April 1944. Here, their Typhoons were replaced with the Spitfire Mk IX.

The groundcrews learnt fast how to arm these new aircraft, which moved to Predannack in preparation for D-Day. P. J. C. Williamson recalls:

On 19 June 1944, the squadron moved to Harrowbeer, near Plymouth, and stayed for only three days, before moving to Detling to combat the V-1. As quite a good shot, I took the opportunity to break the rules and fire a 20 mm cannon, which was manned by an RAF Regiment gunner on the airfield's perimeter, at a 'Doodlebug'. I believe I did have a strike, but it did not alter its course, but did manage to shear the spiral steel rod which supported the barbed wire fence nearby.

I remember that in the woods behind the dispersal, there was quite a lot of unexploded ammunition, including many incendiary bombs from a Molotov cocktail basket. I also had a very near miss at Detling, as a Spitfire taxiing round the dispersal crashed into the one I was working on. The propeller sliced through the cannon barrel on the wing where I was working. How I escaped is still a puzzle to me. It was at Detling that I witnessed the fastest destruction of a flying bomb by one of our fighters, and nearly got hit with a lump of aluminium from it as it exploded in the air. It was not long before we moved back to Lympne on 12 July 1944 to return to Detling on 10 August 1944. The squadron once again was escorting masses of bombers to targets in Germany; we were kept busy, mainly rearming the Spitfires.

Flt Lt Jarman, a pilot with 1 Squadron, remembers the move from Harrowbeer to Detling:

Our time at Harrowbeer was short as we were needed at Detling to combat the V-1 threat; this new weapon could affect the outcome of the war. Detling was back to No. 11 Group where all the excitement was, according to the boys, where they knew their way around and they were all very keen on the move. Personally I couldn't help reflecting that there was enough excitement to keep me from being bored in 10 Group. The arrival of a fighter to a new station is an interesting experience. The squadron is largely judged by its formation flying by the resident personnel and briefed by the CO as to what we will do and heaven help anyone who lets the show down. A typical arrival: in VIC formation with No. 4s in the box, sliding smoothly into three sections of line astern for a low-level run over the mess. This has to be well-judged by the leader, as each aircraft is below the one in front in order to avoid his slipstream and if the leader cuts it too fine, No. 4s are a bit pushed to clear the roof. After this you open out in landing formation and land about 50 yards behind each other.

A traffic-control truck normally leads you to the dispersal pens where the station commander usually welcomes you. At the time it was Mike Crossley, a well-known fighter pilot. After getting ourselves organised we meandered to the mess along a rural path with rustic gates and I was behind the main bunch when they approached the first gate, each carrying a bag of personnel equipment. They were busy arguing and not paying particular attention to what they were doing and after several half-hearted attempts to open it, gave up and started to climb over but as I strolled up I spotted the concealed catch, slid it along and flung open the gate and ambled on. At this there was a roar of laughter and only my acceleration saved my trousers. Outside the mess a crowd of off-duty officers were making punishable remarks typical of which was, 'Did you notice that gaggle of beat-up old aircraft flying in roughly the same direction just now, bouncing about like a lot of kangaroos when they tried to land?' And soon a wild free-for-all was taking place, which served to introduce us formally to our new comrades.

At Detling there was never a dull moment. We escorted bombers and rocket Typhoons and strafed any ground targets that presented themselves. While attacking a train on 1 June 1944, as a section of four we lost F/O F. H. 'Pussy' Cattermoul, who was leading. The first attack out of the sun was OK. Four Spitfires flying along a training line astern, each with two 20 mm cannon and four Brownings, can do an awful amount of damage, but until you actually see troops come pouring out of the windows of the still-speeding train to escape the hail of fire, you somehow do not think of lives being involved. But it was by no means a one-sided business, as the train roof carries much light flack and 'Pussy' made the classic mistake of taking us in for a second attack and paid the penalty. He started spurting glycol and called up that his engine had seized and he was force-landing, which he did successfully in the middle of a large field with undercarriage up.

Any ideas of trying to pick him up were soon dispelled by large numbers of German troops running to the scene, presumably survivors from the train. No. 3, the new leader, said, 'Don't shoot, we'll only stir them up.'

'Pussy' called up and said he was OK. We later heard he was taken POW but died of his wounds on 9 July 1944. Following a similar show, Jimmy Cambell returned with his aircraft covered in oil and hardly any left in the engine. He also had a large hole through the bottom of his cockpit and a corresponding hole through the canopy and we couldn't understand how it had missed him. He was quite slim but even so, when we put a piece of taut string through the two holes, his chin was in the way of the string, so he must have been looking over his shoulder at the time. He was more concerned that his new trousers were covered in oil; although it was pointed out he was lucky to have something to keep in his oily trouser.

On another occasion, 'Mac', one of our pilots, was the first to shoot down a V-1. He was just taking off when the thing appeared quite low and his undercarriage was still retracting when he did a steep turn and had a full 90 degree short burst and the thing turned over and dived in with an almighty bang. But Mac got a strip torn off him by the CO, who said he could have written off the squadron. 1 Squadron took time to get organised at Detling for maximum effect, initially patrolling over the V-1 launching sites, and chasing them to the English coast where they were usually spent of ammunition and were then supposed to hand over patrol to fighters in the Dover area. 'Happy', one of 165 Squadron's pilots, attacked a V-1 at 25 yards; it blew up. I have never seen a Spitfire look sorrier for itself and still get back, black with soot, riddled with holes and with several important pieces missing. But on landing he was still smiling.

On 17 July 1944, the wing moved to Lympne airfield, nearer the coast. The Air Defence of Great Britain flak had been moved and concentrated almost overnight to the south coast. It was not long after this that the anti V-1 patrols were taken over by faster aircraft, Tempests and the new Meteor jets. The wing returned again to Detling on 10 August 1944. Back at Detling, pilots were sent on an engine-handling course at Derby a few at a time, due to the large number of engine failures they were experiencing. Flt Lt Jarman described the situation:

On return to Kent one of the squadron's pilots got married and was sent a telegram, which read, 'Press tits (jargon for engine starting) at 10.00 p.m. and cover target to limit of endurance.' Memories of this period at Detling include visits to many pubs and I couldn't find my way to any of them now as we were always packed in the back of somebody's blacked-out car like so many sardines. One of the pubs had a magnificent collection of hunting horns, which were quite a challenge to the budding musicians amongst us. In fact we must have been a bit of mixed blessing to the locals as we were a pretty wild bunch, but we were always greeted with open arms by all and sundry and always paid for any damage done.

We would return to camp in the wee small hours as drunk as skunks and, led by the CO, we usually raised more mayhem such as singing the squadron song – 'The Gay Desperado' – over the station Tannoy and having all personnel ringing up to see if the war was over, or raiding the ground officers' room. Continuing the off-duty activities, I gave our medical officer, Doc. Wallace, some more lessons in the Tiger Moth and in reply to the CO's query said that in my opinion he was ready for a solo and the boss tested him and sent him solo and this called for a party. One day, while waiting for a squadron patrol, we were three aircraft short, then with the 'Irks' working frantically a tenth became serviceable, then an eleventh, and with about ten minutes to go the fitter of the twelfth leaped aboard to run up the engine – with the CO, who had done enough operational flying by this time, biting his nails down to the elbow and cursing everyone in sight. And then, as the engine roared up to full power, the chokes slipped and the aircraft surged forward with the airman on the tail just managing to leap clear before it crashed into the two that had just been made serviceable. I wouldn't have been in that poor devil's shoes.

During a mission on 14 October 1944 escorting Lancasters to Duisburg, my engine packed up. I radioed my section leader, who gave me some useful advice suggesting I should return to Detling. I tried to locate an ALG in the invasion area, but by now my radio was dead. I remembered that a Mustang pilot had the same problem and by pumping the priming pump he made it back from Berlin. Pumping frantically I was losing height and decided to bail out when I broke cloud. I found I was over an airfield. Unfortunately on trying to land the aircraft looped and came to a stop. I got out and saw several men with guns running towards me; they were British. The Army major in charge was not pleased; as I had turned up the runway his men had recently repaired bomb damage. After Cognac, I was told I was at St Omer and that a Dakota ambulance would take me back. Following more drink, wounded soldiers were put into the Dakota and we took off from Ghent and headed home. A card game was in swing at the back of the aircraft and the pilot who wished to join the game gave me control of his aircraft and returned later. 'OK,' he said, 'ask the Navigator to give me a course and ETA for Detling.'

It was not long before we were circling home, where it was by now dark. Despite this I managed to make out enough to point out the best approach and by this time some of the people below had lit up the Summerfeld tracking with their vehicles' headlights and we were down, and the flight sergeant pilot, leaving me to book him in, had roared off. I had been reported missing, missed a party, and the only souvenir I had was a sore thumb. The cause of the engine failure was a sheared drive to the fuel pump.

Of the five bombs destroyed by 1 Squadron on Wednesday 28 June, one is remembered clearly by LAC Phil Williamson, stationed at Detling:

This chap had just taken off and this V-1 came over. Our pilot got round onto its tail and opened fire and it took a dive right above us! I jumped into a Nissen hut, hit the floor with my hands over my ears, but nothing happened. I came out again and the V-1 had circled round the other side of the airfield and then exploded in a ball of flame.

Our pilot pulled round and landed within seconds and we could see all the fabric had gone from the tail plane. A great lump of aluminium from the V-1 suddenly landed near us, clanging along on the concrete.

The pilot was F/O E. G. McIntosh flying a Spitfire LFIXb. Unfortunately for him, the kill was shared with a pilot of 322 Squadron. Flt Sgt Weller recalls one of the many hazards associated with fighters attacking the V-1s:

The closest call I had with one was the day I was vectored towards one in cloud. Control kept saying our two radar plots are together, you must be right on top of it. I just said, well, I am in cloud and can't see a bloody thing. Suddenly the V-1 came right at me, within feet of my Spitfire and immediately disappeared again. We patrolled over the Channel, sometimes as far as the French coast, trying to pick them up. They would come over at speed, so we were trying to get around 2,000 feet higher than they flew so we could pick up some speed to catch them. Then we got 150-octane petrol, which gave us another 30 mph or so. But it was necessary for our Spits to have an engine change about every sixty hours.

An unusual event happened on Wednesday 5 July when Wg Cdr Peter Powell DFC, who was Wing Commander Flying at Detling, borrowed a Spitfire of 1 Squadron to have a crack at a V-1. In fact, he shared one with F/O P. E. Crocker, who may have been a bit upset at the intrusion of the high-ranking officer. Meanwhile, Flt Sgt Iain Hastings chased another to the fringes of the balloon barrage before he sent it down near Gatwick, but was unable to avoid hitting a balloon cable.

I broke away to avoid barrage but hit cable, which spun aircraft round. I managed to restore aircraft to an even keel but saw that the outer section starboard wing-tip was cut off. I headed for Gatwick, landing safely, but found two opposite blades of propeller damaged.

Not content with his earlier success, Wg Cdr Powell took off again for another anti-diver patrol in the company of disgruntled pilot F/O Jack Batchelor. Like Crocker earlier that day, they had to share a V-1 destroyed.

One incident that should be mentioned in the context of 1 Squadron's temporary stay at Lympne occurred on 24 July. F/O Ken Foskett shot down a V-1, which crashed on railway lines near Ashford. To his horror, Ken realised a fast-approaching train would collided with the debris of the explosion – the driver had not seen the crater caused by the explosion. Ken immediately tried to attract the driver's attention by flying alongside the engine and waggling his wings. Fortunately the engine's crew realised in time and pulled up just short of the crater. Foskett was a hero, and apart from receiving many letters, the incident was reported in the national press.

On 10 August, the squadron was moved back to Detling and resumed its offensive role. The crews had expected to be moved to Hawkinge. During the remainder of August, No. 141 Wing at Detling continued escort operations and the occasional armed reconnaissance flights, attacking barges south of Dixmude. The month ended with the wing acting as withdrawal support for attacks on sites near Abbeville, where V-2 rockets were being stored. WO J. W. McKenzie returned to Detling following his forced landing on the Isle of Thanet, as did WO Neil Howard, who evaded capture in Europe after having crashed in March.

The bombing offensive intensified in September and 1 Squadron took part in 'Big Ben' (codename for the V-2) patrols. As there was no defence against the V-2, it was in fact the first squadron to destroy one of these sites. Squadrons at Detling were also involved in Operation Market Garden – the airborne assault on the bridges at Arnhem. During a fighter sweep over Holland in poor weather on 27 September, several aircraft were seen and mistaken as German. The Spitfires duly jettisoned their long-range fuel tanks to engage them. With the weather getting worse, both F/O Tommy Wyllie and WO E. R. Andrews were last heard calling Manston for a course home. Both pilots were never seen again and it was thought that they had collided over the Channel. It was a tragic loss for the squadron and all at Detling, as both pilots were much liked.

Following another operation on 7 October, all flying was cancelled due – yet again – to the weather. So everyone set off for The Star, a favourite pub used by pilots at Maidstone. A great party was had, with Wg Cdr Michael Grossley helping the proceedings by playing his saxophone. He was also competent on both the guitar and the harmonica. The evening was rounded off when 1 Squadron challenged 165 Squadron to 'mess rugger' and won 2–1. On 10 October, Wg Cdr Powell was involved in a road accident when his car collided with an Army truck. He was injured, but, sadly, the passenger, Flt Lt T. D. Lindsey of 165 Squadron, was killed. As a result, Bobby Oxspring took on the role of No. 141 Wing Leader.

With the successful attacks on the V-1 sites, everyone was shocked when, on the evening of 8 November, no less than a dozen V-1s flew over the airfield. It was believed they had been launched from Heinkel 111 bombers, which still had the capability mount such missions. The airfield at Detling was fast becoming a quagmire and most operations had been cancelled. However, Flt Lt W. S. Wallace, the squadron doctor, was taking flying lessons from Flt Lt J. J. Jarman, and after nearly eight hours' flying he went solo – not bad for a 'rookie' pilot, although he did have to buy everyone a pint in the bar that evening. As November progressed, more operations were cancelled or delayed due to poor weather. Although there were occasional improvements, morale was at low ebb.

Early in December, things were looking up, and the new Spitfire Mk XXI visited Detling for all to have a close look. However, despite 1 Squadron's dire need for the new type, they would have to wait five months before being re-equipped with the powerful Griffin-engine Spitfires. But following flight tests with the airframe modified to accommodate the new engine, the aircraft was considered to be unstable. The Detling Wing took off again in poor weather for another operation, but had to land at Manston due to the fog. However, landing there was assisted by FIDO (Fog Investigation and Dispersal Operation) – which meant fuel was burned to clear the fog. On 9 December, having stayed overnight at Manston, the squadron attempted to return to Detling. A dangerous situation developed, with several near misses. F/O P. W. Stewart decided to return to Manston, and successfully landed at Detling on a third attempt later the same day. Bobby Oxspring had a narrow escape. When he was about to take off, his engine cut, and he was unable to prevent his Spitfire drifting in front of Pat Lardner-Burke. Just in time, he managed to pull back on his stick and hop over the other aircraft, preventing what could have been a major accident.

After a further two weeks of stop-and-go operations, the wing learnt it was to move to Manston; its sister unit, 165, was off to RAF Bentwater, Suffolk. During the previous six weeks, they had destroyed no less than forty-six V-1s. 1 Squadron was to remain at Detling until 18 December, when they were moved to RAF Manston, which at the time was very crowded. The good news was that Wg Cdr Oxspring would remain boss. It was not long before both pilots and groundcrew alike were missing the comforts of RAF Detling, which had proved to be one of the better stations, despite the mud and the weather.

Flt Lt Bob Spurdle was posted from 130 Squadron to 80 Squadron in May 1944, becoming 'B' Flight Commander. He had settled well into 80 Squadron, which was comprised mostly of Commonwealth pilots. The squadron had been formed at Montrose in Scotland on 10 August 1917 and its first CO was a Maj. V. D. Bell. The unit's logo was a bell and understandably they became known as 'the Bell Boys'. They arrived at RAF Detling on 19 May 1944, and remained until 22 June 1944. Their main role was to fly bomber escorts, sweeps and armed reconnaissance flights in preparation for D-Day. The CO, a Norwegian, Maj. Bijon Bjornstad DFC, was not a patient man, but he was well liked by those who served under him. For pilots, like Bob Spurdle, May passed quietly with only seven operational sorties escorting bombers over France.

It became obvious to all pilots of 80 Squadron that something big was about to happen. Several times they were alerted to be ready for an early morning 'scramble'. Leave at Detling was stopped and they were sent on more patrols to protect shipping. The squadron's Spitfire Mk IXs had by then been painted with black and white bands under the wings and around the rear fuselage for ease of identification. Bob recalls:

It made little difference. Pongos (the Army), being trigger happy like the Navy, always blasted at any aircraft foolish enough to fly near them! Late one evening the CO drew me aside and his mangled English told me to organise a strong team for the morning and to see that they got to bed early.

Getting hold of 'Slim' Burbridge, our 'A' Flight Commander at Detling, we tossed a coin as to who would stand down so that the CO could lead the squadron. I won the toss and knowing all the pilots' abilities thoroughly, got 'Slim' to help me sort out a good bunch. All night heavy aircraft droned overhead; the invasion was on! Early the following day, 6 June, we were awakened by an excited batman; we scoffed our breakfast and tore off to the dispersal area. There we waited and waited and pestered the Ops Room for a job. Our job was to stand by; we were being held in reserve. However, shortly after noon everything changed and we were running across the dispersal area to our kites. We strapped ourselves in and took off from Detling to join a glider train of Albemarle's towing gliders, later being joined by Sterling bombers towing Hamelcar gliders.

During this flight, 80 Squadron attacked ground targets, destroying vehicles and generally harassing the enemy. Nearing the English coast, on the return flight, they were short of fuel and decided to land at Hawkinge. It was getting dark before they were rearmed and fuelled, so they stayed the night and joined many other pilots in the mess in the same situation, many having also been shot up by ground fire. The next day, following the previous night's party and nursing headaches, 80 Squadron headed back to Detling for debriefing. Flt Lt Bob Spurdle later went on to command 80 Squadron, having been promoted by 'Hawkeye' Wells, the Wing CO at Detling. Bob remained with the squadron until January 1945.

During their brief stay at Detling, there were only two aircraft lost. On 10 June, F/O G. A. Bush was on an early beach patrol when his Spitfire Mk IX, serial no. BS462, suffered a glycol leak. He bailed out over Le Havre and was rescued unhurt. The same day, F/O J. L. Foubert RCAF also suffered a glycol leak. His Spitfire Mk IX, serial no. MA842, ditched in the sea off Hastings, and he was rescued unhurt. By 11 June 1944, most of 80 Squadron's Spitfires were unserviceable; tests were carried out to prevent the re-occurrence of glycol leaks. Following a patrol over the Western Reaches on 20 June, it was thought doubtful that the patrolling Spitfires could land back at Detling, due to cloud. The whole wing had to land in Sussex. On 22 June, it moved to the airfield at Merston near Chichester.

Six non-operational flights were made on 26 June, plus fifty-two operational flights consisting of twelve aircraft on an escort mission with Halifaxes and forty aircraft on diver patrols. The area of operation was Gravelines. The height of patrol was 16,000 feet. Flt Sgt R. Hughes shot a V-1 down at about 4.00 p.m. and his companion F/O S. H. Chambers bagged one twenty minutes later in the Tunbridge Wells area. That evening, the squadron intelligence officer gave a lecture on the operation of the V-1 and how its propulsion unit worked.

118 Squadron's duties at Detling were for a short period; it was moved from Peterhead on 20 June 1944 and stayed at the airfield for three days. It returned to Peterhead to be re-equipped with Spitfire Mk IXcs and returned again to Detling on 5 February. The squadron's records show that it moved to Skaebrae in March, returning yet again to Detling on 12 July, where it remained until leaving for the last time on 9 August 1944. The squadron's main role at Detling, early in 1944, was to escort B-24 Liberators, Marauders and Fortresses of the 8th USAAF as they continually pounded German targets.

Detling sorties of the social kind involved nights out at the Star pub in Maidstone; some of the squadron reached as far afield as Sittingbourne. On one memorable occasion, 118 Squadron had all its eggs stolen. This may seem trivial by today's standards, but during the war, eggs were as scarce as hen's teeth. On some missions, 118 Squadron flew as many as twenty-four Spitfires; sometimes they would have to land at RAF Manston to refuel. On 4 March, Wg Cdr R. D. Yule was awarded the DSO on the same day as the squadron was to move for a spell to Skaebrae in Scotland for gunnery training. When it returned to Detling, it was tasked with escorting bombers attacking No-ball targets in Germany. These were the bases from which V-1s and V-2s were launched.

At the beginning of August, the CO of 124 Squadron, Sqn Ldr T. Bamforth DFC, wrote:

This month saw a great increase in the operational work of the squadron and an increase in the enthusiasm of the pilots. We carried out a number of sweeps and close escorts of Lancasters and Halifaxes bombing No-ball sites and in particular the large dumps in the area of Crail, north

Flt Lt Jack Douay crash-landed at Detling on 27 July 1944. Jack, a French pilot with 274 Squadron, is seen here at RAF Manston in 1945. The day he crash-landed, his family in France were liberated by the Allies after four years of German occupation.

of Paris. On 5 August the wing at Detling was moving back to Peterhead, 504 Squadron to Manston and we to Westhampett to form a wing with 303 (Polish) Squadron.

Jack Douay MBE flew with 274 Squadron from 17 May to 24 June 1944 and was based at Detling with the unit for a short period:

We returned from Naples on 23 April and went directly to RAF Hornchurch to take delivery of our Spitfire IXs and get accustomed to UK flying conditions. We transferred to Detling on 17 May and took up our operational flying straight away. It was during the last days of May that we first encountered a V-1 flying bomb, commonly called Doodlebug at the time. We were not fast enough to deal with them. On 5 June, after having the previous days given air cover to some of the numerous convoys making their way through the Dover Strait towards the future beachheads, we were confined to camp to give a hand all evening to the ground staff to paint the black and white stripes on the wings and fuselage of all the aircraft.

We covered the Normandy landings and carried out fighter sweeps until on 24 June we moved to Merston. We were billeted near the airfield, but spent most of our free time in Maidstone. To the airfield was quite an uphill effort, only to be considered if a very promising end to the evening justified it. We were on readiness from the dawn to dusk, and in June of course the nights are the shortest. My last connection with Detling airfield was on 28 July 1944. I was flying target cover in Spitfire JJ-S, and in fact it could well have been my last connection with everything. We were based at West Malling at the time. On returning from a sweep on the Continent my engine started losing power and I wouldn't make West Malling airfield. I headed for Detling. I also had an empty 45-gallon auxiliary tank under the belly. When I tried to lower my undercarriage it refused to unlock. Under normal circumstances there are a number of more or less violent actions that can be taken, such as inverted flying while unlocking the wheels, but as I was still losing height with a failing engine I had very little time to indulge in such manoeuvres, and realised I would have to belly-land.

Having an empty 45-gallon auxiliary petrol tank under the aircraft, I quickly took the necessary action to jettison it before coming in on my emergency belly-landing beside the runway. As I was informed by flying control that the auxiliary tank had not jettisoned, I had hardly slid to a stop before I was out of the cockpit like a jack-in-the-box. But it wasn't my day; the tank didn't explode. That was my last visit to Detling.

Ashford was a positive Godsend to pilots returning to Detling and other airfields in Kent. The railway line that ran east from Ashford towards Tunbridge Wells is the only long, straight railway line in the south of England. Therefore, when returning in bad weather (which was frequent) one could fly in from the Channel cross the coast and fly up to the railway line, which couldn't be missed, turn right and then it was easy to get to either Detling or West Malling.

On 26 July 1944, Colin Gray was called to the 11 Group Headquarters at Uxbridge and was appointed Wing Commander (Flying) at Friston, Sussex. The three squadrons were to be detached to Detling, where he was told to report. He rushed back to Milfield to collect his Spitfire IX – RM787 – and flew down to Kent the following day. Wg Cdr Mike Crossley was CO of the airfield at the time and the three squadrons he was to command came under the control of RAF Biggin Hill sector. 118 Squadron was under the command of Sqn Ldr P. W. E. Heppell DFC; the other two, 124 and 504 squadrons, were under the command of Sqn Ldr Banning-Lover. It was not long before Wg Cdr Gray was back in action – the following day he led the wing on a target support mission, with Mitchells bombing Pont-Authou.

The same week he flew eight operational sorties over Europe, mostly Ramrods (the term used for bomber escorts). Regarding the beginning of the V-1 campaign, he recalls:

> Detling was right in the firing line of the flying bombs directed at London. A bevy of these came over the day I arrived, but fortunately kept on flying.
>
> A couple of days later I was playing a game of cricket on the local Maidstone ground when another batch came over. I was keeping wicket at the time and just as the bowler started his run-up, I was horrified to see a 'Buzz Bomb' appear just over his shoulder, hotly pursued by a Tempest. Just at that moment he opened fire. I did not see how he could miss as eleven fielders, including two bowlers and two batsmen, hurriedly hit the deck, but fortunately he did and the thing roared across our heads, heading for the nearby balloon barrage. By now the Allies were breaking out of the beachhead in Normandy and just as I was settling in at Detling my squadrons were posted away to commence operations in support of the 2nd Tactical Air Force. The units they went to had their own wing leaders. So on 11 August I was posted to Lympne as the wing commander.

The period from the beginning of July 1944 was busy for 504 Squadron, as it had recently been detached to Digby. The weather was fine on 11 July when it was preparing to move yet again, this time to Lympne. In fact, the squadron was complying with an HQ Air Defence of Great Britain directive dated 5 July, requiring nineteen pilots to proceed to Lympne to take over the Spitfire Mk IXfs of 310 (Czech) Squadron. At the time, Detling airfield had no space for these aircraft, so the move from Lympne to Detling, planned for the evening, was delayed until the following day. In the event, eighteen of these aircraft took off for Detling at 2.00 p.m. One pilot was unwell, and joined them later. On arrival, three of these pilots returned to Lympne by road to collect the remaining aircraft. The remainder of the day, everyone was unpacking and settling into the new base. On the same day, 118 Squadron arrived to form, with 504 Squadron, the Detling Wing.

The following morning, a briefing was held by Wg Cdr M. Crossley DSO DFC, who gave the pilots information on local conditions. However, at this point the newly formed wing had no Wing Commander (Flying).

Much to the horror of all, on 13 July the wing was informed that it would not be keeping the recently acquired Mk IXf Spitfires. As it turned out, the wing was to re-equip with the much sought-after Mk IXe, which was faster and arrived at Detling the same day. The same afternoon, the crews were airborne and practising formation flying. The weather was bad the next day and the wing was told that it would come under the control of the North Weald sector; crystallisation was carried out on the new aircraft.

The wing took off on its first operation on 16 July at 3.32 p.m. With 118 Squadron, it was to escort thirteen Lancasters and two Mosquitoes to a No-ball target in the St Omer area. Due to heavy cloud, the bombing results could not be seen and all returned without incident. Although WO W. Stevenson returned early due to engine problems, he landed safely. That day the Spitfires had been fitted with 15-gallon drop tanks.

Later in the afternoon, P/O W. J. J. Warwick was posted away to Catfoss; he had been with the squadron for some time and was very popular.

On 17 July, the squadron was ordered to stay the night at Ford following a No-ball mission. Earlier the same day, WO Stevenson and P/O Warren had to fly to Northolt to act as escort for a Dakota en route to B14 and an Advanced Landing Ground in Normandy. While taxiing, Warren burst a tyre and Stevenson completed the mission alone. Early the next morning, flying from Ford, the squadron escorted bombers to targets south-east of Caen. Due to poor weather they had to land at Manston, and returned to Detling at midday. F/O J. I. Mclachlan returned to base with mechanical problems. Sqn Ldr Banning-Lover, the CO of 504 Squadron, led another escort mission on 20 July, which was uneventful. All returned to base unscathed.

Returning from an air test on 24 July, a Canadian pilot, F/O J. Waslyk, scored the only victory of 504 Squadron at Detling when he shot down a V-1 in the neighbourhood of Hailsam, Sussex. As Waslyk reports:

> Over the south coast I was overtaken by a Diver. It was above me so I had to climb quickly. Got a burst in at 200–400 yards. It caught fire and exploded on the ground.

It would appear that other aircraft keen to fire at the V-1 were in the area and it may well be that this kill could have been shared, which was often the case. In the evening, pilots were told that a big operation would take place the following day, so it was an early night.

The morning dawned bright and the squadron prepared for Operation Ramrod 1127. The squadron was to provide cover and withdrawal for a force of thirty Lancasters and three Mosquito Pathfinders for a raid on a V-1 site near Neufchâtel, France. They took off from Detling at 8.05 a.m.

and returned at 8.50 a.m. Later, the squadron took part in a similar raid on a target near Versailles, during which P/O Byehart's aircraft sustained damage from accurate ground fire. Both he and the CO landed back at base safely.

An unfortunate incident occurred on 3 August when, returning to base due to engine problems, Flt Sgt Blalby and F/O Faith were fired at by a Naval ship as they flew over the Channel. Blalby's aircraft was damaged; both pilots made it home.

The following day, four pilots and the CO took off for Northolt. From there they were to escort a Dakota, which was taking Winston Churchill, the Prime Minister, to A9 – an airfield in Normandy. But the weather in the area was so bad that they returned to London and the frustrated Spitfire escort returned to Detling. The same day, Wg Cdr Gray led the remainder of 504 Squadron on yet another escort mission without major incident. On 7 August, 504 Squadron suffered its first casualty during an operation in the vicinity of Falaise. Flt Sgt G. R. Claydon of 'A' Flight radioed that he was turning back without giving a reason. His number one, F/O 'Bish' Bishop, turned to look for him but he had disappeared. However, a pilot of 124 Squadron reported seeing a Spitfire diving vertically out of control and saw a parachute.

Claydon was actually captured and taken POW, only to be rescued by advancing Allied troops. At Detling, pilots of 504 Squadron took off to escort Admiral Ramsay to Thorney Island and later Sir Trafford Leigh-Mallory to an ALG in Normandy. The remaining time at Detling was spent packing and preparing for a move. On 13 August, 504 Squadron was moved to RAF Manston and 124 Squadron was sent to its next temporary base at West Hampett. By September 1944, Luftwaffe fighter squadrons were being rapidly decimated by Allied air supremacy and had mostly retreated within the German borders. Bomber Command was able to switch from night operations to daylight bombing. As a result, RAF Fighter Squadrons were assigned to escort missions. No. 141 Wing, under the command of Gp Capt. Bobby Oxspring DFC AFC, was disbanded.

Oxspring was given command of the Detling Wing, which comprised 1 Squadron, led by Pat Lardner-Burke DFC, and 165 Squadron, led by Jas Storrer. On escort duties, it soon became apparent that the wing's biggest problem was the short range of the Spitfire, which was partially solved by either 45- or 90-gallon fuel tanks being fitted under the fuselage. However, although the 45-gallon type gave the aircraft an additional thirteen hours' flying, the larger tanks reduced the Spitfire's performance. A possible solution was to install an internal fuel tank behind the pilot, as in the P51 Mustangs, but this was not successful as it altered the aircraft's centre of

Pilots of 504 (County of Nottingham) at ease in June 1944. Flt Lt Ken Bishop is leaning over the chair on the left. On 31 August 1944, he was killed while flying from RAF Manston during a routine flight-test. Ken had also flown in Murmansk, Russia, and in the desert war. Many pilots were killed on non-operational flights.

gravity. The problem was later solved when Advanced Landing Grounds were constructed in Belgium.

Detling airfield was handed over to a Care and Maintenance Unit on 1 January 1945. 1336 Wing RAF Regiment moved in to run the Air Disarmament School using 2814, 2878 and 2749 squadrons, using the RAF Regiment as staff. The government thought that Nazi fanatics would continue resisting Germany's downfall and, accordingly, the airfield was laid out as a demonstration centre, with booby-trapped buildings and equipment. To add to the proceedings, German-speaking personnel dressed in German uniforms gave Air Disarmament Unit trainees a taste of confronting situations they may find in Germany. Locals agreed that the whole scene resembled that of an Elstree Studios film set, which kept them amused for many hours. On 12 January, 16 Group Communications Flight was moved from Detling to the Short Brothers airport at Rochester.

Following the hectic days of the Second World War, the future of RAF Detling was very much in the balance. Its use as an airfield was not certain. No. 1336 Wing Headquarters had been moved from RAF Kenley to Detling on 9 January 1945 for the purpose of organising a Weapons Training School. The unit's role was to train personnel in how to deal with a variety of situations connected with taking over materiel and installations from the Luftwaffe. Wg Cdr Fowler and F/O Fleming had received verbal instructions to make a reconnaissance of the existing camp and the local area to find suitable locations for lecture rooms and school accommodation.

Sqn Ldr Coakes, HQ 11 Group (Armament), also visited Detling for the purpose of inspecting a proposed grenade range on a site adjacent to the Bomb Dump Road. During February, No. 13 ADMD – commanded by Gp Capt. R. A. T. Stowell DFC and comprising thirty-four officers, thirty-six senior NCOs and 126 ORs – attended the newly formed Weapons Training School. On 5 February, No. 1 WT Course commenced. The school took charge of a 5 cwt jeep, which was collected from 16 Motor Unit, Stafford. Later the same week, a 15 cwt Ford Tender and two Ariel motorcycles were collected from 241 MU Norton. Gp Capt. T. Healey OBE (Armament) visited Detling in connection with Special Disarmament Exercise due to take place on 16 February 1945. A succession of weapons training courses at Detling were held until July 1945, when the school was disbanded. Headquarters 75 Wing was in fact renamed Southern Signals Area at the beginning of November 1945. By the end of the month, the unit comprised eighty-nine officers, nine WAAF officers and 1,200 ORs. Instructions were received regarding the reorganisation of the wing within 90 Group.

Two years after the war had ended, the RAF was still using the airfield at Detling. On 1 October 1945, the station was taken over by 60 Group. 75 Signals Wing was established there in April 1946. Shortly afterwards, No. 141 Gliding School was formed, and Southern Signals Area replaced the wing at the end of 1946. The winter of 1947 will always be remembered for the heavy snow and freezing cold. For one of the NCOs still based at Detling, the winter brings back memories of that period. Now a retired flight lieutenant, Jim Baldwin was there during the 'big freeze':

I have never seen so much snow and the cold was unbelievable. I recall a small wiry warrant officer, Eric Rubio, who kept us all on the run with organised chores. Many of us were lovers of the classics and would periodically gather to play whatever we had recently bought. A favourite was Marian Anderson singing 'Softly Awakes My Heart' … [I] bought my first recording of Jessie Boerling singing 'Ideal'. Temperatures were so low that units began to close down to save energy and electricity. Eventually Detling closed down. Most servicemen went home, but a small number of us stayed on to keep the station going.

We cut down small trees and chopped them up for fuel; we even put up a Christmas tree, and made all the decorations. One evening we sat in the sergeants' mess until the early hours. One by one they drifted away until only two of us were left in the mess. We decided to get back to quarters about 3 a.m. and as we left the mess, the snow was belting down and was very thick underfoot. We wandered towards the airfield, but we walked and walked and were getting nowhere. I think we were dangerously exhausted by 4 a.m. Had we fallen asleep we could have died, but in the distance we saw a light, and we gathered strength and walked towards it. In some places the snow was up to our hips. When we got there, we found it was our own quarters, and the light was a mate who could not sleep, and had decided to get up and do his laundry.

We estimated that when the light came on, we were at the far end of the runway and God knows where we were heading! In the New Year, I received an award. It wasn't a medal, it was some new idea of a certificate of excellence awarded by the Air Office Commanding. [I] received a telegram. A few days later there was a parade for the presentations. I also was recommended for officer training and following interviews I was sent off to Cadet College. So, all in all, Detling was good to me.

CHAPTER 10

1946–1950s

*Peace returns to Detling – the ATC and RAF Gliding School is
formed – the Kent Gliding Club moves to the airfield*

Royal Aircraft Establishment apprentices from Farnborough were some of
the first people to use Detling as a base for gliding in 1946, and it was not
long before senior students were on their way to the airfield. One of these,
A. J. Barter, shares his memories:

We all assembled at South Gate to board the vehicles, looking forward
to a welcome break from studies. The convoy consisted of two jeeps,
balloon winch and two 60 foot 'Queen Mary's' with the gliders packed
on board. The Kranich (a German glider) was to be towed down by the
Fieseler Storch flown by Bob Smythe. One lucky member of the flight
flew down, while the rest of us draped ourselves around any convenient
vehicle. Stopping the convoy at a pub on the way down caused the
landlord some consternation, but he was soon happy when the hoard
descended on the bar. The rest of the journey was completed in a very
satisfactory warm glow.

The airfield was situated on a high ridge close to Maidstone. On
passing the guardroom at Detling, we parked the trailers and were given
a short lecture by the Camp CO – no girls on camp and, if there were
any signs of shooting, the guard would be turned out. Our billet was
the usual wartime wooden hut with a couple of cast-iron coke stoves in
the middle. The airfield had changed little in the five years since the end
of the war and there was plenty of evidence of the previous occupants
about. In places bullet and bomb splinter holes could still be seen in the
sides of the hanger and the place had a rather haunted air about it at
first. We had not been in our billet very long when an RAF sergeant came
in to give us the 'gen' – mostly what were the best local pubs and how to
get your girlfriend into camp without passing the guardroom.

Gliding instructors and vehicles of RAE. Much of the site at Detling was still usable and in reasonable condition in the late 1940s; many of the original buildings were intact.

Many of the buildings erected for the RAF are seen in this photograph taken by the pilot of the impressed Fiesler Storch VP546, which was used to tow RAE gliders. The main building on the left is Binbury Manor; the Church Army hut is to the right with the barrack huts and sleeping quarters.

I also discovered that the reference to shooting alluded to an incident the previous year. Apparently, a night rabbit shoot was arranged on the airfield, armed with whatever 'ironmongery' they could get. An apprentice managed to be shot in the process and the authorities were not amused – hence the lecture. After eating, we went to the hangar to unpack the gliders and get ourselves sorted out for the following morning.

The next two weeks were marvellous. We flew as much as possible during the daylight hours and in the evenings some undertook repairs while the lucky ones went to the pub. How many apprentices one jeep could carry had been in contest for some time and on one memorable return from the pub up Detling Hill, the police were not too pleased to find a jeep underneath a swaying pile of bodies. (I can't remember what the record was, but I think it was eighteen achieved on the way to the Apprentice Hostel at Farnborough.)

Our days consisted of flying, retrieving, signalling or just loafing about awaiting our turn – hoping all the while that the aeroplane did not get bent before it got to your turn. You were very unpopular if you caused any damage. After a couple of circuits in Kranich VP591 with T. I. Q. Hall and a number of 'high hops' with 'S' turns in the Cadet, I was elected to go for the first solo circuit of the new intake. I had been hoping someone else would get the pleasure, but was out of luck. I climbed into the Cadet and Robbie checked the cable release while I tried to conceal the fact that my knees were shaking. The instructions were simple – climb to the edge of the ridge, keep your speed up in the turn, follow the road downwind and watch for a signal to turn in and land. I climbed to 700 feet and managed to drop the cable well enough, but got a bit of a shock when I looked down. With the high ridge you appeared to gain several hundred feet very suddenly. Remembering Robbie's warning about not stalling in the turn, I stuck the nose down and practically went into a dive to get round the corner.

After this I followed the road with one eye on Robbie a couple of hundred feet below me. He waved and I fumbled the turn to find two large trees in front of me, well short of the landing zone. I managed to get between these by banking very steeply and was just feeling rather pleased with myself when I noticed a concrete gun emplacement right in front of me. Too low to bank into a turn, I shoved on the rudder pedal and landed in a sideslip. I just missed the pillbox, but it didn't do the landing skid much good. It was a much-chastened 'ace' who returned to the launch site – especially when it was pointed out that I did not need to go into a vertical dive just to turn the corners. I felt a bit better later when someone forgot to jettison the wheels on the Kranich until at about 700 feet. Much to our delight they made a loud whistling noise on

The Church Army canteen in 1947; this was where RAE Gliding Club members met for meals and a break. The Church Army, whose sign remains, provided sustenance during wartime. Seated on the jeep, left to right: R. 'Bob' Ward, Terry Beasley, Cyril Hughes, Sid Taylor and Mike Caiger. In front of the window: Art Keeler. In the doorway: Albert Rouse.

RAE members relax after lunch on a warm afternoon in 1948. The glider is a German Grunau Baby, serial no. VP587. Note the blister hangar and various other buildings remaining from RAF occupation. The winch can also be seen in this view.

the way down and a large dent in the road outside camp. The Storch had to fly the axle back to RAE to get the forge to straighten it out.

Just after this I had my first flight in the Storch with Arty Ashworth. It was an incredible aeroplane, as it took off in a very short run and was almost impossible to stall. Arty let me stand up behind his seat and fly with the stick while he operated the rudder pedals. I clearly remember doing a tight turn and looking down on the bald head of an old gentleman working in a greenhouse in Maidstone. We also did a 'recce' of the pubs at low altitude to plan the evening foray. I thought that the test pilots were great and was very proud when I was to fly with Bill Bedford in the Kranich. I was heading for the rear cockpit when Bill said, 'No, in the front, you're flying this thing.'

Late one evening I had to do a quick repair on the rear fuselage of the Kranich after the wheels hit the ground and bounced up awkwardly to punch a hole underneath the fuselage, just in front of the tail plane. Albert showed me how to scarf round the hole, cut a panel to fit and then strap heater pads on to ensure that the glue cured properly. Another job I did for a while was to act as the intermediate signaller. The airfield had a hump in the middle so that there was no direct line of sight between the launch site and the winch. Some unfortunate, with a battery and Aldis lamp, had to stand on this very lonely hump and relay the lamp signals. It was a very quiet spot and the only sound was a loud strumming from the cable every time a glider was launched. During one launch the cable disturbed a large wasps' nest and I had to make a hasty retreat when the strumming noise turned nasty.

On another occasion, the parachute on the end of the cable came off. All I could hear was the heavy shackle whistling down over my head and wondering which way to run, as I couldn't see it. Much to my relief, the shackle buried itself in the ground about 10 feet away and I found a funk hole under a thick wooden plank just in case it happened again.

One morning we were all working in the hangar when someone started to sing, 'We're poor little lambs who have lost our way.' I think it was called the Wiffenpoof Song. We all joined in and harmonised wonderfully in the acoustics of the hanger. It was one of the most moving experiences I have ever had and I have never forgotten it. We were later asked to perform in the officers' mess, but knew that we could not repeat the performance without the acoustics of the hangar. Once or twice we had to wait for the morning mist to clear before we could operate, but we were lucky enough to be able to fly every day. Sadly A. J. Barter died in 2008.

The idea to form the Royal Aircraft Establishment Gliding Club was the brainchild of Harry Midwood, who had joined the company in 1941.

He had managed to form the club with the support of the college and the RAF. The gliders were to come from a collection of German aircraft, which RAE had for evaluation. This later included the use of a Fiesler Storch, serial number VP546. Five German gliders arrived consisting of a Kranich (Crane), Olympia, Grunau and two SG38s. Following a meeting with the RAF CO at Farnborough, the newly formed club was given the use of a Bessonneau hangar, a jeep and a balloon winch, and an instructor from the Experimental Flying Department, Flt Lt Ron Walton DFC.

Harry, or 'Hum', as he was called, was elected president with 'Tommy' Atkins as secretary. Operations started on 10 February 1946 ... [Later] Lorne Welch joined. He was at Colditz and was involved in the building famous Colditz Cock, a glider. Lorne felt that the club's progress was too slow so set about organising a week's camp at Detling. By this time Ray Clackett, a Halifax pilot, joined the membership.

By mid-July 1946, the RAE Gliding Club had set off for Detling. Some travelled in the winch, which towed a large caravan containing much of the club's equipment.

Art Keeler travelled down in the back of the Kranich glider flown by Flt Lt Sullavan of the Technical Training Flight. He was attempting a full circuit of Detling for his 'B' Certificate when things went wrong. He left the cross-wind turn too late and found himself on the wrong side of the down-wind boundary, clipping the fence on approach and catching the skid. The glider turned over and Art landed upside down.

Feisler Storch VP546. This German aircraft was recovered after the war and was used by the Aerodynamics Flight RAE in 1946–56. These aircraft were used as spotters and were well known for their incredibly short take-off and landing characteristics. This particular aircraft is on display at the Royal Air Force Museum, Cosford.

The following year there were problems with the winch. The nose hook of the Grunau, designed for aero towing, meant that two-thirds of climb the cable started to pull the glider down. During one winch the operator tried to hold on to use every last foot of the cable. The cable released directly above the winch, which came crashing down on its occupants. Fortunately the safety cage prevented any injury.

One of the instructors, an ex-RAF pilot, learnt to drive at Detling using the club's jeep, following driving lessons organised by the RAE. He enjoyed visiting local pubs and was a bit of a womaniser and was pleased as punch when he got his own jeep, as he had to rely on other club members to ferry him around. Living off the camp he was joined in his exploits by another bomber pilot ... they soon added midday sorties, not returning until late afternoon. This meant much valuable flying time was lost, not popular with those wishing to fly. By 1948 the club had increased its stay at Detling from one week to two, and the club became a flight and gliding part of the RAE College curriculum.

The weather that year was poor and the club managed only 300 launches during the fortnight. The Kranich was later borrowed by the ATC instructors' course at Detling, an arrangement that meant that two of the club's members would also join the course, which was run by a famous name in gliding, John Furlong, a squadron leader in the ATC. Don Minterne finished his apprenticeship in 1948 and joined the RAE Photography Division. He managed to acquire an F24 hand-held camera, which he used at the camp for aerial photography. Some of these photographs appeared in early editions of the *Sailplane & Gliding* magazine. Short Brothers Ltd of Rochester later selected him for sixty hours' primary flying training with the RAFVR School, No. 24 RFS.

This school used Detling as an auxiliary field for landing practice, particularly emergency landings. When the pupil reached a height of 600 feet after take-off, crossing the upwind hedge, the instructor cut the throttle and he had to make a dead-stick landing. On his final flight of the course, Don made a mess of things and had to open the throttle to avoid a nasty undershoot. During the camp of 1950, the Fiesler Storch towed an Olympia glider of the RAF Gliding & Soaring Association from Farnborough to Detling with Norman Kearney in the glider. He released without landing on the airfield, allowed himself to get too far back behind the ridge, lost control and crashed. The glider was smashed to pieces and Norman did not fly again for several months. Another near miss happened in 1951, when Arthur Dearden, flying the Grunau, undershot at the north end of the airfield. The glider's wing tip clipped some small branches of a

Sgt Jim Baldwin receives his Meritorious Service Medal from AVM Addison at RAF Detling during a special parade for the AOC's inspection on 9 May 1947. Jim is standing front row, left. Next to him are Flt Sgt 'Nan' Stockley (WRAF) and Cpl Bass (WRAF). On the right are Sqn Ldr Cooper and Gp Capt. Elliot.

tree outside the boundary fence, which pulled the glider round, but it did no damage and he landed safely.

In 1952, RAE apprentice gliding would fall victim to economic pressures. However, on 5 July, Dennis Fielder asked Don Minterne if he would fly him down to Detling in a T21, with Bill Bedford (the famous test pilot) towing with a Storch. Despite the strong wind blowing from the north, the glider released and both it and the Storch landed safely. After refreshments at a local pub, they set off back to Farnborough. Between September 1951 and August 1952, the RAE Gliding Club had made over 3,000 launches. On 24 July 1952, the club's gliders were ferried back to Farnborough. These were happy days at Detling; the apprentices looked back on the long summer evenings at the Hook & Hatchet pub in Hucking with affection.

In 1947, Jim Baldwin was a supply sergeant at Detling as part of the station's base headquarters. The Supply (or Equipment) Branch had the responsibility of supplying everything that anyone required. There were 'Married Quarters' on the outer fringe of Detling, close to the road running by the airfield, where Jim and his wife were accommodated. There was a café here, where the staff could enjoy things like egg and chips or other non-rationed items for a few pence. While Jim served at Detling there was very little aircraft activity. In fact, he recalls not seeing any aircraft based there while he was on the staff.

Most probably the only exciting event that happened was when he received his Meritorious Service Medal from AVM Addison during a special parade for the AOC's inspection on 9 May 1947. The winter

Sgt Jim Baldwin is collecting wood for the mess fire during the severe winter of 1947. As can be seen, Detling airfield is covered in the heavy snow of that year. Were the trains still running?

of 1947 is famous for the freezing cold and the snow, and Baldwin remembers the staff devoted much of their time at Christmas to scouting the surroundings for suitable timber to burn on their fire and stoves. By the time LAC Kingman was posted to Detling in January 1949, the station was non-operational, but it was administered by a Care and Maintenance party. The CO was F/O Beesley; second-in-command was WO Thomas. There were two sergeants, one being Sgt Singleton, and two corporals, Vidler and Maison, along with a medical corporal and ten other airmen. This was the full complement.

LAC Kingman was DMT (Driver Mechanical Transport) and one of his duties was to collect the ATC cadets from Rochester and Maidstone stations that were sent to Detling for glider training. He recalls that there were two types of glider used, Slingsbys and single-seaters. During a heavy thunderstorm and strong wind and hail on 2 April 1950, people at Folkestone saw a glider suddenly appear from the direction of the sea and land on the shingle beach close to the harbour, not more than 10 yards from the sea. The pilot, Flt Lt Miller, an instructor at the glider school at Detling, stepped out of the open cockpit of the glider, which was practically undamaged.

He had taken off from Detling airfield in an attempt to attain a height of 10,000 feet, and he made for the coast at Folkestone, which he reached when the storm broke. He made an unsuccessful attempt to land at Hawkinge airfield, two miles from Folkestone, and he was flying virtually blind when he discovered that he was over two miles out at sea. *The Times* reported that:

> The Channel was crossed twice in April by gliders piloted by Mr Lorne Welch, chief instructor of the Surrey Gliding Club, and Flt Lt Miller, of Detling (Kent) Glider School. Mr Welch, who took off in the morning from Redhill and arrived in Brussels in the afternoon, piloted a sailplane of a German design. Flt Lt Miller landed at Coxyde on the Belgian coast. The first sailplane crossing of the Channel was made by Mr G. H. Stephenson, who flew from Dunstable to Calais beach in 1939.

Unfortunately, the same pilot was killed on 10 May 1950 when he crashed his glider in a field near Stockbury; he was forty-six years old. On another occasion, an ATC cadet and his instructor were both killed in a gliding accident while flying from Detling. The Care and Maintenance party at Detling was supposed to ensure that no one trespassed on the airfield; on one occasion a small group of travellers did so, but after being talked to by the airmen they left peacefully. However, it was not all doom and gloom.

Staff of 5131 Bomb Disposal Squadron with the much-loved QL truck in the background. Top, left to right: unknown, Tom Bugler. Middle row, left to right: Wally Marshall, unknown, WO Bill Bailey, unknown, Keith Hyatt, 'Peck' Peckham. Bottom, left to right: Ronnie Barnes, Bob Turner, Tom Wilman.

There was an abundance of rabbits on the airfield and the CO was in possession of a .22 rifle; occasionally everyone had decent meals.

Daily existence at Detling was very basic as there was no NAAFI or any form of camp entertainment like that enjoyed by airmen at other RAF stations; trips to Maidstone were essential. The weekly rations were not delivered, so LAC Kingman had to drive to RAF West Malling for them and all mail was picked up from Maidstone post office. A variety of RAF units were based at Detling during the 1950s, and one such was 6226 Bomb Disposal Flight, 5131 Bomb Disposal Squadron, which served there in 1952–53. LAC 'Bill' Mayes recalls his memories of that time:

It was during my National Service as an armourer when Detling became part of my service life. After trade training at RAF Kirk Holm I was posted to 5131 Bomb Disposal Squadron at RAF North Coates as an AC1. The squadron had, I think, six flights, one in Germany, the others in the UK. As I came from Sussex I was detached to 6226 BDF in Kent at RAF Detling. Other flights were, as I remember, at Hornchurch, Waterbeach, and Driffield. 6226's bread and butter job was, between other calls, clearing a disused bombing range on the Downs at the back of Ashbury, near Shrivenham and Lambourne. (We got tips from the stable lads at the racing stables.) For this we had our hut at RAF Watchfield, which was used as a parachute training landing ground, and had a large army presence. We drew our rations from the cookhouse at Watchfield for our midday meal, which we cooked at a hut by the side of the bombing range.

As my mate 'Chalky' White's family ran a café, he was given the job as cook, and I assisted. Sometimes we would do a day on Salisbury Plain when the RAF and USAF fired rockets etc. on the ranges in front of VIPs; also a few weeks at RAF Old Sarum when some US ammunition was getting ploughed up. During this time 'Chalky' and I were both promoted to LACs and, after a further course at North Coates, to SACs.

Detling's area, loosely, was south of the Thames and Severn. All our heavy equipment was at Detling in huts north-west of the camp; here we stored timber and pumps. We had a Coventry Climax pump trailer fire brigade type, sludge pumps, drilling equipment etc. Our transport consisted, when I first arrived, of a large Thornycroft 4x4 wagon, soon replaced by a Bedford 4x4 QL, a Fordson 30 cwt truck, and a Hillman Utility, the CO's runabout. We also had a water bowser that we filled and cleaned weekly to give us a supply of water for cooking and washing on the job.

Our billet at Detling was brick-built but damp and we were allowed extra fuel rations to keep a fire permanently going. We were adjacent to the cookhouse, very handy. Our office and the CO's office were in the station headquarters building and had a flight bicycle to use locally. The CO, a flight lieutenant, was jealous of other flight commanders, as they had new Standard Vanguard pick-ups, and he only had a Hillman. However, we had two large German bombs at the entrance to our site, and one day one of the lads ran the Hillman into one of them, so the CO finally got a Vanguard.

ATC cadets, and also a fair proportion of auxiliary officers, overran every so often at Detling. They came for the gliding, which were launched by winches. The cookhouse facilities got overrun on occasions when the cadets were there. The cadet NCOs thought they could have precedence over us airmen, but they soon got put in their places (get back in the queue!). Sometimes, I don't remember why ... no airmen under the age of twenty-one was allowed to be off camp after midnight, unless he was married and had a sleeping-out pass. Something to do with the local clergy and their concern for the airmen's morals. Our flight consisted of about twenty/twenty-five people.

The CO back at Detling, WO Bill Bailey – mostly shared between Detling and wherever – a clerk GD at Detling HQ, an MT driver

This is perhaps one of the finest aerial views taken of Detling airfield during the 1950s. At the time, Kent Gliding Club was based on the airfield. As can be seen by the two gliders in the left-hand corner, most of the RAF buildings are still standing, including the Bellman hangar.

wherever we were working, a couple of corporals and the rest of us LACs and SACs were detached to our work or back at Detling ... when my father Bill 'Tubby' Mayes was station WO at RAF Coltishall in Norfolk during the Second World War, Bill Bailey was a sergeant armourer there and they knew one another. I remember that not far from our store at Detling were parked a few service families in caravans and sometimes we would be asked to babysit for them in caravans. Nothing of great note happened to me at Detling as I recall. I arrived in April 1952 and stayed until November 1953. Wherever we used our transport, we were instantly recognised by our red mudguards ...

Having been conscripted into National Service with the RAF in 1950, Keith Hyatt completed training as an Armament Mechanic (Bombs) at Kirkham. He was then posted, with others, to North Coates near Grimsby. Here, he and his companions were told their duties would involve bomb disposal. It was a dangerous assignment, and they would receive danger money. For further training, Keith was sent to Bomb Disposal Flight Feltwell, Norfolk, mainly a flying training school. To his surprise, one of the lads had been at school with him during his grammar school days in South East London during the 1920s. The following day, he met members of the flight, which was headed by a flight lieutenant and a warrant officer:

In early May we completed the BD course and were allocated to our flights. About five of us were to go to Biggin Hill, only 12 miles from my home. At the last minute we were informed that our team was moving to RAF Detling, which was then home to Royal Air Force Volunteer Reserve officers doing gliding. We new arrivals joined the other members of 6226 Bomb Disposal Flight in their brick-built billet and settled in. This was to be my base for the next fourteen months, and it was a most enjoyable time. Detling was just 30 miles by road from my home at Blackheath and the first Friday I travelled home on the train. At Whitsun I decided to cycle home – thus began a regular routine of cycling home from Detling most weekends and Wednesday afternoons (sports afternoon), returning early Thursday morning.

Of course, when we were away from Detling on a job, I forwent those rides, but usually took my bike on our QL (truck); one of my mates took his motorcycle. My job at Detling was to maintain the many portable water pumps and generators; for this task I would draw a jerry can of petrol from the station supply every so often and would follow a routine of running and servicing the equipment. I recall that that our electrician made a good job of rewiring the flight lieutenant's car, which pleased the CO, but the latter wasn't very pleased when he drove off in our Hillman pick-up and the wheels nearly came off. Well, he shouldn't have taken it before our MT driver, who'd been changing the wheel, had tightened the nuts.

On bomb disposal we were able to have extra rations and if we returned from a job late in the day, a meal would be provided for us. We were issued with old khaki uniforms and denims for fieldwork, black plastic cap badges, gumboots and sea-boot stockings, and extra boots and shoes. The first job my group did away from Detling was a farm near Ashford where the farmer reckoned he had an unexploded bomb on one of his fields. On the second day of our soggy digging activities the press arrived and a photograph of us duly appeared in the *Kent Messenger*. Needless to say, he didn't have a bomb, just a collapsed land drain. From Detling we made several trips to more distant locations, such as Boscombe Down. Our task was to disarm on Salisbury Plain.

What turned out to be out last trip from Detling was to RAF Eynsham near Oxford; here we were to dispose of aircraft ammunition, which would take us about ten days.

The weather was poor so we demolished the ammunition in small quantities, burying them deep in the ground. It was not long before a local 'bobby' arrived, complaining we had broken windows in Eynsham; this was caused by low cloud affecting the blast.

After which, it was back to base at Detling for the remaining seven months of my National Service. I don't recall much activity during my final months at the airfield.

When it was announced on 6 February 1952 that King George VI had died, the Detling flag was hoisted to half-mast, but it had to be lowered again until the official order was given to do it ceremonially.

One day our CO asked if any of us wanted to go to North Coates for promotion to LAC; I was demobbed there on 25 June 1952, then it was home and back to Civvy Street. I wouldn't have missed it for anything, despite the fact that I had already commenced my scientific career when called up. I felt that if I hadn't already got a job, it was the RAF for me. One of my colleagues at Detling was an orphan – what better life for him than the services? I haven't mentioned the corporal with his unruly ginger moustache, which we nicknamed 'US Shredded Wheat'; or my flight mate, who requested a compassionate posting back to North Coates, only to find, when he arrived there, that his intended was going out with another; or our pre-war corporal, who was always 'scrounging' junk that looked useful ... we reckoned he and his wife lived in a Nissen hut.

Following a 'joy ride' in a Tiger Moth at Rochester Airport in 1949, Edward Day, then aged twenty-three, couldn't wait to get airborne. His pilot that day was 'Tubby' Dash. After some local flying, Tubby asked

Edward what he wanted to do. It was suggested they fly to the family farm in Collier Street, for a cup of tea. They landed behind the farmhouse. After tea, they took off again for Rochester. Tubby was impressed by Edward and offered to teach him to fly in ten hours for £30 – £3 per hour. Edward's flying exploits were recorded by him and have since been published by Marden History Society, but it's worth mentioning that he did participate in the 1950 King's Cup Race.

During the 1950s, he visited Detling to find out about the Kent Gliding Club, and with the same enthusiasm he showed for powered flight, he learned to fly gliders. He quickly discovered that, unlike landing in an aircraft, you could not make a mistake when landing, as you had to put down the first time. This was usual practice in a large field like Detling, but if you crossed country you were often as not committed to land in a small field. At Detling, there were a couple of tractor-engine-driven winches, which often broke down, and it was not unusual for members to have to visit local scrapyards to look for spares. The chief instructor, whose responsibilities included safety at the airfield, taught Edward in a twin-seater glider how to take off, do a circuit and, of course, land. After each flight the pilot would return the glider to the take-off point, ready for the next pupil.

Edward later bought a Sky sailplane to enter the Gold 'C' competition. The Sky was fitted with a detachable undercarriage that was released on take-off; it had been entered into the World Gliding Championships, which it won. It was fitted with VHF radio. A large trailer was later made at his farm for transportation; the wings would be dismantled and put on the trailer. Edward recalls one day when he was waiting for good weather and talking to other members of KGC at the café; one of his chums came running over from the airfield:

'If Ted wants some 'Gold C' lift, tell him to come to the field *now*.'

I rushed over to my car and went back to the field. Approaching fast was the daddy of a thunderstorm. A crew had already lined my Sky up, switched on the oxygen, started the barometer, and hooked the line to the winch. 'Get in Ted.' Everybody was watching and I really had myself painted into a corner with my impatience.

They hooked up my parachute and I waved to the winch man and was off. By the time I got to 600 feet, the storm grabbed me. The speed was getting to be excessive; I dumped the winch wire and pulled out the spoilers to protect the airframe from structural damage due to overspeeding when the storm literally sucked me into its bosom. The artificial horizon gyro that I needed to fly by … had toppled and was of no use and the glider was now completely out of control. I was being tossed around in the storm cloud like a piece of paper; never knowing which way was up. The altimeter was winding up and down in a blur and it was clear that I was going up forever.

The lightning started and hail was battering the canopy until I thought it would fracture and I was drawing on the oxygen. I went up and down inside the storm forever and finally it tossed me out of the side over Faversham at 1,400 feet about 20 miles from Detling airfield. The recorder showed that at least I had achieved my 'Gold C' altitude to complete the badge. I cast around wondering what to do with all this altitude and at one point wondered whether I should set off for France – I had enough altitude to do that without any more lift but I would have to go through the expense of getting the car and trailer across the Channel. When I arrived back at Detling the police were there, I had been gone an hour and twenty minutes and they had their force and the AA out looking for me. I hadn't experienced fear before because I didn't fancy getting into my parachute in a hailstorm. I really wouldn't recommend the experience to anyone. I was later accused by the authorities of being in the middle of an air corridor without clearance.

Back on the ground, the damage to Edward's prized sailplane was evident; the hailstones had damaged the fabric, some of which you could pass your arm through.

Later, with television and press interested in his exploits, he had to get the glider repaired in time for the 1957 National Gliding Championships, which took place at Lasham. Edward, our intrepid pilot, won the championship, and the prize was presented to him by the Duke of Edinburgh. It was an impressive achievement, as he beat the RAF at its own game. Edward's father, Capt. James May DFC, who had been a pilot in the First World War, surely would have been proud of his flying son.

In February 1955, No. 1903 Flight (Air Observation Post) – as part of 1913 Light Liason Flight, which worked with the Army in Korea – was due to return to the UK. Capt. R. D. Wilkinson, who was to take over 1903 Flight on its arrival, paid a short visit to the squadron. Maj. Walton and Capt. Wilkinson visited Detling to make domestic arrangements for the flight, which was to be stationed there in support of Royal Artillery No. 3 Infantry Division.

The majority of the personnel of 1903 and 1913 flights returned from disembarkation and privilege leave during the month. One Auster Mk VII was allotted to 1913 Flight; this aircraft was later reallocated to 1903 Flight. The flight spent the month settling in at Detling, obtaining publications, receiving stores, taking over a share of station duties, and generally coping with the score or more problems of building up a new

Detling, as seen during the 1950s from one of KGC gliders. At the bottom of the picture are the cottages, which were once airmen's married quarters and later the WAAF's quarters. Just above them are Hazel Dene and Binbury Lodge, with stores and sleeping quarters behind. Opposite the curved trackway, centre, there was once a blister hangar. To the right is the A249.

station. Driver training went ahead as far as the vehicle situation permitted, and one exercise was held for the drivers. No signal training was possible, due to the total absence of wireless sets. On 19 February, the squadron took part in the ceremonial parade on the occasion of an inspection of the station by Air Cdre Hogan ADC 81 Group RAF.

Shortly after another further Auster Mk VII was delivered to the unit, all pilots returned from leave. This coincided with good weather conditions, so many hours of flying were achieved. Morale was boosted when the unit was informed that it would receive other Austers, which were en route back from Japan. In fact, two DH Chipmunks (on loan) and one Auster Mk VII arrived, followed by five more Austers, which were available at RAF Middle Wallop, still in their crates. By 15 February, long-awaited spares had also arrived and Capt. Culless assumed command of 1913 Flight from Capt. Bellamy, who was to return to another posting in Korea. By July 1955, 1903 was again fully operational.

Capt. Brown and Capt. Pink carried out air shoots with 663 Auxiliary Air OP Squadron at Otterburn Ranges. Capt. Henry took a section and acted as umpire to 1957 Air AOP Flight during Exercise Dover Castle on Salisbury Plain. Exercises were carried out using local fields near Detling; other flying included field reconnaissance and photographic sorties. All aircraft were serviceable except Auster Mk VII, serial no. VF663, which had been struck off charge and sent to the manufacturers for essential repairs.

Prime Minister Sir Anthony Eden was flown by Maj. Begbic and Maj. Spittal on 3 September from Chequers to Colchester to visit the Army garrison; he returned the same day. On 25 September, the flights moved to RAF Wrougton and later to Shrewton for Exercise Searchlight, returning to Detling on 5 September. Pilot training continued and various field exercises were undertaken, but the writing was on the wall and 1903 Flight 657 AOP was eventually disbanded on 1 November 1955 and renumbered No. 651 AOP Squadron.

The Air Training Corps continued to use the airfield, and in 1955 ATC squadrons held a two-week summer camp. 'Jock' Manson remembers his time as one of the lucky boys attending the camp – he was fourteen years old:

> I can still hear the whining of the gear box of the Bedford QL truck that picked us up from Maidstone station. It crawled up the famous hill to the airfield. I found a tremendous atmosphere existed at Detling; the place seemed steeped in history. By then the Home Command Gliding Instructors School were based there. I flew in Slingsby T21b and Sedbergh gliders WB925 and WG947. There were also DH Chipmunks at Detling and 'Jock' was lucky to fly in WG323, WG350 and WZ866.
>
> HCGI School arrived on 1 August 1950 and remained at Detling until 1 September 1955. The 'Chippy', as it was affectionately known, was the RAF/ATC Trainer at the time and remained so until they were grounded in the 1990s.
>
> The unit also flew two German gliders, a Grunau Baby and the Rhonbussard, both of which were impounded after the war. By coincidence 'Jock' became the historian for 53 Squadron, who were based at Detling.

CHAPTER 11

The 1950s

RAF Detling closes – Care and Maintenance – de-requisitioning

In 1942, when Air Cadet Gliding was formally established, one of the first schools formed was 141 Gliding School at RAF Kidbrooke in South London. On 1 December 1945, it moved to Gravesend, from where in June 1946 it went to RAF Detling on the North Downs and then to RAF West Malling for the period between September 1949 and September 1950. Following a short stay, it returned to Detling, where it disbanded. Later, it was merged into 146 GS and 168 GS. In 1956, this unit became 615 GS at RAF Kenley, which remains in operation today.

Derek Piggott joined the RAF in 1942. After a posting in Burma, he was posted to Central Flying School and later the Gliding Instructors School at Detling as chief instructor. He had attended a week-long detachment to the ATC Gliding School. At the time, Detling consisted of half a dozen officers and forty airmen. It was both an ATC Gliding School and a school for gliding instructors. There were three glider pilots, Flt Lt Jock Forbes, Peter Mallet and Charmin Thomas. However, none of these pilots were particularly good as instructors, although Derek learned a lot during that week. Later, he decided to return to Detling – he thought it a worthwhile job to teach voluntary gliding instructors, which he did. His first task at Detling was organising guidelines for instruction in two-seater gliders. Until this introduction, trainee glider pilots were put into a single-seater glider and towed along the ground while trying to keep the wings level.

Following a few exercises like this, Derek was told how to take off and land, eventually becoming airborne for a brief period, landing after release of the cable. He introduced many changes and wrote a booklet, which was used for several years as the basis for instruction. Derek remained at Detling, but got a bit fed up when, each time a new CO was drafted in, he had to teach him about basic gliding. Each CO knew that it was a temporary posting that would not do his career much good. Christmas at Detling was

Enthusiastic children helping to recover a Sky 1 glider that has landed away from the airfield at the lower end of Detling Hill, at the rear of the Dennis Monkton Centre. The cockpit canopy has been removed. The pilot was not injured.

very entertaining and one year the CO – a former champion boxer and an Irishman – visited all the shops in Maidstone to get prizes for the Christmas draw and he collected enough prizes for all the officers and airmen at the station. After completing three years at Detling airfield, Piggott left Detling to become the chief gliding instructor at Lasham in Hampshire.

The Kent Gliding Club of today was formed on 26 April 1956 with the amalgamation of the Royal Engineers (RE) Gliding Club and the old Kent Gliding Club, based on Detling airfield. In May 1961, the land at Challock was purchased, but it was another two years of preparation before the field could be used for gliding.

Detling airfield was to have a new lease of life when, shortly after the Second World War, the well-known newspaper owner Lord Kemsley, who had an interest in gliding, set up a charitable trust fund with the sum of £100,000. The idea was to make loans available to gliding clubs, giving them the opportunity to expand their activities. To enable this, Sir Basil Meads was given the role of administrator, and he spent much time visiting gliding clubs and attending meetings of those recently formed to assess whether or not they deserved the investment. Fortunately, the Kent Gliding Club, which held its inaugural meeting at the Royal Star Hotel, Maidstone, on 26 April 1956, was one of the lucky ones.

A gentleman by the name of Hugh Gardiner helped to form the gliding club. The RE Club consisted of Roger Neame of the Shepherd Neame Brewery, 'Nobby' Clark, George McPherson and 'Tug' Burne.

Some seventy people attended the meeting, forty of whom decided to join. Thus the Kent Gliding Club was reborn from the ashes of the original club, founded by Lowe and Wylde in 1930. A loan of £1,497 was secured for the club, with which it was to purchase a T21 glider and a suitable winch. Also available were the RE's T31 and Prefect gliders. Kent Gliding Club came under the umbrella of the British Gliding Association (BGA) and the club's first president was Sqn Ldr Furlong. Hugh Gardiner became chairman, and Ken O'Riley was the chief flying instructor.

On 12 May 1956, work commenced on a clubhouse, which was on the top floor of an old coach house on a farm half a mile from the airfield, and it was rented for only 5s a week. The fuel and spares store was a converted pig shed. The club gained momentum and in August that year it had achieved 1,807 launches and was making plans for the first club party, which took place on 25 August. In September the Tudor House at Bearsted was the venue for the first club dance. A new appointment was made when Peter Crabtree became the deputy chief flying instructor.

Although the club was praised for its progress, it had to arrange for security of tenure. Until this was achieved, no further loans were available. As with many airfields after the war, Detling's future was uncertain. No longer being required by the Air Ministry, it was likely to be sold off as farmland. So arrangements were made with the Royal Engineers for the Kent Gliding Club to have full use of their gliders. In return, the club would be responsible for the administration and maintenance of the site. The gliders were purchased, following Messrs Day, Smith and Hunter being appointed accountants. As a result of the Suez Crisis in October 1956, petrol was rationed; the BGA managed to arrange for an allowance for the club, which, coupled with car sharing, enabled it to continue its activities.

The club's engineer, Roy Hubble, while repairing the T31 glider, had managed to rig its wings onto the Tutor fuselage, allowing solo flying to continue for those pilots who were not ready to fly the Prefect. Kent Gliding Club had achieved so much in a year and by the end of 1956 had become a limited company, with full membership of the BGA. After 3,705 launches, and with membership increasing, gliding courses had been planned for New Year 1957. At the beginning of the year, Roy Hubble had completed his 'C' certificate, and Ted Day had completed his first five hours' gliding. Flushed with success, the membership organised another dance. Membership had risen to 100 flying members and fifty associate members. By March, the club was also operating five gliders: the T31, the Prefect, the T21, and two privately owned types, the Olympia and the Sky, whose owners had granted limited club use.

Roy Hubble was busy, not only with Certificates of Airworthiness, but also with fitting a Perspex canopy to a new instrument panel in the Prefect.

A busy day for Kent Gliding Club. The glider in the foreground is a T21 twin-seat trainer.

A visitor to the Kent Gliding Club at Detling was this T21, type registration SE-SHM, later BGA 969. Note the KGC's trailer to the right, which appears to be an ex-RAF Queen Mary aircraft transporter. On the left is a glider winch. This glider was destroyed by fire at Spalding on 21 March 1999.

Over seventy people attended a party given at Detling by the Kent Gliding Club on 27 April, to celebrate the club's first anniversary. The evening's entertainment was shared by a number of visitors from most of the southern gliding clubs. In the club's first year, thirty-four members had flown solo, a number had gained 'C' certificates, and some of the more experienced pilots had flown on cross-country and duration flights. The total flights in the year amounted to nearly 5,000. Another winch was being constructed and the club hoped to exceed these figures in 1957.

The spring weather meant that auto-towing could begin. Club member 'Mickey' Gilbert returned from the BGA ball the proud possessor of the California in England Trophy, for the best female flight of 1956. Mickey had flown from Lasham in Hampshire to Castle Bromwich, a distance of 98 miles. She was later to lose her life in a mid-air collision when flying in a competition in Austria. In April 1958, the chairman of the British Gliding Association attended the club's first birthday party and was impressed by the progress made. One improvement being worked on by Ken O'Riley and Frank Tiley was the construction of a twin-drum winch to increase the number of launches even further. That same month, Ted Day was awarded the club's first Silver 'C' for his flight to Tangmere, which was

Preparing to move the Sky 1 glider is the faithful Fordson Tractor, itself a vintage vehicle and property of KGC during the 1950s at Detling.

swiftly followed by Ian Abel's flight to Ramsgate, also achieving the Silver 'C'. Other successful flights were by 'Nobby' Clark and Bill Bailey.

The problem of tenure remained. It affected many gliding clubs located on redundant RAF airfields. On 21 May, a report was published on the future of gliding. The main topic was how to help gliding clubs in the acquisition of such airfields and the effect of gliding on civil aviation. The same month, a new glider joined the ranks, a Skylark 3b, which was owned by a syndicate. The chief flying instructor, Ken O'Riley, gained a new speed record of 100 km/h for a two-seater flight with Dr Brenning James. Later, with Ted Day, Ken entered the National Gliding Championships. Ted won the Furlong Trophy. New launching equipment was purchased at the beginning of 1958 for the sum of £25 from government surplus. This included two 15 cwt trucks for cable retrieval, with the option of buying another two. A much-needed 3-ton truck was included in the bargain. It was needed for the completion of the twin-drum winch. The Tiger Moth Club visited Detling on 15 February. Later, glider pilots were introduced to the aero tow, which became a popular fortnightly event. The aircraft would tow its glider to 2,000 or 5,000 feet at very little cost to the club.

To increase revenue from gliding, an award was given to duty pilots who managed to rustle up 100 or more launches per day. This consisted of a carved wooden fish and half a pint of Red Barrel beer. To create interest and recruit more members, evening lectures began on various aspects of gliding. During the August Bank Holiday of 1958, the club took part in the flying show at Ramsgate Airport, at which they gave a spectacular aerobatic display, earning much-needed publicity.

Events were overshadowed by the urgent need to find a suitable home for Kent Gliding Club. The time was fast approaching when the Air Ministry would have to dispose of the airfield and buildings at Detling. In November 1958, it sold the site to Mr Mackleden of Bobbing Farm. It was to be the club's last year at Detling.

In 1959, Kent Gliding Club was offered a lease on the facilities at Lympne until it was able to find a permanent home. Eventually, this was achieved and the club established its own airfield on a 90-acre site at Challock, near Charing on the North Downs. The following year, a tragedy occurred when Mickey Gilbert was killed in a mid-air collision while gliding in Austria. In her memory, several annual trophies were established: the Instructors Trophy, the Ab-Initio Trophy, the Cross-Country Trophy and the Aerobatic Trophy. Since those days, Kent Gliding Club has gone from strength to strength. It is without a doubt one of the UK's most successful and respected gliding clubs and can be proud of its achievements.

Alan Simmunds describes his first flight in a glider:

Micky Gilbert and Owen Maddock moving a T31 glider from the Bellman hangar during a club day in 1956. Note the tyre, which took the weight of the wing when parked.

The damage caused by hailstones to Edward Day's Sky glider can clearly be seen in this photograph. The preceding adventure is worthy of a place in the annals of gliding history.

... a winch launch with the ATC Gliding Instructors School at Detling, near Maidstone in Kent ... I well remember feeling rather exposed in the open cockpit sitting on the bare plywood seat alongside my pilot, John Furlong. John was one of the people who first developed the Ottfur release hook for safer winch launching.

Up to that time, there were a number of fatal accidents caused by being unable to release the cable; it incorporated a spring-loaded gate. Of course my first launch ever was a cable break, just as we were pulling up into the full climb, which seemed to me, a mere power pilot, incredibly steep. However, we recovered to normal flight without any difficulty and landed straight ahead. With only the tyre to absorb most of the shock it seemed rather heavy and I was surprised that there was no damage to the front skid. My main impression of the landing was the noise as we hit the ground, and the sensation of speed sitting so close to the ground. That was my only flight that day as it was to have been a hangar flight. Next morning I met the instructors, Flt Lt Jock Forbes and F/O Peter Mallet, both of whom had been instructors at British Forces Gliding Clubs (BAFO) in Germany and had flown in the British team in the World Championships. Pete took me for three or four winch launches to get me familiar with the Sedburgh.

The first were up, round and down, lasting about four minutes. On the last one we flew into a thermal and climbed up to about 2,000 feet. This was the first time I had climbed more than a few feet in a thermal and I was able to grasp the rudiments of soaring techniques. But I was learning a great deal by just watching the others fly. Unfortunately, we then had several days of unflyable weather, so it was taken up with lectures. At the time I had been on the staff of the Central Flying School (CFS) at Little Rissington for several years at that time when there was an opportunity to go gliding for a week. I managed to get a place on what was an instructors' course for civilian instructors from the Cadet Gliding Schools, which operated all over the UK at weekends and holiday times.

I was not at all impressed by the ground instruction. In fact I was staggered by the arguments between the students and instructors, largely caused by lack of basic knowledge by the staff. The one or two people who understood the need for teaching the correct facts kept catching them out. Usually I was called in to settle the discussions and as a result I quickly found that although I didn't know much about soaring, I was given the course to run for the rest of the week. So I ended up doing almost all the talks and also flew with the students teaching them instructional patter, while being able to watch them and pick up tips on how to fly the T-21.

I never did go solo that week but went back a week or two later and flew a Slingsby Prefect for my A, B and C badges, which included an eighteen minutes thermal flight. On 9 September 1945 I made a flight of thirty-eight seconds (followed by a normal landing) so obtaining my 'A' Certificate and that would have been the end of my involvement with gliding in the ATC. However my friends and I had been bitten by the bug and, when we learned that John Furlong was organising a course for ATC instructors at Detling in Kent the following Easter, Mark and I asked whether they would like help on the ground. This offer they were pleased to accept. So Easter 1946 found us at Detling driving Beaverettes. As well as another flight in the Falcon 3 we were also given a flight in the Slingsby Gull II, a side-by-side two-seater which had an enclosed cockpit and cantilever gull wing.

My memory of that aircraft was that the controls were very heavy. One day during the weekend, the wind was quite fresh from the south-west. John Furlong thought he might be able to soar the Falcon 3 over the adjacent slope but after a couple of attempts he found he could not get sufficient height and had not enough penetration to reach it. However there was a dispersal area nearer the edge with an approach in line with the runway, but it was on the other side of the main Maidstone-to-Sittingbourne road. The plan was, when he was ready to be launched, to stop the traffic on the main road and when the Falcon was nearly over the winch (which was on a lorry chassis) it was to be driven across the road towards the slope into the dispersal area. When it was tried there was a short delay between the winch being stopped and it being driven forward. As a result, the occupants of the waiting cars were treated to a few choice words from above. By this time, the wind had dropped and he failed to soar.

It was 1942 when Air Cadet Gliding was formally established; one of the first schools formed was 141 Gliding School at RAF Kidbrooke in South London. On 1 December 1945, it moved to Gravesend, from where in June 1946 it went to RAF Detling on the North Downs and then to RAF West Malling for the period between September 1949 and September 1950. Following a short stay, it returned to Detling, where it disbanded and later merged into 146 GS and 168 GS. In 1956, this unit became 615 GS at RAF Kenley, which remains in operation today.

Gliders first flew above West Malling between 1930 and 1933 when Mr 'Jimmy' C. H. Lowe-Wild designed and built his own primary gliders. He operated some from the local airfield at West Malling, which at that time was called Maidstone Airport. In 1930, the Kent Gliding Club was formed.

After the Second World War, the club moved around various airfields in Kent, including a spell at West Malling, before finding a permanent site at Challock. Following the US Naval Facility withdrawal from RAF West

Malling in late 1963, the airfield was given Care and Maintenance status. No. 618 GS moved from Manston into West Malling in March 1965 and made its headquarters in the old dispersal spider complex near the threshold of Runway 07. Its aircraft and equipment were stored in one of the large T4 hangars, where they remained until 1992. Then, in 1964, Short Brothers' servicing section arrived from Rochester Airport. The company had the contract for servicing RAF Chipmunks and other aircraft. The Gliding School had a very good relationship and worked side-by-side with Shorts, as they performed very few movements that would hinder 618's operations. In 1968, the company lost the service contract and unpowered aircraft used West Malling exclusively for some years.

The first gliding induction course for a cadet was flown on 3 September. Further staff members were recruited, and the third and final Vigilant arrived from Kinloss in November. New staff were recruited during the first few months and instructor training began and continues today. After many months of operating without mains power and water, the installation of services was completed in late 2001 and staff were able to begin improving the briefing and living accommodation.

In May 1950, *Flight* magazine reported on a successful cross-Channel flight from Detling in a glider flown by Flt Lt L. A. Miller. The pilot recalls the events of this record-breaking flight in his own words:

The location of the Reserve Command Gliding Instructors School at Detling, some 30 miles west of the Strait of Dover, makes long-distance flights to the Continent a frequent possibility in unstable westerly to north-westerly winds. Tentative arrangements were therefore made some weeks ago for aero-tow retrieving facilities from the Continent to be available should a successful Channel crossing be made.

On Wednesday 12 April, the personnel of RAF Station Detling were on delayed Easter leave, and at 10 a.m. on that day I saw that conditions seemed favourable for a high, long-distance flight towards the east. Arriving at Detling at 11 a.m., I prepared for a winch launch in an old Gull I – a sailplane of pre-war vintage by Slingsby's, and of similar design to the one flown across the Channel in 1939 by Mr Stephenson. As most of RAF Detling was on leave, it was not until 12.15 p.m. that I was able to get away, being winched off to 1,000 feet by the Kent ATC wing adjutant, Flt Lt Emberley. After releasing, I circled to cloud-base at 4,000 feet and then found that the wind was carrying me too far northwards of my desired track to Folkestone. From a position three miles north of Canterbury, therefore, I started to work my way south. This proved a difficult operation in the Gull I, which has limited powers of penetration (it was designed in 1937, I believe), and at one time I thought I would be forced to land However. Soon after 1.15 p.m., I found a narrow but strong thermal, which took me to cloud-base at 5,000 feet, by which time I was seven or eight miles south-west of Folkestone. I eventually reached the coast north of Folkestone at 2 p.m. and flew two or three miles out over the Strait of Dover.

I was experiencing very slight icing just beneath the cloud, and recalled that the meteorological forecast had given severe icing in cloud above a freezing level of 3,000 feet. However, conditions were such that I could utilise the cloud lift to gain height, and this I decided to do. Entering cloud, I climbed in smooth lift of about 6 ft/sec to 900 feet, at which height the turbulence became quite severe. As the machine was then heavily iced, with clear ice an inch or more thick on the leading edges and struts, I straightened up on a course of 120° magnetic. The cockpit cover was, of course, also coated with ice, and the air-speed indicator had stopped working. Instruments remaining in use were the electric turn-and-slip indicator, altimeter, inclinometer, variometer and compass.

Under these conditions I descended to 7,000 feet, and saw that I had left a line of cumulus clouds, which extended up the Strait of Dover. I checked the surface wind from the whitecaps and found that in order to reach the French coast – which I could see beneath a clear blue sky some eight miles to the south – it was necessary to make good a track almost at right angles to the wind. My position at that time was approximately north-west of Calais. The coast looked very far distant in view of the ice, which the machine was carrying, the strong crosswind, and the probable performance of the Gull I under such conditions. Still without ASI, I flew to get a rate of sink of 2 metres down on the variometer (about 4 ft/sec). Keeping Calais in view, I finally crossed the coast west of Calais at an indicated height of 900 feet above sea level. After flying over the wide stretch of sands, I found a thermal and climbed to cloud base at 3,800 feet, whence I made off down a wind which was blowing straight up the coast towards Belgium. The actual Channel crossing had taken slightly over one hour.

The late start, which I had made from Detling, now prevented further flight for, at 900 feet with nothing but dead sky, I was forced to look for a landing place. I saw an airfield below (Coxyde) and landed at 3.50 p.m. at a dispersal point near to the runway in use. I found that Coxyde was a Belgian Air Force base, commanded by Col. Arends, and I became the guest of No. 1 Fighter Squadron (Commandant Roger de Weser) during my enforced stay there. An Auster … later retrieved me … In the past I have been employed for some years as a long-range heavy-transport pilot on trans-ocean flights. The weather experience, which I gained during that time in the Bay of Bengal during the monsoons, coupled with two years' transatlantic flying, has helped considerably in my gliding activities. To others who will undoubtedly wish to attempt long-distance flights to Europe, I would stress that instrument flying experience is essential. Given a sound knowledge of meteorology, good instrument flying and good planning, even low-performance sailplanes are possible record-breakers in the higher wind speeds and unstable conditions of winter weather.

It is sad to recall that on 10 May 1950, shortly after his cross-Channel flight from Detling airfield, Flt Lt Leslie A. Miller was killed in a gliding accident. He was forty-seven at the time of his death and was chief flying instructor of the RAF Gliding Instructors School at Detling. He was sadly missed by all who knew him. Two days later, a Court of Inquiry was held and continued for two days. Presiding over the inquiry was Wg Cdr Keddie, HQ 61G, assisted by Sqn Ldr Thompson and Flt Lt Hyde. The funeral of Leslie Miller took place the following day at Detling church and a Coroner's Inquest was held in the officers' mess.

The same year, ATC gliding instructors were to have the opportunity to receive standardised training in two-seater gliders so that they could be better qualified to train cadets up to the solo-circuit stage. Training was given at Detling. Instructors were able go there whenever they could take time off work for one or two weeks at a time. On joining the RAF, a cadet's gliding was virtually over unless he was lucky enough to be posted to one of the stations at which gliding was officially organised.

The newly formed RAF Soaring and Gliding Association hoped to overcome this problem. It had already been operating at Detling, and planned to start clubs at Mildenhall, St Athan, Boscombe Down and Warton. It was hoped that eventually any member of the RAF who wished to do so would be able to glide at or near his home station. The association itself also provides more advanced facilities. To help those unable to visit Detling, staff instructors from the school occasionally visited gliding schools at weekends to upgrade instructors. The grading scheme was revised to provide a clearer indication of ability, and to give instructors a more definite aim. The result was a higher gliding standard throughout the ATC.

A Detling Defence Force was formed in March 1954 to take part in an operation to simulate an enemy attack. It consisted of four units: Home Command Gliding Instructors School, VR (T) Administration School, HQ Kent ATC Wing, and No. 6226 Bomb Disposal Flight. The idea was that this force would defend the airfield from ground attack; this would assist the Army, who would already be heavily committed. It was one of many exercises undertaken in the Cold War climate of the 1950s.

CHAPTER 12

Echoes from the Past

The airfield today – memorials and war graves –
buildings and further evidence

There are many stories of equipment and aircraft remains being buried at Kent's disused airfields. Most of these have yet to be located and recovered. However, in August 1989, a bizarre and potentially lethal find was made on the site of Detling airfield. Mines were found that had been laid during the Second World War so that the airfield could be destroyed should the expected invasion take place. It seems incredible now, but in 1940, following Dunkirk and the Battle of Britain, the nation was bracing itself for Hitler's attempt to conquer the British Isles. The operation, undertaken by the 33rd Royal Engineers Battalion based at Chattenden near Chatham, took five days to complete. A 3,000-metre exclusion zone was necessary to eliminate any risk to residents and workers, and during the operation some 230 police officers were used to stop the public from entering the site.

Maj. Harris, in charge, said that the risk would not be from any unexpected explosive blast but from flying pieces of flint and glass. He went on to say:

> There is always an element of risk with any clearing operation like this but provided everything goes to plan there shouldn't be any danger.

The Army bomb disposal team used remote-controlled diggers operated from within an armoured van to unearth the nine pipe-mines, which were up to 70 feet in length. Two of these were known to have explosives in them and it was thought possible the others could have too. Once the pipes were uncovered they were broken into manageable lengths with the explosive charges and any gelignite inside was removed and later burnt. Since this episode, no other mines or bombs have been discovered.

Peter Hubbard, who was in charge of an MoD research team, recalls his memories of the Events (he was later awarded the OBE for his work):

The saga of the pipe-mines started back in the days when it looked as though Hitler would invade any day. In those days of great anxiety, it was decided that the last thing we wanted was for our advanced airfields to fall into the hands of the Germans. Therefore a dangerous plan was put into place on the English side. Thirty-four airfields that lay close to or even within parachutist range of the south and east coasts would be mined. These mines had to be particular as it was essential that the airfields remained usable by our aircraft until the last moment, but as soon as it looked as though they might fall into the hands of the enemy, bang! This was complicated by the fact that a fighter airfield in those days did not just launch its aircraft off from the runways. Any stretch of flat grass would serve. Therefore it was essential that the whole usable area of the airfield had to be destroyed.

Hydraulic rams were brought in and long metal pipes were driven at a slight downward angle into the ground. A lattice of pipes was formed so that they lay for 150 feet under the ground, at one end about 3 feet down and at the other perhaps at 6 feet. The metal tubes were 3 inches in diameter at the bottoms and 2 inches at the tops. Once these had been positioned about 12 feet apart, they were filled with cartridges of the most readily and cheapest explosive available, nitroglycerine-based blasting gelignite. Each of the pipes was primed with detonating cord and then awaited the Nazi onslaught. It would be the work of a few minutes to connect the tails of the Detonating Cord and set the whole series of charges off. The airfield would have disappeared into so much ploughed mess. As we are all aware, the invasion did not occur, therefore sometime towards the end of the war the decision was made to remove the pipe-mines.

I do not know what the pilots who had been merrily using the airfields for active duty themselves thought of constantly flying on fields under which there were several hundred pounds of explosive, but maybe nobody told them, which is the usual way. A Canadian sapper unit was given the job of clearing the pipe-mines and told that it could only go home once the job was done. Strangely enough, the job was completed in quick time and the various clearance certificates logged for each of the thirty-four airfields. Cut ... to some forty years later, to a solitary figure excavating a hole on Lympne airfield in Kent, one of the thirty-four airfields originally mined.

The solitary figure is Ukrainian, and one of the Legions of the Lost attached to the British Army for range-clearance duties. At the end of the Second World War, a whole Ukrainian SS unit was drafted into the British Army as the alternative was to send them to their homes where they would be summarily executed by the Communist authorities. Their fate was not exactly brilliant as the job they were given was to go around clearing unexploded ordnance left over after the hostilities. But it was better than certain death. The Ukrainians served as civilians, worked under the direction of British sappers, and most religiously sent home a proportion of their pay to their homelands, which is an interesting thought all through the Cold War.

Our solitary individual had found a long metal tube in the ground and proceeded to investigate it with the aid of a hammer. The resulting explosion unfortunately killed him. The subsequent court of enquiry uncovered the facts about the pipe-mine saga of which he was unaware and introduced into everyone's mind the fact that the Canadian sappers might not have been quite so thorough as had been first thought. A programme of additional searching was put in hand but it was acknowledged at the start that this could take some time. Simultaneously my group was tasked with assisting initially the RAF EOD teams, as all forms of EOD on RAF property were an RAF responsibility.

The initial studies were conducted at Tangmere in Sussex. I remember Ron telling me that he was stood at the bottom end of one of the tubes while water was gently washed down its length. Very glutinous-looking sausages of forty-year-old Polar Ammon Gelignite were slowly plopping out of the end of the tube and Ron was catching them one at a time. In between this process he happened to glance down at the considerable puddle he was standing in, the water table at Tangmere being only inches below the surface. He noticed a peculiar oily sheen to the water surface. He was standing in a pond, the top surface of which was a layer of nitroglycerine.

A method of dealing with the problem that kept most of the operation remote was devised jointly by my troops (Terry and Ron) and the RAF EOD boys. Basically it consisted of using a remote-control Hymac, a hydraulic digger, to excavate down to the buried pipes. Once uncovered, the pipes would have small charges of linear cutting charge attached to them at intervals. These would be designed to weaken the pipes without actually penetrating them completely so should not have set off the explosive contents. Once weakened, the remote-control equipment would again be used to break the pipes into sections. Low-pressure water would then be used to ease the ancient explosive cartridges out of the tubes. The explosive would then be burned under precautions.

Now this all sounds reasonably sensible and it was. But there were complications. Commercial nitroglycerine-based explosives are designed to be used weeks or at most months after manufacture. They are not designed to sit in metal pipes under the ground for more than forty years. Consequently some of the NG-based material was now a horrible mush of God knows what composition. Surprisingly not all of it was supersensitive. One solution tried in the early days was to put countermining charges on the pipes when they were discovered and just blow them. On nearly every occasion the explosive reaction faded out quickly and left us with scattered unreacted explosive. But as Ron (and the Ukrainian gentleman) had discovered, on some occasions there were pockets of nitroglycerine that had become disassociated from their normal desensitising matrix. Then things got more exciting.

This is more or less where I came on the scene personally. Some, in fact many, of the wartime airfields were no longer under the control of the RAF. Therefore the responsibility for clearing them passed over to the sappers (remember the complicated turf war associated with all forms of EOD). As a further complication, some were not even airfields anymore. Some were factory sites and at least one was a large housing estate. We will deal with how these were tackled later. The sappers needed someone to give them guidance on what could be considered safe working distances for dealing with the pipe-mines.

That someone was me. If I had wanted to be really pedantic, I could have stuck to the normal 1,000 yards radius that most use as the safe radius for confined explosives up to the sort of scale we were thinking of. But there were additional considerations such as the age of the material: by this time we knew that it was unlikely to all detonate in one go from our various experiments. It was also underground to the extent of at least 3 feet and hence the distance that a detonating pipe-mine could throw metal was restricted. I did some sums and came up with 500 metres as the safety distance. However, life is never simple and there were several occasions that I was invited to attend a site meeting to discuss particular aspects of an airfield clearance that could only be considered by viewing the problem first-hand.

The first of these was at HMS *Daedalus*, a Fleet Air Arm aerodrome near Lee-on-Solent. There the complication was several high-priced dwellings with enormous picture windows overlooking the Solent right on the perimeter of the airfield. The effects of a blast on large areas of unsupported glass is hard to predict even at ranges normally considered safe (remember the headmaster and his little darlings at Hemswel). It only affected work on a proportion of the pipes but while that was going on, I suggested that the houses within an extended safety trace be evacuated. That was reinforced during the clearance operation by a particularly vigorous bang during one of the clearances, which broke a window or two in the control tower. This caused no casualties as it had been evacuated but proved that some of the charges in the pipes still had some zing in them.

Another interesting series of dilemmas arose when Eastleigh came to be cleared. By this time my military chums had got used to the idea of 500 metre safety traces and had produced a plan of the site with nice circles drawn around the pipe-mines that had been identified. Even that is not simple as the pipe-mines were linear features and ran in a far from regular pattern despite the original intention of the installers. On this occasion I found that the safety traces took some decidedly strange variations when it came to one particular perimeter.

'What has happened here?' I enquired.

'Oh, that is the London-to-Southampton main line railway,' replied the major.

'What! And why the big kink here?' – indicating another deviation from the 500 metre trace.

'Oh, that is the M3/M27. We obviously can't shut down the M3/M27 and the mainline railway – just as we can't shut down Ford's factory, which is in the airfield area.'

'Have I got news for you,' [was] my brisk reply.

There was much weeping and wailing and gnashing of teeth but I refused to have my name associated with the safety plan until they agreed to close the railway line, the M3/M27 and Ford's factory. There was a relatively painless way of doing it which involved working over the weekend and shutting the factory when there were only maintenance men there anyway. The closure of the railway and the motorways was an inconvenience to many, I am sure, but less so at the weekend. But not such an inconvenience as having large amounts of metal or great clods of earth flying at users of them.

I suppose I should mention my brush with the Palace too. We knew that Detling, long since disused as an airfield, had pipe-mines under the surface, but as these were not to be disturbed, the clearance awaited resources some way down the line. However, parts of what had been the airfield were to be used by the Kent County Showground and Her Majesty the Queen was to open the Kent Show. Some bright spark had mentioned to the Palace that we suspected there were unexploded pipe-mines under the area that was to be traversed by the Queen. I was asked to assure the Palace that there was absolutely no chance of one of the pipe-mines detonating while she passed over them. Now, being a scientist, I could not give this assurance as there is no such thing in risk analysis as zero risk if there is even the faintest chance of something happening. I could make assessments of millions to one against but I could not give assurance of zero risk.

The pressure I was put under to bend the rules. But I didn't. I think they eventually rerouted the Royal Party so that she came nowhere near the buried nastiness. Risk is a funny business. People driving to the Kent Show were subjecting themselves to infinitely higher levels of risk from injury or death from road accidents than they were from dormant pipe-mines buried under the surface of the showground. So was Her Majesty. But it was out of the ordinary so needed separate consideration. The last of the pipe-mine saga that I was concerned with personally was at Gravesend. This was the airfield that now was a large housing estate. I again attended a site meeting after the sappers had been in and sought the remaining pipe-mines with their special magnetic anomaly detectors. There was another carefully drawn map with all sorts of deviations from the 500 metre safety traces, most of the deviations occurring when the safety traces cut across the hundreds of houses in the estate.

'What is this?' I queried.

'Well, we cannot throw out hundreds of people from the estate. Where will they go? It will be a logistic nightmare!'

'Get them out!'

The solution was not mine, only the prompt that it was necessary. On day one of the five days set aside for the clearance of Gravesend, a fleet of coaches turned up. Roll up! Roll up for the magical mystery tour! The clearance was to be conducted from Monday to Friday from 9 a.m. to 5 p.m. Hence a fair proportion of the potential evacuees had already gone to work. The mothers, children under school age and old-age pensioners were mainly quite happy to be taken out for the day at the government's expense. One or two of the older souls who had not been inclined to move when Hitler bombed them expressed an obstructive view to having to move for the removal of some explosive unpleasantness associated with the war against him. It happened that one of the pipe-mines dealt with on the first day had a quite large chunk of active ingredient associated with it. It objected to the removal process, which made quite a good-sized bang. Everyone was on the coach the next morning. The sapper gentlemen worked solidly through the week and actually finished the job by Thursday. There was a near riot on the Friday morning when it was announced that the expected coach trip was cancelled as there was no need.

Shortly before the magnificent memorial was unveiled in Detling village in 1998, some interesting artwork was revealed at Thurnham Old Rectory, or Little Dane as the house was known. The then-owners, Steve and Sonia Ashdown, were renovating the rambling old rectory, which had to date taken them two years of hard work. While removing paper from the walls of a ground-floor room, which they were aware was used as a bar by airmen at RAF Detling, they were delighted if not somewhat embarrassed

Above: This is believed to be the entrance to an ammunition store – one of few structures still to be found on the airfield site.

Right: This tariff board from the NAAFI was recovered some years ago by aviation enthusiasts. Despite the author's best efforts, its fate remains unknown.

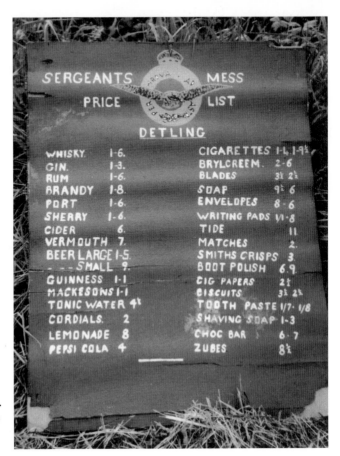

SERGEANTS MESS PRICE LIST

DETLING

WHISKY.	1-6.	CIGARETTES	1-4. 1-9½
GIN.	1-3.	BRYLCREEM.	2-6
RUM	1-6.	BLADES	3½ 2½
BRANDY	1-8.	SOAP	9½ 6
PORT	1-6.	ENVELOPES	8 - 6
SHERRY	1-6.	WRITING PADS	1/1-8
CIDER	6.	TIDE	11
VERMOUTH	7.	MATCHES	2.
BEER LARGE	1-5.	SMITHS CRISPS	3.
---SMALL	9.	BOOT POLISH	6.9.
GUINNESS	1-1	CIG PAPERS	2½
MACKESONS	1-1	BISCUITS	3½ 2½
TONIC WATER	4½	TOOTH PASTE	1/7- 1/8
CORDIALS.	2	SHAVING SOAP	1-3
LEMONADE	8	CHOC BAR	6. 7
PEPSI COLA	4	ZUBES	8½

The Detling grave of Lt Norris Felix Perris, who was killed when his aircraft collided with that of 2Lt T. Wright. Wright was buried in his hometown of Fleetwood. Several airmen and pilots from both world wars are buried in the village cemetery.

On Sunday 6 September 1998, a service was held close to the Cock Inn at Detling village to mark the unveiling of a memorial dedicated to the RNAS, RFC, RAF, FAA, and all who were based at RAF Detling.

to uncover an almost full-size drawing of a naked young lady. To the right-hand side of the work of art were caricatures of airmen peeping around a door with rather smug smiles on their faces.

No less than eight cartoons were exposed, and it was suggested that aircraft paint had been used to draw them. A hidden signature revealed that the artist or artists were members of the RAF regiment. Work had to be halted on Mrs Ashdown's office, from where she ran the Montessori Nursery School for up to twenty-five infants.

In an interview for *Detling Village Mail*, Sonia Ashdown said of the cartoons:

> They cause a lot of interest and I now feel a great responsibility for them.
> We have to give them very careful thought in the future.

Other wartime memories uncovered at Little Dane were the air-raid shelter in the garden and the RAF store sign in the cellar.

In October 1959, Kent County Council purchased land from the original owner and established the County Agricultural Show Ground. Pye Ltd later took over the Wireless Telecommunication Station and an Airways VOR/DME Transmitter was set up for navigational purposes. Today, Detling is a shadow of its former self, although, thankfully, the old Bellman hangar has been spared and is still used for shows and storage. Small industrial businesses occupy some of the smaller buildings. As with many deserted airfields, the pillboxes and air-raid shelters remain, but many of the original buildings have disappeared. An event that takes place every year is the Military Odyssey, which is spread over a few days in late summer with many military enactment groups and side stalls.

The Kent County Show, a major event in the area, is also held at the airfield, and the Antiques and Collectors' Show brings many people into the area. Apart from the memorials on the old airfield and in Detling village, and the war graves at the church, there is very little to remind the public of the important role Detling played in the history of aviation. The airfield at Detling has a complex past, which is all the more reason to record some of the events and stories associated with it. Given the disappearance of so many airfields throughout the UK, it is a comforting thought that recording their histories helps maintain the memory of those who served.

Squadrons and Units Based at Detling, 1915–1959

First World War RAF Squadrons

- RNAS Strategic Bombing Wing – 1915–16
- No. 3 Wing RNAS – 1916 – Curtis JN3, Sopwith 1½ Strutters
- 50 Squadron – October 1916 to March 1918 – Be2c, Be2e, Be12, AW FK8
- 112 Squadron – 25–30 July 1917 – Sopwith Pup, Sopwith Camel – formed from 'B' Flight, 50 Squadron, at Throwley
- 143 Squadron – 14 February 1918 to 31 October 1919 – AW FK8, Sopwith F1 Camel, Se5a, Sopwith Snipe

Second World War RAF Squadrons

- No. 11 Group – 1944
- No. 35 (Army Co-operation Wing) Southern England – 22 August 1941
- 500 (County of Kent) Squadron – 28 September 1938 to 30 July 1939, 13 August 1939 to 30 May 1941 – Avro Anson, Blenheim IV
- 235 Squadron – 26 May to 10 June 1940 – Blenheim IV
- 59 Squadron – 25 June to 22 July 1941 – Blenheim IV
- 53 Squadron – 3 July to 24 November 1941 – Blenheim IV
- 280 Squadron – 10 February to 30 July 1942 – Avro Anson
- 239 Squadron – 19 to 31 May 1942 – Mustang Mk I
- 318 Squadron – 20 March to 5 August 1943 – Hurricane Mk I
- 26 Squadron – 13 January to 1 March 1943, 22 June–11 July 1943 – Mustang Mk I
- 655 Squadron – 7 April to 12 August 1943 – Auster Mks 1 and 3, Tiger Moth Mk II

- 48 Squadron – August 1939 to January 1940 – Avro Anson Mk I
- 4 Squadron – May 1940 – Lysander Mk II
- 132 Squadron – 12 October 1943 to 17 January 1944, 10–13 March 1944, 19 March to 18 April 1944 – Spitfire IXb
- 184 Squadron – 12 October 1943 to 6 March 1944 – Hurricane IV
- 602 (City of Glasgow) Squadron – 12 October 1943 to 17 January 1944, 12–13 March 1944, 20 March to 18 April 1944 – Spitfire IXb
- 567 Squadron – 1 December 1943 to 14 November 1944 – Hurricane Mk 1, Martinet Mk I, Spitfire VC, Oxford Mk I, Vengeance Mk IV – formed from 1624 AACF
- 453 Squadron RAAF – 19–21 January 1944, 4 February to 13 March 1944, 19 March to 18 April 1944 – Spitfire IXe
- 118 Squadron – 20–23 January 1944, 5 February to 10 March 1944, 12 July to 9 August 1944 – Spitfire IXc
- 80 Squadron – 19 May to 22 June 1944 – Spitfire IX
- 1 Squadron – 22 June to 11 July 1944, 10 August to 18 December 1944 – Spitfire LF-IXb
- 13 Squadron – July 1941 to August 1942 – Lysander Mks I, II and III, Blenheim Mk IV
- 229 Squadron – 19 May to 22 June 1944 – Spitfire IX
- 274 Squadron – 19 May to 22 June 1944 – Spitfire IX
- 165 Squadron – 22 June to 12 July 1944, 10 August to 15 December 1944 – Spitfire Vc, Spitfire IXb
- 504 (Nottingham) Squadron – 12 July to 13 August 1944 – Spitfire Vc, Spitfire IX
- 124 Squadron – 26 July to 9 August 1944 – Spitfire VII, Spitfire IX
- 75 Wing – 1 November to 1 December 1946 – Blenheim Mk IV, Tiger Moth Mk II, Hornet Moth
- HQ No. 15 Wing – 12 October 1943 to 15 April 1944 – Spitfires
- HQ No. 125 Airfield Headquarters – 12 October 1943 to 4 May 1944
- No. 125 Wing – 12 May 1944 – Auster Mk III

Second World War Fleet Air Arm Units

- 801 Squadron – 31 May to 23 June 1940 – Skua Mk I, Roc Mk I
- 806 Squadron – 7–31 May 1940 – Skua Mk I, Roc Mk I
- 812 Squadron – 27–28 August 1940, 27 December 1940 to 12 March 1941 – Swordfish Mk I
- 815 Squadron – 27 May to 5 June 1940 – Swordfish Mk I
- 816 Squadron – 12 March to 4 April 1941, 11–16 April 1941, 23 April – Swordfish Mk I

- 819 Squadron – 21–23 May 1940 – Swordfish Mk I
- 821 Squadron – 1–14 July 1941 – Swordfish Mk I
- 825 Squadron – 18–28 May 1940, 1–5 July 1940 – Swordfish Mk I
- 826 Squadron – 31 May to 1 June 1940 – Albecore Mk I

Miscellaneous Units

- No. 1624 (Anti-Aircraft) Co-operation Flight – 14 February 1943 to 1 December 1943 – Defiant TT1, Barracude Mk II, Hurricane Mk I, Martinet Mk I, Oxford, Gladiator Mks I and II – formed from 567 Squadron
- No. 1493 (Target Towing) Flight 3 ADF – 26 July to 7 October 1943 – Lysander Mks I, II and III, Master Mk III, Martinet TT1
- No. 1 Coast Artillery Co-operation Unit – 12 Jan 1942 to 11 October 1943 – Avro Anson Mk I, Blenheim IV, Defiant Mk I, Spitfire Mk II, Skua Mk I
- No. 6 Anti-Aircraft Co-operation Unit – 18 September to November 1943 – Blenheim Mks I and IV, Battle, Lysanders Mks II and III, Martinet, Hurricane IV, Tiger Moth, Rapide
- No. 2 'D' Flight, Anti-Aircraft Co-operation Unit – 11 June 1941 to 14 February 1943 – became 1624 Flight
- No. 1 'K' Flight, Photographic Reconnaissance Unit – 23 January to 1 August 1942 – Spitfire PR No. 8 (Coastal) Operational Training Unit – 1 August 1942 – absorbed 'K' Flight No. 1 PRU
- No. 16 Group Communications Flight – 1941 to 8 January 1945 – Proctor Mks I and III, Dominie, Anson, Oxford
- No. 3 Aircraft Delivery Flight – 23 July to 20 September 1943 – Dominie Mk I, Spitfire Mk IIa, Tiger Moth Mk II, Oxford, Magister Mk I
- No. 4 Aircraft Delivery Flight – 21 September to 20 October 1943 – Dominie Mk I, Defiant Mk I, Oxford, Magister Mk I, Mustang Mk I
- No. 403 Repair and Salvage Unit – September to October 1943 – Hawker Typhoon
- No. 405 Repair and Salvage Unit – 26 January to 16 April 1944 – Mustang, Hurricane, Proctor, Auster, Spitfire
- No. 410 Repair and Salvage Unit – 6 November 1943 to 26 January 1944 – Hawker Typhoon, Hurricane, Spitfire
- No. 401 (Air Stores Park) – 28 July 1943 (Vinters Park), 1 July 1943 (Park House, Maidstone), 25 October 1943
- Boxley No. 4018 Anti-Aircraft Flight RAF Regiment – 1942–43
- No. 4138 Anti-Aircraft Flight RAF Regiment – June 1943
- No. 4207 Anti-Aircraft Flight RAF Regiment – June 1943

- Southern Signals Area – November 1946 to January 1950
- No. 1336 RAF Regiment Wing HQ – January 1945 – formed at Detling
- No. 1338 RAF Regiment Wing HQ – January 1945 – formed at Detling
- No. 5004 Airfield Construction Squadron, No. 34 Works Flight – 1941

Service Echelons and RAF Regiments

- No. 6132 Servicing Echelon – 22 March to 18 April 1944 – attached to operational squadrons, e.g. 132 Squadron.
- No. 6453 (RAAF) Servicing Echelon – 22 March to 18 April 1944
- No. 6602 Servicing Echelon – 22 March to 18 April 1944
- No. 6080 Servicing Echelon – 19 May to 22 June 1944
- No. 6229 Servicing Echelon – 19 May to 22 June 1944
- No. 6001 Servicing Echelon – 22 June to 12 July 1944, 10 August to 16 December 1944
- No. 6165 Servicing Echelon – 22 June to 12 July 1944, 10 August to 15 December 1944
- No. 6504 Servicing Echelon – 11 July to 13 August 1944
- No. 6118 Servicing Echelon – 12 July to 9 August 1944
- No. 6124 Servicing Echelon – 26 July to 9 August 1944
- No. 6274 Servicing Echelon – 19 May to 22 June 1944
- 2709 Squadron RAF Regiment – dates unknown
- 2746 Squadron RAF Regiment – 1944–?
- 2793 Squadron RAF Regiment – 1944–?
- 2828 Squadron RAF Regiment – 1944–?
- 2877 Squadron RAF Regiment – July 1943–?

Post-War

- No. 141 Gliding School – October 1951 to September 1955 – Cadets Mks I and II, Prefect TX1, Falcon Mk III, Grunau Baby, Sedbergh TX1
- No. 168 Gliding School – 30 June 1949 to 1 September 1955 – Cadet Mks I, II and TX3, BAC VII, Sedbergh TX1
- Reserve Command Gliding Instructors School – 1 July 1949 to 1 August 1950 – Cadet Mks I and II, Prefect TX1, Sedbergh TX1, Grunau Baby, Gull 1, Rhonbussard
- Home Command Gliding Instructors School – 1 August 1950 to 1 September 1955 – Cadet TX3, Prefect TX1, Sedbergh TX1, Grunau Baby, Gull 1, Rhonbussard

- (No. 1) Home Command Gliding Centre – 1 September–1 December 1955 – Cadet TX3
- 615 (Volunteer) Gliding School – dates unknown – Cadet TX3, Prefect TX1, Sedbergh TX1, Viking TX1
- 655 Squadron – April to August 1943 – Auster Mk III
- 651 Squadron – November 1955 to April 1957 – Auster Mk III
- 657 Squadron – September 1951 to November 1955 – Auster Mk III
- No. 1903 Flight – February 1955 to January 1956

'Clipped, Clapped and Cropped'

Tommy Thommerson of 602 (Glasgow) Squadron RauxAF invented the term 'clipped, clapped and cropped' to describe the Spitfire Vb.

'Clipped'

For its clipped wings. In order to increase the aircraft's speed and lateral manoeuvrability, the Vickers engineers reduced the wingspan by about 4 feet by suppressing the wing tips, which rounded off the Spitfire's famous elliptical wing.

'Clapped'

Expressed the general opinion among pilots of the Vb that, although extremely fast at ground level (350 mph straight and level), the aircraft became lumps at 10,000 feet – the height at which escort missions had to operate. The square wings also meant the aircraft lost the Spitfire's main advantage – the ability to turn right.

'Cropped'

For its reduced-diameter Merlin 45 engine. It was only an RR 45 with supercharger turbine, allowing the power to be increased below 3,000 feet from 1,200 hp to 1,585 hp. As the volume of supercharged air was reduced, the power curve fell rapidly from 8,000 feet; at 12,000 feet the engine produced about 500 hp. These engines had a reduced service life.

Air Raids Involving 50 Squadron

5 June 1917
Daylight Gotha Raid – twenty-two Gothas, target Sheerness
Detling 'A' Flight – Be12 No. 6183 (pilot 2Lt W. R. Oulton), Be12a No. A6313 (2Lt. C. C. White)

13 June 1917
Daylight Gotha Raid – twenty Gothas, target London
Detling 'A' Flight – Be2c No. 2711 (pilot 2Lt W. R. Oulton took off at 11.07 a.m. and force-landed at Kingsnorth, Isle of Grain), Be12a No. A6313 (2Lt C. C. White), Be12a No. A6309 (2Lt. L. Lucas)

7 July 1917
Daylight Gotha Raid
Be12a No. A6313 (2Lt L. Lucas)

22 July 1917
Daylight Gotha Raid
Sopwith Pups of 'A' Flight took part in five sorties against the enemy.

19–20 October 1917
Night Zeppelin Raid
L54 tried to bomb Detling, but missed its target and did little damage.

Selected Aircraft Movements, 1915–1918

Curtis JN3 – Tractor Biplane

- No. 8399: Delivered to Detling on 31 December 1915 and to Eastchurch on 12 March 1916. Returned to Detling on 16 March 1916.
- No. 8403: Delivered from Eastchurch Night Flying School to Detling on 23 November 1915. Due to low cloud, the aircraft landed at Birling 10 miles west of Detling. The engine failed and the aircraft tipped over into hedge, smashing the undercarriage. The aircraft returned to Detling by lorry on 6 December 1915.
- No. 8408: Delivered to Detling 21 November 1916. En route to Grain on 7 July 1916, it force-landed in a ploughed field at Stockbury. Flt Lt A. F. Buck and FS R. H. Horniman were uninjured. The aircraft was repaired and flown to Manston on 31 March 1917.
- No. 8398: Delivered from Eastchurch to Detling on 23 November 1915 On a routine flight, the engine failed and the aircraft force-landed 2 miles west of Detling on 28 November 1915. FS D. H. Whittier was uninjured. During landing on 2 September 1916, flight sergeants G. K. Williams, Smith and Webber ran into a hedge. The aircraft's undercarriage was damaged. Deleted on 9 March 1916.
- No. 3393: Delivered to Detling on 31 December 1915. Flown to Eastchurch on 20 March 1916.
- No. 3420: Delivered to Detling on 13 July 1916; coded No. 5.
- No. 3423: On flight to Detling, became lost and crash-landed in marshes 2 miles from Wrotham on 27 November 1915.
- No. 3422: Delivered on 27 November 1915. Damaged chassis and wings while landing on 14 December 1915.
- No. 3453: Flew to Detling on 21 September 1916; in transit for Eastchurch.

Detling Airfield: A History, 1915–1959

- No. 3447: Flew to Detling on 18 May 1916; in transit for Manston on 9 June 1916.

Curtis JN4 – Tractor Biplane

- No. 8802: Dual-control aircraft delivered from RAF Hendon to Detling on 17 May 1916.

Be2c – Tractor Biplane

- No. 8415: Visited Detling on 8 July 1916 from Brooklands.

Avro 504 Scout – Tractor Biplane

- No. 8574: Deleted at Detling on 7 May 1916.
- No. 8577: At Detling on 24 December 1916, en route to Eastchurch.
- No. 8582: New engine fitted at Eastchurch on 16 January 1916; sent to Detling on 9 June 1916.
- No. 8628: Delivered to the Isle of Grain by rail for erection on 12 September 1916 and fitted for night-flying. En route to Detling on 27 December 1917, force-landed at Four Elms piloted by FS G. M. F. O'Brian. Arrived at Detling on 28 December 1917.

Bristol Scout Type D – Tractor Biplane

- No. 8965: Delivered from War Flight Eastchurch to Detling on 22 December 1916.
- No. 8969: Delivered from Eastchurch War Flight to Detling on 20 December 1916.
- No. 8970: Delivered from Eastchurch War Flight to Detling on 15 February 1917.
- No. 8973: Delivered from Eastchurch to Detling on 15 February 1917. Set off for Manston on 1 March 1917, but returned to Detling due to bad weather. Returned to Manston on 1 March 1917.
- No. 8989: Delivered from Eastchurch to Detling on 7 December 1916.
- No. 8990: Delivered from Eastchurch to Detling on 22 December 1916 and collided with 3052 Bristol Scout Type C; propeller and wings damaged.

Albatross B2 – Tractor Biplane

- No. 890: Visited Detling on 8 February 1917. Impressed in August 1914.

Bristol Scout – Tractor Biplane

- No. 3052: Arrives in Detling on 20 December 1916. Hit By Bristol Scout Type D No. 8990 on 24 December 1916.

Henry Farman – Pusher Biplane

- No. 3150: Delivered to 4 Wing Eastchurch for erection on 6 September 1915. To Detling on 14 December 1915; to 3 Wing Detling in April 1916. Deleted 28 June 1916.

Burges Type Gunbus – Pusher Biplane

- No. 3659: Arrives in Detling on 5 January 1916; in transit to Eastchurch on 6 January 1916.

Sopwith Admiralty 806 Type (Gunbus) – Pusher Biplane

- No. 3833: Flies from Brooklands to Detling on 10 February 1916. Wrecked in gale while pegged out.
- No. 3835: Delivered to Detling on 13 December 1915. Chassis and one wing smashed on 28 December 1915. Wrecked in gale while pegged out on 16 December 1916.
- No. 3836: Delivered from Brooklands to Detling on 3 January 1916. Chassis and propeller damaged.
- No. 3838: Delivered from Brooklands to Detling on 10 December 1916. Wrecked in gale on 16 February 1917.
- No. 3841: Delivered from Brooklands to Detling on 9 January 1916. Wrecked in gale on 16 January 1916.

Sopwith 1½ Strutter Tractor Biplane

Between 11 May 1916 and 25 May 1916, nos 9400, 9401, 9407 and 9408 were delivered from Brooklands to Detling to join 3 Wing RNAS.

Sopwith 1½ Strutter Tractor Biplane

• No. 9891: Prototype for proposed version of 1½ Strutter accepted at Brooklands and delivered to 3 Wing RNAS Detling on 18 May 1916. Moved to Manston on 9 June 1916. Returned to 3 Wing Detling on 11 June 1916.

Bristol Scout 'D' Tractor Biplane

• No. N5392: Delivered from Eastchurch to Detling on 15 May 1917.
• No. N5395: Delivered from Eastchurch to Detling on 15 May 1917.

Sopwith Camel F1

• No. D6639: Lt W. D. H. Baird of 112 Squadron, Throwley, was killed at Detling on 22 November 1918 while doing a 3,000-foot loop.
• No. F2181: Passed from 143 Squadron to 75 Squadron, Elmswell; left Detling on 23 January 1919.
• D6407: Flew from Norwich AAP to Lympne; landed at Detling due to mist on 28 February 1918.

Selected Presentation Aircraft at Detling

Aircraft were usually constructed by public subscription and fundraising; many were named after the town or borough that paid for the aircraft.

Assam V Lakhimpur – Spitfire Mk IIb – No. P8548

Delivered to No. 1 CACU, Detling, on 20 July 1942. Aircraft lost its port undercarriage leg during landing at Detling on 20 September. Piloted by P/O R. Turner, repaired by No. 1 Civilian Repair Unit, Cowley. Returned to Detling on 29 January 1943. Later collided with Spitfire AD388 *Ambala II Punjab* Spitfire Mk Vb during practice attack and crashed at Yew Tree Farm, Frinsted, near Sittingbourne. Flt Lt Henry Lloyd David Tanner was killed. He was buried at Streatham Park Cemetery, Mitcham, Surrey. The pilot of AD388, also killed, was buried at Brookwood, Woking.

Assam VI Lakhimpur – Spitfire Mk IIb – No. P8543

Delivered to No. 1 CACU, Detling, on 3 April 1942. Returned to No. 33 Maintenance Unit on 10 June 1942.

Banda – Spitfire Mk IIb – No. P8333

Delivered to No. 1 CACU, Detling, on 28 October 1942. Returning from an abortive night co-operation flight with Coast Artillery on 9 November 1942 in poor visibility over the Channel, the aircraft flew into the ground while crossing the coast near Church Hunton, Kent. Sqn Ldr David John Hamilton was killed and is buried at Brookwood, Woking.

Barnsley Chop – Spitfire Mk IX – No. MA819

Delivered to No. 410 Repair and Salvage Unit, Detling, on 18 December 1943; also flown by 19 Squadron, Newchurch Advanced Landing Ground.

Basoko – Spitfire Mk Vb – No. AR396

Flew with 132 Squadron at Castleton on 13 February 1944. This unit moved to Detling in March 1944 and was taken over by 504 Squadron (County of Nottingham) – which flew convoy patrols and similar operations – until 23 July 1944.

Bellows Brazil – Spitfire Mk IXc – No. BS545

Originally a Mk Vb, the aircraft was taken to Hucknall to be converted into a Mk IX with a Merlin 61 engine. By 19 June 1943, it was flying with 229 Squadron, Detling, piloted by Flt Sgt Thompson. The aircraft was damaged when the drop tank fell off, and had to be repaired.

Borough of Edmonton – Spitfire Mk IX – No. MA845

With 3501 Servicing Unit at Cranfield before passing on to 80 Squadron, Detling, in March 1944. Coded EY-N. First operation flown by Flt Sgt C. W. Jarrod.

Canadian Pacific I – Spitfire Mk IX – No. BS474

Operated with 501 (County of Gloucester) Squadron at Hawkinge on 8 March 1943. Moved to Detling on 29 May 1944 and flew with 274 Squadron until 21 August. Coded JJ-N. Moved to Fighter Leader School Milfield.

Ceredigion I – Spitfire Mk IIb – No. P8691

Moved from 46 MU Lossiemouth to No. 1 CAAU, Detling, on 22 March 1943. F/O P. F. Sewell overshot his landing and hit a barbed-wire fence. The aircraft was repaired the following day and returned to 59 OUT on 27 April 1943.

Chatham – Spitfire Mk Vb – No. BL956

Donated by Chatham & Sheerness Dockyards. Flew as NX-J with 131 (County of Kent) Squadron in March 1942, later with 3501 Service Unit. On 8 October 1943, the aircraft was transferred to No. 125 Wing, Detling, to fly with 80, 229 and 274 squadrons.

Elcardo the Thistle – Spitfire Mk Vb – No. BL525

On 9 September 1943, the aircraft joined 132 Squadron Newchurch ALG with 602 Squadron. It was taken over by 118 Squadron on 13 March 1944.

Ethel Marsden – Spitfire Mk IX – No. MH486

Joined 132 Squadron Newchurch ALG on 26 September 1943. Inspected at Detling on 15 December 1943 by Sir Hugh Grant. The aircraft moved to 83 Group, Redhill, on 15 June 1944.

Forward V – Spitfire Mk IX – MH873

In Gravesend from 1 November 1943 with 65 Squadron and 122 Squadron. Later joined 80 Squadron at Detling. Flt Lt L. G. R. Smith made a heavy landing on 29 May 1944, tearing off the tail wheel on the Sommerfeld Tracking. Repaired by 3 June 1944. On 8 August 1944, the aircraft suffered a glycol leak and the undercarriage collapsed. An emergency landing was made at Friston ALG. P/O F. G. Ealder (RAAF) was unhurt; the aircraft was not repaired.

H. E. H. Nizam's State Railway No. 2 – Spitfire Mk IX – No. MA747.

274 Squadron arrived in the UK from overseas. It was first based in Hornchurch, and then moved to Detling in April 1944. MA747 joined 274 Squadron on 29 May 1944.

Hunter – Spitfire Mk IIb – No. P8534.

On 29 January 1942, moved from No. 6 MU Brize Norton to No. 1 CACU Detling. Undercarriage collapsed as P/O P. F. Sowell landed on 25 March, but was repaired. The aircraft was moved to No. 1 CACU on 12 April 1942.

Kenya Daisy – Spitfire Mk Vc – No. BM271

Based with 65 Squadron Kingsnorth ALG on 15 July 1943. Moved to 130 Squadron West Malling on 17 August 1943. On 31 January 1944, moved to 453 Squadron, 125 Wing, Detling, for forward operations.

Lombok – Spitfire Mk IIb – No. P8341

Allotted to No. 1 CACU, Detling, on 7 May 1943 from No. 9 MU Cosford. Joined 2nd TAF on 19 June 1943.

Lusambo – Spitfire Mk Vb – No. BL696

602 Squadron moved to Detling from Scotland on 12 March 1944, leaving behind this aircraft for 118 Squadron. In July 1944, 118 Squadron moved to Detling and again the aircraft was left behind at Skeabrae, this time for the use of 313 Squadron.

Melton Mowbray & District – Spitfire Mk Ia – No. P8522

Moved from No. 37 MU Burtonwood on 10 April 1942 to relocate with No. 1 CACU. On 3 May 1942, F/O H. L. D. Tanner made heavy landing at Weston Zoyland. Returned to Detling on 15 May 1942. Sqn Ldr D. J. Hamilton made a wheels-up landing on the airfield. A month later, on 29 September 1942, he collided with birds. The aircraft was damaged again when it was tipped on the nose at Detling, following spotting for artillery. It was repaired on 2 October 1942 and damaged again on 29 January 1943. The aircraft was sent to 2nd TAF.

Metabox – Spitfire Mk IIa – No. P8389

Delivered to No. 6 MU Brize Norton. Joined No. 1 CACU at Detling on 25 February 1942. Transferred to No. 61 OTU at Rednal on 9 October 1942.

Nabha III – Spitfire Mk IIIb – No. P8518

Moved from 46 MU Lossiemouth to No. 1 CACU, Detling, on 8 April 1943. Flt Lt F. H. James forgot to lower the undercarriage. The aircraft was repaired at Detling and returned to duties on 13 May 1943.

North West Surrey – Spitfire Mk IIb – No. P8641

Moved from No. 6 MU Brize Norton to No. 1 CACU Detling on 17 February 1942. Damaged on 9 March 1942 when P/O H. L. D. Tanner got lost and, out of fuel, force-landed. The aircraft hit a ridge and overturned; it was taken to Air Service Training at Eastleigh for repair.

Rootes Snipe – Spitfire Mk Vb – No. BM132

Allocated to 118 Squadron Detling on 25 May 1944 from No. 33 MU Lyneham. Engaged in bomber-escort operations over Europe.

Rossendale – Spitfire Mk Vc – No. AB196

Moved to 80 Squadron, Detling, on 29 May 1944 and was damaged during bombing practice. Flt Sgt N. J. Rankin was injured.

Southampton – Spitfire Mk Ia – No. R7059

Moved from No. 8 OUT at Fraserburgh, where photo-reconnaissance pilots were trained. On 3 July 1942, Sgt G. Etherington undershot his landing at Detling and hit the embankment, ripping off the aircraft's undercarriage.

Yaounde – Spitfire Mk Vb – No. A979

Transferred from 610 Squadron, Bolt Head, to 602 Squadron, Detling, on 4 March 1944. When the squadron was re-equipped with Spitfire Mk IXs, the aircraft moved to 313 Squadron, Skeabrae, Scotland.

Spitfire Mk IX MH486 FF-F *Ethel Marsden* flown by Flt Lt Wooley of 132 (Bombay) Squadron. At Detling in 1943.

Bibliography

Books

Boot, Henry, and Ray Sturtivant, *Gifts of War: Presentation Aircraft in Two World Wars* (Air Britain Historians, 2005).

Brooks, Robin J., *Kent's Own: The History of 500 (County of Kent) Squadron Royal Auxiliary Air Force* (Meresborough Books, 1982).

Caygill, Peter, *In All Things First: No. 1 Squadron at War 1939–1945* (Pen and Sword, 2009).

Cole, Christopher, and E. F. Cheesman, *The Air Defence of Great Britain 1914–1918* (Putnam, 1984).

Cornwell, Peter D., *The Battle of France: Then and Now* (After the Battle, 2008).

Cull, Brian, and Bruce Lander, *Diver! Diver! Diver! RAF and American Fighter Pilots Battle the V-1 Assault over South-East England 1944–45* (Grub Street, 2008).

Gray, Colin F., *Spitfire Patrol* (Hutchinson, 1990).

Listemann, Phil and M. Laird, *No. 453 (RAAF) Squadron 1941–1945: Buffalo, Spitfire* (Listemann, 2009).

McLachlan, Ian, and Russell J. Zorn, *Eighth Air Force Bomber Stories: Eye-Witness Accounts from American Airmen and British Civilians of the Perils of War* (PSL, 1991).

Minterne, Don, *Detling Diary: An Account of RAE Technical College Gliding 1946–52* (2005).

Olmsted, Bill, *Blue Skies: The Autobiography of a Canadian Spitfire Pilot in World War II* (Stoddart, 1987).

Onderwater, Hans, *Gentlemen in Blue: The History of No. 600 (City of London) Squadron Royal Auxiliary Air Force and No. 600 (City of London) Squadron Association 1925–1995* (Pen and Sword, 1997).

Piggott, Derek, *Delta Papa: A Life of Flying* (Pelham Books, 1977).

RAF Flying Review (1950–60).

Rawlings, John R., *Fighters Squadrons of the RAF and Their Aircraft* (rev. edn, Macdonald 1992).

Rochford, Leonard H., *I Chose The Sky* (William Kimber, 1977).

Rootes, Andrew, *Front Line County: Kent at War 1939–45* (Robert Hale, 1980).

Shores, Christopher, and Chris Thomas, *2nd Tactical Air Force* (4 vols, Classic Publications, 2006).

Simpson, Bill, *Spitfire Dive Bombers Versus the V2: Fighter Command's Battle with Hitler's Mobile Missiles* (Pen and Sword, 2007).

Spurdle, Bob, *The Blue Arena* (William Kimber, 1986).

Sturtivant, Ray, and Gordon Page, *Royal Navy Aircraft Serials and Units 1911–1919* (Air Britain Historians, 1992).

Warner, Graham, *The Bristol Blenheim: A Complete History* (2nd edn, Crecy Publishing, 2005).

Websites

www.bbc.co.uk/ww2peopleswar
www.epibreren.com/ww2/raf/index.htm
www.telegraph.co.uk